Higher Education and
Social Change

Kenneth W. Thompson
Barbara R. Fogel

Published in cooperation with
the International Council for
Educational Development

The Praeger Special Studies program—
utilizing the most modern and efficient book
production techniques and a selective
worldwide distribution network—makes
available to the academic, government, and
business communities significant, timely
research in U.S. and international economic, social, and political development.

Higher Education and Social Change

Promising Experiments in Developing Countries

Volume 1: Reports

PRAEGER SPECIAL STUDIES IN INTERNATIONAL ECONOMICS AND DEVELOPMENT

Praeger Publishers   New York   Washington   London

Library of Congress Cataloging in Publication Data

Thompson, Kenneth W   1921-
    Higher education and social change.

    (Praeger special studies in international
economics and development)
    Includes bibliographical references and index
    CONTENTS: v. 1. Reports.—
    1. Underdeveloped areas—Education.   I. Fogel,
Barbara R., joint author.   II. Title.
LC2605.T45   378'.009172'4   76-14474
ISBN 0-275-23150-X

PRAEGER PUBLISHERS
111 Fourth Avenue, New York, N.Y. 10003, U.S.A.

Published in the United States of America in 1976
by Praeger Publishers, Inc.

789   038   98765432

"Higher Education for Development" is a phrase that hides important problems, a slogan that requires careful analysis, and a source
of hope for a majority of the world's people struggling for a respect-
able future. Recognizing the pivotal importance of this source of hope,
12 donor agencies (public and private, national, regional, and international) agreed to sponsor a study of current efforts in this area and
to make recommendations to all parties on how higher education in
developing countries could improve its contribution to their social
progress. The International Council for Educational Development was
invited to design and manage the inquiry.

The International Council for Educational Development had the
good fortune to secure Kenneth W. Thompson to direct the study as a
new division director. Upon his arrival, a scenario with appropriate
guidelines was prepared, regional teams were organized under the
chairmanship of outstanding indigenous leaders, a budget was prepared, and the complicated task was started. This report and its ac-
companying regional reports and case studies are the result of two
years of joint effort by donor agency staffs and educators from developing countries, of the benign interest of the trustees of the International Council for Educational Development (two of whom were
chairmen of regional teams), and of particularly the skillful meshing
of all these gears by the study director, Kenneth Thompson.

A word about the style and content is in order. From the beginning the study was designed as a joint effort of donor and donee, of
agencies and institutions, of governments and experts. It was widely
and wisely recognized that the day of donor omniscience and single-
handed initiatives was over and that the new international environment
called for joint effort, a commonly designed approach, and consensus
on recommendations. While we do not claim uniqueness, we like to
think the conduct of this study of higher education for development is
a good example of a new style.

We should also point out the importance of the words "higher
education" and "development." In many parts of the world, traditional
universities are almost the sole agencies for postsecondary education.
But as countries develop, the needs for talent become more diverse,
students have increasingly different aspirations, and academic programs and institutions become more specialized to take care of these
specialized needs. Higher education embraces the new diversity of
institutions, of which the university becomes the most important.

Many developing countries are in a state of transition, moving toward systems of higher education that require both specialization and coordination—a requirement that is an organizational problem for both developed as well as developing countries.

The world "development" also has broadened to include social concerns and the very quality of life as well as the traditional preoccupation with economic growth. But, as the definition of development has broadened, the responsibilities of higher education have become more complicated. The professoriat of institutions of higher education are reluctant to take on tasks for which they were neither selected nor prepared. Once again the debate on the proper role and measure of higher education is a universal one. Instruction, research, and public service—in what proportions? The advancement or application of knowledge—in what measure? With their rising demand for social progress, the developing countries' pressure for the social performance of universities and colleges is intense.

Not the least of the difficulties created by the evolution of systems of higher education and the broadening of the definition of development is the necessary rethinking of the role of donor agencies, particularly those that primarily represent the developed world. External assistance is a tricky business even when confined to narrow economic issues. But when the effectiveness of assistance must be measured by its impact on a total culture, outside involvement becomes extremely sensitive. This fact alone requires maximum local participation if projects are to be constructive rather than abrasive.

The study and this report, it can be seen, deal with highly important and complicated matters. The International Council for Educational Development is pleased with the results, plans to continue its interest, and will be responsive to opportunities to pursue the many questions that are posed. It only remains to thank once again Kenneth Thompson as director of the Higher Education for Development study, Barbara Fogel as the coauthor of the report, and Helen Danner as Mr. Thompson's chief assistant and expert manager of the logistics of the study. This trio sat as the nerve center of the enterprise working effectively with the regional chairmen. Together they made a unique international team.

CONTENTS

Page

FOREWORD   v
James A. Perkins

LIST OF TABLES   xi

LIST OF ABBREVIATIONS   xii

PART I: HIGHER EDUCATION FOR DEVELOPMENT
PROJECT: FINAL REPORT

Chapter

1   INTRODUCTION   3
Kenneth W. Thompson

The Nature of the Findings   4
Different Circumstances and Different Possibilities
    and Approaches   7
The Real Issues in Higher Education for Development   13
Notes   16

2   THE PROBLEMS: WHAT NEEDS TO BE DONE?   17

Developing Rural Areas   18
Developing Urban Areas   20
Improving Health   20
Educating People More Effectively   22
Creating Jobs and Employment   25
Assisting in Development Planning (Consultancy
    Centers)   29
Notes   31

3   THE INSTITUTION: ORGANIZING FOR DEVELOPMENT   32

Institutional Models   32
Service, Extension, Training, Research   35
The Interdisciplinary Approach   37

Chapter   Page

    Relations with Government   39
    Relations with Private Enterprise   43
    Notes   44

4   LEADERS: HOW TO GET THINGS GOING   45

5   ASSISTANCE   48

    How to Make Assistance More Useful   51

6   GUIDELINES   54

    Recognizing Good Programs in Higher Education for
      Development   54
    Overcoming Obstacles to Success   63
    Note   77

APPENDIXES   79

A   PATTERNS OF EDUCATIONAL DEVELOPMENT   79

B   DONOR AGENCIES   80

C   CASE STUDIES   81

    PART II: SUMMARIES OF CASE STUDIES CONDUCTED
        BY REGIONAL TEAMS

7   AFRICA   87

    Prospects for Regional Universities in Africa   87
    The University Centre for Health Sciences   89
    Functional Bilingualism: An Emergent Issue of the
      African University   91
    The Public Service Role of the University   92
    Technology at the Service of Rural and Industrial
      Development   94
    Higher Education in Mali   96
    Developing a University in a Small Country   98
    Agricultural and Educational Development Roles of
      the University   100
    Staff Development in an African University   102
    Higher Education and Development in Sudan   104
    The University's Response to Manpower Needs   106

Chapter   Page

8   ASIA   108

    Center for Studies in Rural Development   108
    The University's Role in Rural Development   110
    Development of Cultural Unity   112
    Manpower Training Programs in the Philippines   113
    Training Technicians Through Nondegree Polytechnic
        Programs   119
    Maeklong Integrated Rural Development Project   120

9   LATIN AMERICA   123

    Center for Urban Development   123
    Education for Rural Areas   125
    The Research Program for Systems of Health
        Services Delivery   127
    Structure of Higher Education for Development in
        Colombia   129
    Research and Extension Program for Industrial
        Development   131
    Program for Transferal of Technology   133

PART III: REGIONAL TEAM REPORTS

10 AFRICAN REGIONAL REPORT   139

    Background   139
    Major Problems of Higher Education in Africa   140
    Objectives, Approach, and Limitations of This Study   147
    Higher Education and Nation Building   149
    Successful Educational Approaches   153
    Some Characteristics of Development-Oriented
        Universities   156
    Higher Education and External Assistance   158
    Notes   165

11 ASIAN REGIONAL REPORT   166

    The Concept of Development   166
    The Role of the University   169
    The Southeast Asian Region   170
    Some Conclusions   175
    The Role of Donors   184
    The Case Studies   185

Chapter   Page

         The Asian Regional Team   187
         Note   188

12   LATIN AMERICAN REGIONAL REPORT   189

         The Concept of Development   189
         Higher Education and Development   191
         Latin American Development Priorities   193
         The Latin American Programs   197
         Requirements for Development Programs   203
         Suggestions for the Future   204
         Notes   205

      PART IV: PROJECT STAFF, REGIONAL TEAMS, TASK
                FORCE MEMBERS, AND CORRESPONDING
                MEMBERS

         New York Staff   209
         African Regional Team   209
         Asian Regional Team   211
         Latin American Regional Team   212
         Task Force Members   213
         Corresponding Members   215

INDEX   217

ABOUT THE AUTHORS   225

LIST OF TABLES

Table   Page

1   Percentage of Girls in Total Enrollment in Higher
       Education in Africa   141

2   Enrollment of Students in Higher Education: Number of
       Postsecondary Students per 10,000 Inhabitants   142

3   Ratio of Student Numbers to Total 20- to 24-Year-Old
       Group: Enrollment Ratio in Higher Education   144

4   Average Annual Student Enrollment: Growth Rate of
       Higher Education in Africa   146

5   Basic Economic Data on Southeast Asia   172

6   Public Expenditure on Education—Around 1954, 1960,
       and 1967   180

7   Unit Recurrent Costs of Education by Level in Southeast
       Asian Countries, 1965   182

LIST OF ABBREVIATIONS

AIM — Asian Institute of Management, Philippines

ASAIHL — Association of Southeast Asian Institutions of Higher Learning, Thailand

ASEAN — Association of Southeast Asian Nations, (rotating headquarters)

AVRDC — Asian Vegetable Research and Development Center, Taiwan

CASTAFRICA — Conference of Ministers of African Member States Responsible for the Application of Science and Technology to Development

CEDUR — Center for Urban Development, Brazil

CEPAL — United Nations Economic Commission for Latin America

CIAT — Centro Internacional de Agricultura Tropical, Colombia

CIDA — Canadian International Development Agency

CIMMYT — International Maize and Wheat Improvement Center, Mexico

CRC — Center for Research and Communication, Philippines

DAP — Development Academy of the Philippines

ECLA — United Nations Economic Commission for Latin America

ENS — Ecole Normale Supérieure, Mali

EUS — Ethiopian University Service

FAC — Fonds Aide Coopération, (foreign aid branch of the French Government)

GNP	Gross National Product
HED	Higher Education for Development
IBRD	International Bank for Reconstruction and Development (World Bank)
ICED	International Council for Educational Development
ICFES	Colombian Institute for the Development of Higher Education
ICOLPE	Colombian Institute of Pedagogy
ICRISAT	International Crops Research Institute for the Semi-Arid Tropics, India
IDB	Inter-American Development Bank
IITA	International Institute for Tropical Agriculture, Nigeria
IRRI	International Rice Research Institute, Philippines
ITESM	Monterrey Institute of Technology and Advanced Studies, Mexico
IUC	Inter-University Council for Higher Education Overseas, Great Britain
KKN	Kulia Kerga Niata, Indonesia
MUCIA	Midwest Universities Consortium for International Activities, USA
NBP	Net Beneficial Product
NNW	Net National Welfare
OECD	Organization for Economic Co-operation and Development, France
PRIMOPS	Research Program for Systems of Health Services Delivery, Colombia

PROPED	Program of Research and Education for Development, Brazil
RIHED	Regional Institute of Higher Education and Development, Singapore
SEDA	Secretary of Education of Antioquia, Colombia
SMS	Municipal Health Service of Cali, Colombia
TANU	Tanganyika African National Union (National Political Party of Tanzania)
UBLS	University of Botswana, Lesotho, and Swaziland
UCHS	University Centre for Health Sciences, Cameroon
UNACAST	United Nations Advisory Committee on the Application of Science and Technology to Development
UNDP	United Nations Development Programme
Unesco	United Nations Educational, Scientific and Cultural Organization
UNICEF	United Nations Children's Fund
USAID	United States Agency for International Development
WHO	World Health Organization

HIGHER EDUCATION
FOR DEVELOPMENT
PROJECT: FINAL REPORT

INTRODUCTION
Kenneth W. Thompson

At the invitation of 12 major donor agencies (see Appendix B) concerned with higher education in developing countries, the International Council for Educational Development (ICED) undertook, in January 1974, a far-ranging review of selected postsecondary institutions in Africa, Asia, and Latin America. The 18-month study had been preceded by more than two years of discussion by a task force made up of staff members from 15 multilateral, bilateral, and private foreign assistance agencies. The impetus for the effort was 25 years of experience in educational assistance that provided not only a body of knowledge to be studied but a state of mind to be assessed. Disillusionment had spread within the agencies because it was believed that assistance had not yielded the hoped-for results. It was said that most institutions of higher education abroad were ivory towers, elitist in character, and, for the most part, unresponsive to the urgent needs of their people. In the words of a respected official of the International Bank for Reconstruction and Development (IBRD), the two central questions to be answered were: Is the contribution to development by higher education less than it might be? Is something being done about it and can this be further extended?

There can be little doubt of the importance and possible consequences of such an inquiry. Given the facts that the United States Agency for International Development (USAID) alone has contributed more than $1 billion to educational assistance, that the World Bank's projections call for expenditures on higher education of up to $300 million over the next five years, and that the staffs of all major donor agencies are actively engaged in discussions on redeploying and reorienting educational assistance, an audit and review by outsiders was long overdue. Writing of the study, the distinguished New York Times columnist Harrison Salisbury observed: It is "the right kind of exercise in a time when so much time and thought and energy seems to be wasted on nothings."[1]

In accepting the invitation to conduct the study, Dr. James A. Perkins, chairman of the ICED and past president of Cornell University, set out three conditions: (1) that the director should be myself as the former chairman of the task force; (2) that respected educators from the developing countries should be responsible for institutional case studies; and (3) that the ICED reserve to itself independence in planning and coordinating the work and publishing the findings. The ICED was to be a third force serving as the link between teams of developing country educators and the important donor agencies. It was to be initiator, catalyst, and buffer whose past study and publication record would ensure the participants of the integrity of the findings against real or imagined pressures from any quarter.

Three steps were taken at the outset: (1) a small core staff was appointed with headquarters in New York, aided by the lively and continuing interest of the chairman and vice-chairman of the ICED, James A. Perkins and Philip H. Coombs, author of two widely discussed studies on nonformal and rural education; (2) a 50-page guide and study plan was prepared for participants, along with a dozen or more shorter papers on hypotheses, leading questions, and procedural and substantive issues intended to bring unity and a common character to the separate inquiries; and (3) three regional directors were named with authority to select their own team members and the institutions to be studied. It would be difficult to exaggerate the importance of this third step for it represented a sharp departure from the established practice of calling on Western educators for this function. Thus, it signaled the unique character of the study. In accordance with its mandate to listen to developing country voices, the ICED study, with the exception of this introduction by the director, reflects primarily the views of educators from the developing world. For those who have provided educational assistance, it is a graphic illustration of the dividends of experienced and proven indigenous educational leaders. For the Third World, it testifies to its right to be heard. For the worldwide intellectual community, it demonstrates the presence in Africa, Asia, and Latin America of undisputed educational equals.

THE NATURE OF THE FINDINGS

The findings of the study are both simple and complex. There is little doubt that the answers to the two leading questions are in the affirmative. The 23 studies, by virtue of the process of selection, which focused on more successful rather than on less successful institutions, demonstrate that higher education's contribution to development across three continents is less than it could be. By the standards of the relative success stories of the majority of the case studies, it is clear more can be done. The study shows that many institutions are doing innovative things and, by extension, that other institutions could follow their lead. The case studies prove, second, that something is being done about development education and that the ivory tower stereotype does not fit the institutions studied. The last two thirds of the report call attention to steps that might extend what has been tried and tested elsewhere.

On the other hand, more innovative and relevant education is needed even in the so-called successful institutions. Higher education in developing countries is plagued by a host of residual problems. There is a serious erosion of confidence throughout the world in development theories that appear to have been overtaken by major historical events. We need a deeper understanding of the historical and cultural processes in individual countries. There are unsolved problems involved in the transfers of technology. Less in known about how to help weaker institutions and poorer countries that have been largely bypassed by progress in more advantaged places. The increase of indigenous capacity is still spotty within regions and universities. Many universities and numerous faculties in strong institutions are not interested in development. A different selection of case studies would have meant a higher proportion of failures. How are the sources of strength to spread to weaker centers? How can the time be shortened to make institutions willing and able to look at their own problems and aspirations from a national rather than a Western perspective?

All this notwithstanding, the major underlying assumption of the study, and in particular of the regional teams, is that the widespread disillusionment about the results of support to higher education is misplaced. The message conveyed to the friends of higher education, many of whom feel discouraged and frustrated, is don't despair and don't withdraw all support. Often forgotten is the fact that the majority of developing country institutions have at most a few decades of history. They are in their infancy as educational institutions, some still suffering birth pangs. Higher education in the West, by contrast, has over 800 years of history. Yet despite its mounting problems, which crested in the 1960s and 1970s, few call for abandoning educational efforts in the West.

Another assumption of the study is that higher education for development can be characterized and defined. Certain fundamental sectors of development are susceptible to analysis and study. In the developing countries, the focus of development is determined by the rural character of the societies, their relative underdevelopment, and the necessity of grappling with such rudimentary needs as food and nutrition, public health, low per capita incomes, unemployment or underemployment, weak spots in the educational system, the preservation of cultural values, and the movement toward equity and social or ethnic equality. The real issue is what higher education can do and what it is doing about these fundamental needs.

Any such list of basic needs hardly exhausts the main tasks of higher education. As it struggles to meet local problems, it must avoid provincialism. It must attend, withal, to the building of overall educational institutions capable of producing graduates with broad views and sound judgment. Higher education in the Third World, however, operates within a short time span. Unless it can contribute quickly to the amelioration of certain basic and fundamental needs, the societies that nurture it may not survive.

Thus, higher education in the developing countries has a sense of urgency. It isn't enough to plan for the future of countries if the demands of the present are overwhelming. Developing countries cannot afford the luxury of disenchantment or resignation. They must act now, and this need for prompt action involves clarity on development priorities and needs. Effective educational action requires a partnership between governments and universities, whatever the risks.

H. J. Habakkuk, vice-chancellor of Oxford University, warned delegates to the sixth quinquennial conference of the International Association of Universities, meeting in August 1975 in Moscow,[2] that the role of universities as centers for the "unfettered exchange of ideas" was being threatened increasingly by national governments. He said that he was opposed to the principle that universities should be responsive to the needs of society. At issue was who should decide which external demands on universities could and should be met.

However well-placed his warning, the dilemma facing the new nations is that programs of education for development must be placed in the context of their societies' needs and be interconnected with well-conceived development plans. New educational institutions cannot do everything. They, no less than their governments, must strike a balance between what is essential and possible and what is desirable and possible but not essential. There must be a free and open dialogue between educational and government planners. Governments and societies at large are the major consumers of the products of higher education. Their efforts must be linked together. Education for education's sake is not enough.

At the same time, the findings of this study do not support the widespread impression that universities in developing nations have no choice but to subordinate themselves to governments. Ideally, they should be potential centers of independent social criticism. They run the risk of such deep involvement that their human capital and sources of growth may be depleted. They cannot allow themselves to be mere service stations. They ought not to take on the tasks belonging to governments. In the long run, their most enduring development function is to train developers. Even given the assumption that universities have a different role to play in developing countries than they do in developed countries, there are still certain tasks higher education for development can legitimately assume and others that fall outside its province.

Within these limits, the findings of the study suggest that higher educational institutions are appropriately and successfully engaging in service and extension programs, adult education, consultancy centers, assistance to small and medium-sized landowners, health delivery in rural and urban areas, experimental farming, high-priority manpower training, land reform and human settlement, preparation of business technicians and middle managers, and primary and secondary education. Many if not all of these efforts put them in direct contact with governments, and thus there is a need for a sorting-out process and some kind of division of labor. The university can design and carry forward workable projects but cannot replicate them throughout the country.

Through it all, universities must preserve relative independence from interference. There are examples in the study of institutional autonomy even when development-oriented programs must depend on government, but this autonomy calls for vigilance and objectivity on all sides. Some point to the National Agrarian University in Peru, as an institution so dependent on its relationship with government that it may have lost its autonomy, and others say that the Monterrey Institute of Technology in Mexico is subservient to the industrial community. Whatever the verdict, and the case studies appear to substantiate their independence, these institutions have to cope with an ongoing problem that is never solved once and for all.

DIFFERENT CIRCUMSTANCES AND DIFFERENT POSSIBILITIES AND APPROACHES

Participants, including the regional teams, are very much aware of the limitations of the study. A relatively small number of educational experiments has been studied. Most of us view the current effort only as the first phase in a more comprehensive endeavor. It would be unfortunate if the impression were given that the study had arrived at the point of universal generalizations or that its conclusions could be applied to higher education and development everywhere, for the data do not support such assumptions. We are only saying that a limited

number of case studies can generate useful guidelines for similar projects. We have tried to make governments, institutions, and educators
aware of new concepts and patterns of higher education not to prescribe
solutions to their problems. There are a variety of circumstances in
which universities function. Different circumstances require different
policies and approaches. Different views about education are true in
different situations. There is no single principle or monolithic truth.
It is important to identify the circumstances under which the various
concepts and guidelines can be effective, and we have tried to do this
in the report.

The impact of different problems and concerns is evident in the
several regional studies and reports. On government-university relations, the Latin Americans express the most concern that universities
are threatened by those who would make them an arm of government.
The Africans view the problem as less critical, more concerned perhaps by the staggering need for development. The Asians take a position someplace between these two views.

Speculating on the reasons, first we must look to historical and
national experience. Latin America is an area wracked by social conflict and class struggles. It is not surprising that the stronger and
more independent universities, seeking the pursuit of truth and the
advancement of knowledge, should strive to insulate themselves from
some of the conflict. The ordinary business of any educational institution requires some measure of stability and order, and when students
and faculty find themselves continually in a prerevolutionary or revolutionary situation, order is difficult if not impossible. National
universities in particular sometimes have become open battlegrounds
of social conflict--closed down during most if not all of the academic
year. Thus it is understandable that the better educational institutions
should seek to protect themselves. But to this there is a balancing
truth. The criticism is made that some scientifically and administra-
tively superior institutions have shut themselves off from the main
currents of social forces that will shape their nations' future. If isolation goes too far, superior educational centers may risk finding
themselves out of touch with governments and the mass of the people.

For Africa, the situation is different. Not only universities but
whole countries are at an earlier stage of development. The first task
for new governments is to create a sense of national identity. For
some, this may mean demonstrating the capacity to establish a superi-
or traditional university capable, within limits, of matching the standards of excellence of more developed states. To condemn this out of
hand is to ignore the dynamics of modern nationalism and obscure the
vital and important function of institutions such as the University of
Ibadan in "putting Nigeria on the world's educational map" and training
civil servants, government planners, and educators for its own and

other faculties. To jump on the development bandwagon to the extent of abandoning historic educational values would be a serious mistake. Indeed, anyone viewing the world's educational landscape knows there are at least two forms of slavish imitation. One is copying an imported model, such as Oxbridge or Harvard, and the other is to assume that instituting a homegrown variant of the land-grant university will meet all needs of the developing country. Both have lessons for those who will heed them, and the path to avoid is the slavish and unthinking imitation of either.

For countries in Africa the imperatives of national development determine the place of educational institutions. For one thing, the number of institutions of all kinds with capacity to serve is severely limited; higher educational institutions often have the largest concentration of trained manpower. The concept of the umbrella university emerged in Africa because the university provides a workable framework within which both higher education and applied and development-oriented activities are possible. Universities are too important to governments to be left entirely to educators. Both costs and necessity dictate that they serve the state within certain fundamental and well-defined sectors. There are too few trained people and too many urgent problems for universities to remain aloof. Moreover, the risk of government interference for some African countries, such as Tanzania, is mitigated because they have had the good fortune of having leaders, such as President Julius Nyerere, with a clear educational philosophy and the ability to formulate social purposes that education can serve. Africa may reach the point where fear of interference reaches the proportions of the Latin American countries that were studied, but, for the present, the problem seems to be less urgent.

Asia's problems and its stage of development fall somewhere between those of Latin America and Africa. The focus of the present study was on Southeast Asia. If South Asia or certain Middle Eastern countries had been included, the regional conclusions might have been quite different. The issue is one of the relations among problems, resources, and educational capacity. It is important in this connection to comment on the dominant trend of thought in the Asian report on manpower and mass education. The conclusion set forth by the Asian team is that unemployment performs a vital social and economic function. The Philippine case studies, in particular, and the Thai, Malaysian, and Indonesian studies, to some extent, are predicated on the existence of a free market economy with the natural forces of supply and demand and income disparity working themselves out in practice. The Asians, therefore, are less concerned about mass education and temporarily high levels of unemployment because they look forward to natural adjustments within the economy. Whenever there is an oversupply of educated personnel, salaries drop and expatriates, who may temporarily occupy professional positions in the economy, depart, freeing such posts. In the long run, the savings to the country and the resulting social benefits may exceed the cost of training. As countries approach the economic takeoff point, the existence of a reservoir of trained personnel allows them to meet new manpower needs and to move ahead rapidly. This more than overbalances the temporary frustration of those who upon graduation are unable to find employment. Singapore is a notable exception, for there the society has committed itself to the training of a specified number of people for occupations for which there is high demand.

The process of natural adjustment cannot, of course, take place in the absence of a free market economy. In China, salaries are determined not by supply and demand but by government fiat. One legitimate criticism of the Higher Education for Development Study is that it has excluded, with but a few marginal exceptions, such as Tanzania, all-out socialist experiments, such as China and Cuba. The Asian report is but one especially vivid example of the effect of social and economic circumstances on educational philosophy.

These differences persist on another issue that generates widespread controversy and debate. The study has found that the major source of educational innovation is an individual or group of individuals who take the lead. As a corollary, for many developing countries the principal source of resistance is the vested interest of establishment faculties that, for reasons of influence and privilege, fight to preserve the status quo. Students, who have been major forces for change in some Western countries, less often play this role in developing countries. One reason for their lack of influence is the limited amount of time they spend at an institution and another is their exaggerated social and economic expectations given national income and resources.

The principal roadblocks to change, however, are university and administrative structures inherited from colonial systems that are now obsolete because of escalating demands for change. The number of examples of educational innovation taking place outside established structures supports the call for institutional reform. Most developing universities need alternative management patterns. Decisions on development projects must be rapid, but the machinery of university governance impedes this. Too much power still resides in the hands of older traditionalists enthroned in university senates, and the most one can expect are the kinds of palliatives described by Frank Bowles, who wrote: "Educational innovation most often occurs through an infusion of outside aid which takes nothing away from the established holders of privilege and power but adds a new dimension initially financed by seed money."[3] The alternative is to hope that the ethos of change in one faculty will spread to others, as was the case with the medical group at the University of Valle in Colombia.

Governments' contributions to educational innovation and change
also are shaped by time and place. An officer of a leading United States
foundation stated the point most emphatically that, the government of
Peru pulled La Molina kicking and screaming into a program of service
to small and middle-sized landowners. If these are strong words, it
is, nonetheless, true that in Peru the Agrarian Reform Act of 1969
gave impetus to the Program for Transferal of Technology, which resulted in 1,000 students moving into rural areas. The program brought
greater realism to their classroom work and provided advice and consultation to farmers with small and medium-sized holdings. Elsewhere,
government may be less forthcoming, and it would be wrong to seek in
government the main source of innovation throughout the developing
world. It was two successful physicians and a rather traditional rector
who were the driving forces for change at the University of Valle. The
fact that Colombian government leaders such as Lleras Camargo also
backed these efforts gave a provincial undertaking national and regional
significance.

Yet governments in some developing countries may, for their own
good and sufficient reasons, falter at the point of supporting worthwhile
educational change. There are examples of developing countries that
request outside experts from technical assistance agencies but fail to
use their own well-trained leaders within their own boundaries. Often-
times lack of local incentives for innovators stifles initiative. Outside
agencies find that scientific equipment or seeds and fertilizer essential
to production-oriented programs are heavily taxed at ports of entry.
The ultimate frustration may be the isolation and neutralization of
genuine innovation, however urgent the need.

Finally, circumstances affect the responsiveness of society and
the use that is made of profoundly significant efforts, such as work-
study or service programs. "We are all engaged in the introduction of
work-study programs," declared the leader of the African regional
team at a meeting of the African group. The movement he described
has indeed taken on worldwide dimensions. In the United States,
Willard Wirtz, former secretary of labor, has proposed the establishment of community education-work councils in 25 cities and rural areas
to be administered by school officials, employers, members of labor
unions, and public members. The emphasis, James Reston writes:

> would be on local control, thrift and practical career guid-
> ance and counseling—at least five hours per year for all
> high school and college students on the basis of employ-
> ment possibilities, occupation by occupation. . . . one
> option for students might be a year or two of work between
> the ages of sixteen and twenty . . . [with] a careful analy-
> sis . . . of all laws or regulation that now impede the
> movement from study to work and vice versa.[4]

If a rich and powerful country such as the United States can no longer afford what Secretary Wirtz describes as "time traps of youth for education, adulthood for work, and old age for nothing" with "learning and earning passing as totally isolated chapters," how can the poorer countries. Indeed, there is growing evidence that the developing world has much to teach the developed world in this regard. No one has stated the issue more forcefully than the regional director for Asia: "We have been taught that the primary duty of students is to study, in order to render service to society. But, in fact, service itself has become study par excellence, and the simple truth is that a circle exists—study for service for study."

This is not the place to discuss in detail the advances and setbacks that have occurred in this worldwide movement. The report itself, and especially the case studies, throw the spotlight on a wide range of experience. For the purpose here, it suffices to say that local circumstances have shaped the possibilities, limitations, and directions of study and service. In some countries, the same kinds of restrictive legislation and regulations of which Secretary Wirtz spoke have been obstacles. In others, the educational hierarchy has been less than supportive. In traditional and revolutionary societies alike, students have not always welcomed opportunities to work in rural areas. Compulsory student service programs have met with opposition, and the idea of an obligatory period of service, whether during the long vacation or between secondary and tertiary schools, has led to student strikes. University students in both developing and developed countries have often seen themselves as a privileged class who were fleeing the misery and suffering of less privileged rural or urban areas. The choice between dining at commons high table or on the floor of a humble peasant hut was not difficult for some to make. Even in Tanzania, whose educational system was founded to advance a social revolution, President Nyerere encountered widespread resistance that has only gradually dissipated.

The chief source of resistance, however, comes not from the students but from certain faculty and community groups. More traditional, Western-educated faculty members have questioned whether education in the bush was part of the making of a university person. It was said that education's main business was to teach young people to think. The gulf that inevitably exists in most educational systems between faculty and students widened when students returned with experiences that were largely alien to the lives of their teachers. Add to this irritation community leaders' suspicion of young upstarts who knew less than they claimed, expressed radical ideas, and weren't particularly well equipped, and the circle of resistance is complete.

The work-study movement, however, has continued with increasing momentum in many places. It has prospered when the circumstances were ripe and programs were reinforced by human and cultural factors. Some cultures readily find a place for youth and take for granted its ability for early constructive work; others see teaching or rural leadership as immutably the province of elders. For example, it made an enormous difference that in Thailand Puey Ungphakorn accompanied volunteer students to rural areas and worked alongside them. Intelligent and thoroughgoing planning has been essential, and the success of current programs in Cameroon and Thailand can be explained largely on these grounds, whereas some of the recent difficulties in Ethiopia and earlier in Peru stem from planning deficiencies. When well-thought-out efforts have been made to allay community suspicions, acceptance has been more rapid. Successful programs also have had clear and realistic notions of what students can and cannot do.

It is still too early for an assessment of the movement. The recurrent theme in most questioning is, What are the permanent effects on students' attitudes and lives? For some countries, the first very tentative evidence is at hand. In Thailand, 65 percent of the students have returned on graduation to live and work in rural areas. No experiment, with the possible exception of Thailand, has yet introduced a comprehensive system of rewards and penalties, and it is worth noting that even in China strict discipline and controls did not prevent students from seeking to avoid service in rural areas during the Cultural Revolution and perhaps since then as well. There is a need for more tracer studies and more time to assess lasting changes in students' attitudes and contributions. Who can question the evidence, however, that far-reaching forces are at work and that developing countries have lessons to share with the rest of the world.

THE REAL ISSUES IN HIGHER EDUCATION FOR DEVELOPMENT

Apart from the singular lessons and guidelines to be derived from the case studies and reports, at least five central issues emerge and call for further study and deliberation.

First, the study demonstrates the possibility, indeed the necessity, for review and assessment by those who are close to the problem. No Westerner should expect the degree of cooperation and access that regional teams enjoyed in this inquiry. We take this for granted within our own culture. Most of the operating responsibility for equal opportunity programs in the United States is carried by minority people. The real issue for the intellectual community of assistance agencies having called into being a network of highly respected and responsible Third World educators is whether they will be called on again and their membership broadened and expanded. For agency bureaucrats, they are in one sense a rival group. Will donors be prepared to turn to them especially if this time they request a responsibility in planning and policymaking? Or will it be said they are less sophisticated, have less objectivity, and fall on the wrong side of the we/they divide?

Second, it has been said quite properly that the knowledge base of the present study is too limited, that generalizations at best fit a small and narrow group of cases, and that conclusions ought not be carried beyond the data. Participants agree and have for that reason proposed a second phase to the inquiry, increasing the number of case studies, conducting a few in greater depth, and expanding the geographic, political, and institutional bases of the study. A distinguished international advisory committee has been named to oversee the work, and the regional teams have shown a readiness to continue if the agencies should call on them.

Third, the existing data of the present study could be subjected to various types and methods of analysis: behavioral, the use of performance criteria, goal and achievement analysis, educational systems analysis, the use of cross-matrix techniques, cost-benefits, and so on. The present study is, in one sense, an exercise in macroanalysis with each institution being viewed as a unit within its larger society. Experienced educators brought to their task the rare gift of being able to size up an educational problem. Other approaches and techniques are possible, and the case studies in particular may furnish new material for these efforts. A new group of social scientists may be needed to carry out such work.

Fourth, the authors are very much aware that the study, while it may serve to open up important areas for discussion, can in no sense be considered definitive. This is true with regard both to concepts and to data. Conceptually, we have proceeded on the basis of certain broad categories of analysis. In the words of Dr. Gabriel Velazquez, a member of the Latin American team, "We are at an early stage in understanding higher education for development." For purposes of analysis, it was decided to see what higher education has contributed to national development in certain broad areas, such as food, public health, and improvement of overall national education systems. There are limits to such analysis, but the study has served at least to identify trends and benchmarks. The consensus of Third World educators was that these sectors encompassed the most urgent fields to which higher educational and other institutions of society must contribute if society is to survive. A similar view was expressed by developers with whom we talked.

Early on the question was asked, particularly in Latin America, What is the goal of higher education? Is it the development of education, that is, institution building, or is it education for development?

Out of the clash of these two divergent views a creative dialogue emerged. Whatever view prevails, certain central points persist. For either approach, staff development is essential. The first aim of a visiting professor in any developing university is to prepare for his departure by identifying and training his successor. For expatriates, their first mission is to render themselves nonessential. Help to individuals, as to institutions, must proceed on the basis of a plan with a beginning, a middle, and an end. There can be no substitute, however, for judgment on when to cut the natal cord. The most grievous errors occur when people or institutions are cast adrift too early or too late, and the test must be: When are local educators able to carry out alone the task they have set themselves? There are a few rough guidelines: At some point the visitor, if he or she remains, must move decisively into the background, must help to ensure that a sufficient critical mass of trained professionals and innovators is at hand so progress will not be undone, and must work to solidify institutional support.

A similar question arises in connection with institutional capacity. Concern is often expressed that if too much effort is devoted to urgent development needs, an institution may use up its intellectual capital. Often forgotten is the fact that universities in both developed and developing countries have self-sufficiency as one of their goals. They are resource-generating as well as training institutions. In the United States, one extreme example is the Massachusetts Institute of Technology whose teaching budget at one time was said to be only 10 percent of its overall budget. In assessing a developing country institution, it is important to know what success it is having in generating grants and contracts for important services to the community (Monterrey has 64 research contracts with industrial and governmental groups). Self-sufficiency and the ability to help oneself remain important indexes of educational capacity for both individuals and institutions.

The real issue remains: What is the main business of a university? Its leaders, in seeking to generate support, must ask themselves: How does a given project relate to its central purposes and capacities? The large universities in the Western world have sometimes found themselves on a precipice. One educator said that if we take one more government contract we are undone. Universities should not relieve governmental agencies in, say, public health or agricultural extension, or in industry for that matter, of their prime responsibility to carry out constitutionally defined tasks. One Latin American educator warns that we ought not to step out of our shoes and become a substitute for government. The province of universities is to combine training with pilot projects. Once these are tried and tested, it is for governments to replicate and extend them. The university must ask of every new undertaking, how does it relate to our historical values, to training and research, to improving the curriculum? At the same time, the legitimate purposes of universities vary from institution to institution. For example, in the United States, the land-grant universities started with different purposes from those of Harvard or Yale. So did Tuskegee Institute, which from the beginning had extension as one of its central purposes.

Higher education for development, then, is an evolving concept. It is not the same in West Africa and West Germany. The demands of developing countries require higher education to contribute to basic human needs. Failing to do so, higher education will lose public support and its essential constituency. Not every community-oriented problem is an expression of fundamental needs, however, and to certain demands a responsible university must be prepared to say no. There are other postsecondary and noneducational institutions that are better equipped to shoulder certain burdens, particularly as the system achieves greater diversity and maturity (Ngee Ann Institute in Singapore is an example).

Fifth, there remain issues and questions barely considered in the report that should be high on the list of any future agenda. Equity and social equality are such issues, but there are others. Universities cannot determine social mobility as such, but they can contribute to it. The university can join forces with other institutions, as American universities have, in theory at least, with community colleges and vocational schools. More attention must be paid to problems of access. On an even broader front, development-oriented universities must not neglect the training of national leaders who, in the words of William Bradley, president of the Hazen Foundation, "will transform the very fabric of their nation in respect to domestic and international affairs. These leaders . . . are likely to need a very different kind of education than the specialists in any type of technology including economics. . . . Thus we are dealing with people in the humanities and social sciences broadly defined."[5] In short, we are dealing with values. The land-grant and technology universities have moved to respond to this need. The future of developing universities may well depend on their responses to similar fundamental needs.

NOTES

1. Harrison Salisbury, personal letter to the author, August 4, 1975.

2. The Times Higher Education Supplement, September 5, 1975, p. 6.

3. Frank Bowles, discussion at meeting. (paraphrase)

4. New York Times, 7 December 1975, p. E15.

5. William Bradley, personal letter to the author, April 18, 1972.

2

THE PROBLEMS: WHAT NEEDS TO BE DONE?

For 18 months, 17 developing country educators looked within their own regions for programs that are making an impact on national development. They found 24 that face the problems of development and that use the resources of higher education to solve them.

The case studies resulting from this search focus on five major social questions: (1) How can the development needs of rural areas and, in particular, the small farmer be met? (2) How can poor urban families receive better health care, education, housing, recreation, and job opportunities? (3) How can effective health services and agricultural technology be brought to rural areas? (4) How can the formal school systems better educate more people of all ages in what they want and need to know? (5) How can jobs and training be matched to meet a society's need for economic growth and prevent widespread unemployment? Several of the programs, of course, attack more than one problem, and the program emphasis varies; different countries and institutions have different needs at different stages of their development. Most combine training and community service, preparing effective contributors to development and applying knowledge to the solution of social problems. The best programs at the same time define social needs.

Regional teams have reported on new and innovative educational structures that illustrate ways and means through which institutions of higher education are attacking the problems. They include (1) parallel training of professionals and technicians in the same program; (2) work-study programs in which class work and field experience enrich each other; (3) consultancy centers for assisting government, industry, and individual farmers; (4) continuing education programs for adults at both university and nonuniversity levels; (5) extension and summer programs using university faculties to teach university

17

courses at night and during vacations; (6) the year-round university; and (7) the development academy, which trains rural developers, conducts research, and carries out action programs.

Not all these efforts have gone smoothly or achieved their goals, and some have too brief a history for an authoritative judgment. Although many of them have set standards and provided models, they have all had, and still have, many and varied problems, and no one of them is considered by its operators as completely successful. But enough efforts have survived and grown to have created a momentum, and the number of institutions seeking to link higher education more productively to national development clearly has increased in recent years. In this chapter the five social questions and the case studies are described; in later chapters their common qualities are analyzed.

DEVELOPING RURAL AREAS

Most agricultural efforts have been directed at large commercial farmers. Recently, however, a number of postsecondary institutions have turned their attention to the urgent needs of the small farmer or farm worker. Because the problems of rural development involve not only food production but also distribution, nutrition, health, water supplies, housing, and education, the institutions have tried to take a broader and more integrated approach.

Five case studies have been concerned with the complex of problems associated with the well-being of the small farmer. At Gadjah Mada University in Indonesia, the Institute of Rural and Regional Studies is surveying rural patterns in order to help define the ideal local development unit and to encourage village leadership. In cooperation with the government, the National Agrarian University in La Molina, Peru, has designed a plan for services to medium and small landowners under the Agrarian Reform Law of 1969. Farmers, cooperatives, agricultural societies, and rural communities may request help of the University's Transferal of Technology Program, either directly or through the Ministry of Agriculture. Students and faculty volunteer for weekends or vacations to supply practical on-the-spot service and advice. The program not only helps the farmers but also gives the students and staff a new understanding of rural problems and their complex interrelationships. A growing number of student theses are based on practical agricultural problems, and professors from different disciplines have cooperated in giving courses for people from rural areas. The university also prepares pamphlets on farm management, sanitation, and crop technology.

The Institute of Development Research at Addis Ababa University,*
Ethiopia, formerly Haile Selassie I University, sought to define rural
development problems more precisely, but, in addition, under former
President Aklilu Habte, the university as a whole was involved in an
unusual effort to link itself to the rural community. To get their degrees, students were required to spend one academic year using their
university training in rural villages. Most students served as teachers
in local schools, filling a sometimes desperate need and acquiring an
awareness of local community conditions. One shortcoming has been
that students have not always seen the connection between this experience and their course work, partly because of planning and organizing
difficulties.

Three Thai universities in Bangkok—Kasetsart, Mahidol, and
Thammasat—are pooling their institutional specialties in agriculture,
medical science, and social sciences, and cooperating in the Maeklong
Project in rural development. It is a unique experiment in Asia in
interuniversity cooperation. Their goal is to find out what combination
of measures—improved health, sanitation, nutrition, new varieties of
basic crops, better schools, adult education, housing, roads to open
up commerce and trade—can bring a better way of life to the approximately 2 million people in this area. Teams, each made up of three
students and a university teacher-researcher, determine local needs
and enlist the support of villagers and village leaders while living
among them. Interested village residents receive training in health,
literacy, and crop and animal production, and eventually replace team
members as teachers and leaders.

The Institute for Agricultural Research and Special Services at
Nigeria's Ahmadu Bello University, the largest agricultural research
organization in middle Africa, diagnoses plant disease in the field,
organizes pest control, produces improved seed, and has put heavy
emphasis on information services to the farmer, including brochures,
films, radio programs, discussion groups, and demonstration days.
(In fact, a commentator on new agricultural developments, who has
his own television program, has become a folk hero.) The Institute
tries to improve not only cattle and crop production but also the quality
of village life. A rural economic research unit was set up by the University to find out why agricultural research had not brought about
anticipated changes in farming and rural life.

---

*The formal programs of this university have been suspended
since the change in Ethiopia's government in 1974.

DEVELOPING URBAN AREAS

In developing as well as developed countries, large numbers of rural dwellers have migrated to towns and cities, drawn by the glitter of the city and the hope of better living and jobs. Many of these migrants, however, find themselves settling in crowded urban slums under conditions hardly better than those they left. Their plight is both a result of rural poverty and a cause of new urban problems. Those who flee the conditions of the countryside may temporarily improve their life in the town, but children born in the slums face new misery. The problems of country and city life interlock.

The Federal University of Bahia in Brazil has set up the Center for Urban Development (CEDUR) as part of an overall University Program of Research and Education for Development (PROPED). Basing its activities on the earlier experience of a Faculty of Medicine community health program in a poor city district and on comparable experiences in Colombia, CEDUR focuses the resources of medicine, architecture, education, sociology, and engineering on the interrelated community problems of health, housing, education, sanitation, and recreation of 9,000 families in a district of Salvador.

A low-income urban population is also the target of the Research Program for Systems of Health Services Delivery (PRIMOPS) at the University of Valle in Colombia. The program is the outcome of a series of community health programs sponsored by the Faculty of Medicine in Siloé, a district of Cali, in 1955, and in the town of Candelaria, in 1958. The first program was designed to prepare medical students for community practice. As students and faculty started to work in Siloé's health center, they began to see that disease and health had social as well as biological causes, and, in Candelaria, the program broadened its focus to include the interrelations of health problems; teaching had led to research. PRIMOPS, established in 1973, is investigating the most efficient way to deliver health services to 90,000 people in a poor urban community. Both CEDUR in Brazil and PRIMOPS in Colombia will advise government agencies interested in community development, and both are trying to create an interdisciplinary model that can be adapted to similar areas. It is hoped that the results will be similar to those at Candelaria where mortality was reduced by about half.

IMPROVING HEALTH

One of the most difficult problems facing developing countries is how to bring effective health services to those who need them most, the majority poor. There are not enough physicians, nurses, or technicians, and those who do have medical training are reluctant or ill prepared to work in rural areas. Medical schools traditionally have emphasized hospital practice and research to the neglect of rural health and preventive medicine.

Important changes are taking place, however, within institutions of higher education. Programs have been developed to make better use of scarce health personnel by training and assigning them in teams that sometimes include community members. Research focused on community needs feeds back into teaching, and medical students learn clinical work in villages and farm communities. New training concepts—the umbrella university, for example, in which common courses for professional and technical personnel are attracting more nurses and technicians by bringing them into the university—are changing fundamental attitudes toward health practice.

Three case studies have focused on how to prepare health personnel for rural medicine. Each has, in the process, designed model systems of health care that government agencies have helped to introduce into other areas.

The University Centre for Health Sciences (UCHS) at the University of Yaounde in Cameroon trains doctors, nurses, and medical technicians side by side in a pioneering health program that bridges the gap between professional and technical workers. Students share common core courses, and all meet in rural community health assignments where, working as a team, they help run health services for a village or group of villages. The Centre was originally proposed by two Cameroon professors and developed with the support of the World Health Organization (WHO), the United Nations Development Pro gramme (UNDP), and the Cameroon government's National Planning Commission. It has been designed to change basic attitudes toward health practice and medical education through interdisciplinary study and public health orientation; its principal research is a continual evaluation of the country's health situation. It has already made an impact on students, teachers, the University, the government, and the public. The University launched a staff development program for the Centre four years before it opened. WHO and other donors helped Cameroon physicians take postgraduate training abroad, and the National Planning Commission identified qualified staff. Technical assistance agencies, including UNDP, WHO, Fonds Aide Cooperation (FAC), the Canadian International Development Agency (CIDA), and USAID, have supported training for other staff.

The health extension program at Ahmadu Bello University in Nigeria, geared to putting medical faculty and students in touch with community needs, runs its own small factory, which produces needed medical instruments and supplies. It has found that major health problems in rural areas are primarily the result of waterborne diseases and has taken the lead in a campaign for potable water. It has established health demonstration centers throughout the region that are similar to those in Cameroon.

PRIMOPS at the University of Valle in Colombia seeks not only to build a model of urban health care but also to redefine the basic medical group (public health specialist, medical doctor, nurse) for the delivery of health services. The program has set up a total system of health services for maternal and child care, from home visits to hospital care, and has so far trained 11 nurse's auxiliaries, 40 midwives, and 30 health promoters (primary school graduates living in the community who, after six weeks of training, give primary health care). The program is based on university study of community conditions.

Support for the project has grown. Government agencies were originally suspicious of the University's role, but University officials established better relations through clearly spelled-out agreements and monthly meetings with representatives of participating government agencies. The case study points out the advantage to the program of having, in government offices, physicians from the University of Valle who understood and agreed with the program's approach.

EDUCATING PEOPLE MORE EFFECTIVELY

"Increasingly," said Soedjatmoko, prominent Asian educational philosopher, "the need is being felt for a continuous effort to strengthen what might be called 'the learning capacity of the nation.'"[1] To bring knowledge and skills not only to an elite but also to the mass of people in developing countries, many formal systems of education will need radical reform. There is a widespread feeling that resources for education must be redeployed, curricula must be redesigned, teacher training must be restructured, and methods for engaging student interest and concern must be explored to meet this need.

There are, moreover, basic questions about the systems as a whole: How should investment in primary, secondary, and post-secondary education be balanced to meet the needs for more education for more people and for leaders and experts to manage the complexities of a developing society? How can learning be improved at all levels? How can formal systems provide for lifelong learning and a flexible relationship between classroom work and practical experience? How can access to education become more equitable?

The case studies seem to indicate that institutions of higher education have an essential role in performing the research that answers these questions and in implementing the answers. These institutions are beginning to look at national systems of education and offer curriculum guidance and help in teacher training. A few are taking the lead in school reform.

Everywhere there is a shortage of primary and secondary school-teachers, and often available teachers are inadequately trained for their jobs. To help solve Ethiopia's chronic shortage of secondary school science teachers, a special committee, representing the Faculty of Education, the Faculty of Sciences, and the College of Agriculture at Haile Selassie I University, developed an accelerated science teacher training program. Selected secondary school students combined university classwork and full-time teaching in Ethiopian schools. Students could then return to the University for one year to complete the requirements for the B.Sc. degree.

The University of Botswana, Lesotho, and Swaziland (UBLS), before its dissolution as a single institution, offered both content and methods courses in development studies for prospective teachers, based on a curriculum designed at Swaneng Hill School in Botswana. The University also established a program for primary school head-masters and, with the Botswana Ministry of Education, a joint program of primary school improvement.

To upgrade teacher training throughout the Nigerian states, the Institute of Education at Ahmadu Bello has encouraged the approximately 80 teachers' colleges to become affiliate members of the Institute. Among teachers of the affiliated colleges, the Institute organizes boards for curriculum study, provides subject areas specialists, moderates examinations, and sends mobile teacher training teams from one college to another to advise, assist, and train as required. The Institute also provides vacation refresher courses and training in educational administration. Recently, it took over from the Faculty of Education the one-year postgraduate diploma of education course in which practicing teachers alternate two summer school periods at the Institute with teaching under professional supervision and guidance.

A number of institutions of higher education are taking on responsibility for the total educational system of their countries. Tanzania's University of Dar es Salaam prepares and grades national examinations and is beginning to evaluate Tanzanian educational practices. Ahmadu Bello's Institute of Education acts as a coordinating agency for research in all matters pertaining to education and development of education in the northern region of Nigeria. It advises the ministries responsible for education in the region and collaborates with the ministries in planning and extending educational facilities.

With Unesco-UNICEF support, Ahmadu Bello also is experimenting with innovations in primary school curricula. The Institute prepares and tests teaching materials and textbooks and develops curricula in all subjects through teachers' workshops. It trains teachers in the use of the new curricula and teaching materials and operates 30 model primary schools.

Universities also perform a research and experimental role in national education. At the Federal University of Bahia in Brazil, a team of psychology students and education professors is working with 650 first-graders in state and municipal primary schools to develop vocabulary, writing skills, motor coordination, time and space perception, and math and social studies skills. The project grew out of an exploratory study in 1973 to find out why there were so many repeaters in the first grade; ten psychology students and a professor looked for ways in which teacher attitudes and teaching methods in the first grade affected student behavior. Almost 700 elementary students took psychological tests, and elementary schoolteachers answered questionnaires asking, among other things, their reaction to introducing change in the elementary schools. Government agencies do not participate in the project but support it indirectly.

Furthermore, universities may play a role in creating new institutions and methodologies. At the University of Antioquia in Colombia, the Department of Research and Extension of the Faculty of Education, along with the state secretaries of education of Antioquia and Sucre, initiated two primary school programs: one to improve the quality of rural five-grade schools, composed of about 30 students and one teacher, and the other to adopt flexible schedules and teaching methods in poorly attended rural schools so that children needed at home can study part time at home. Although the Faculty of Education is oriented to secondary education, it saw rural primary education as a major problem of the country. Rural teachers were inadequately prepared and had few materials to rely on. Normal schools, which train primary teachers, needed help.

The department brought together university, government, and normal school representatives with teachers, programmers, and illustrators to design and produce teaching materials and to improve teaching techniques. To help teachers manage five grades, the program set out to train them in group dynamics, psychology of learning, and evaluation. Teachers were also supplied with programmed course material and suggestions for activities in which students do practical tasks and actively observe their environment rather than merely sit at their desks.

So far, this project, called the One-Teacher School Program, has produced instruction materials for the student and guides for the teacher in the first four years of school and hopes to create a model of a one-teacher school program for normal schools' use. At present, 70 primary schools are using these materials. Teachers who have received training meet about four times a year to discuss the materials and their use.

The Program on Individualized Instruction and Flexible Schooling was designed as another experiment in programmed instruction for the rural schools and a way of meeting the problem of low attendance rates. It set up a primary school model that requires children to attend class only three days a week. During the remaining two days some school work is done at home. The days on which children will attend school are chosen in consultation with their parents, according to when they will be needed at home or to help out on the farm. The program has also modified the One-Teacher School materials and has set up a system of teaching cards to help individualize instruction.

Both programs have attracted widespread attention and public pressures for their extension in Colombia and in other parts of Latin America as well. The University of Antioquia, however, believes the programs require further study and evaluation before being applied on any large scale.

Continuing or adult education programs have introduced profound changes in the concept of higher education. A number of African universities provide evening classes for young people and adults who wish to complete their secondary education, study for university entrance examinations, or procure better employment. Courses include history, economics, shorthand and typing, accountancy, bookkeeping, mathematics, and English. Some departments organize seminars and workshops for farmers, small businessmen, lawyers, engineers, and others who wish to update knowledge or skills. The Institute of Adult Education at the University of Dar es Salaam in Tanzania produced a mass health campaign designed to reach 2 million people. It distributed over 2 million booklets, trained 75,000 discussion leaders, and created supplementary materials.

University extension services also add to lifelong learning facilities. The University of Nigeria, Nsukka, invites farmers to a week's conference to learn better ways to grow maize or yams. The Extra-Mural Department at Nigeria's University of Ibadan, in collaboration with Unesco, ran a functional literacy program for tobacco farmers. At the University of Ife in Nigeria the Department of Extension Education runs the Isoya Rural Development Project to serve as a laboratory for training rural development and agricultural workers and to serve as a research center on community development. The department helps farmers market their products and runs health and nutrition programs and a functional literacy program.[2]

CREATING JOBS AND EMPLOYMENT

To what extent should higher education be related to employment? Many developing country planners and educators are convinced that students should be trained for specific manpower needs because these needs are so urgent. There is an acute shortage not only of doctors but also of teachers, medical technicians, agricultural extension agents, managers of rural cooperatives, and engineers. At the same time, students graduating from many institutions of higher education have unmarketable skills and cannot find jobs.

Views differ on what should be done about such manpower discrepancies. There are those who think that institutions of higher education should produce higher level manpower to meet a country's employment needs and that governments should have the right to restrict enrollment on the grounds of opportunities and efficiency. Others see high-level manpower as only one of several purposes for higher education (such purposes include transmittal of knowledge and culture, and service to the community), and they are likely to differ on the relative importance of these purposes. Still others doubt that institutions of higher education should be required to produce high-level manpower in immediate response to the demands of the market. The Asian team's report, with some reservations, has taken this latter position.

Taking the first view, the minister for national education and culture in Burundi, Gilles Bimazubute, said that Burundi must build up a work force, "not of intellectuals primarily but rather of the technicians, specialists and civil servants that the country needs. Only in this way," he said, "can we justify the enormous funds spent on education every year.[3] The view is illustrated by case studies in Tanzania, Singapore, and, to some extent, in Thailand Malaya, Monterrey, Mali, and Mauritius.

In Tanzania, controls are exerted at a preuniversity level where quotas are established on the basis of need. As demand requires, students are channeled in secondary education not only toward broad areas such as science but also more specifically to chemistry or physics. In Singapore, the Ngee Ann Institute downgraded itself from a degree-granting to a diploma-awarding institution to meet demands for middle-level manpower. It prepares a specified number of personnel for subprofessional and technician posts, predetermined by government and educational planners. Singapore's manpower needs have determined both the nature and number of its institutions of higher education. "The overall philosophy guiding the planning for higher education is one which aims at selective as opposed to mass access,"[4] said Dr. Toh Chin Chye, former vice-chancellor of the University of Singapore and minister of science and technology.

Other systems geared to selective access are Mali and Mauritius. Malian higher education developed not through the establishment of a traditional university but rather through five institutions intended to meet special employment needs: the Higher Teacher Training School, the Rural Polytechnic Institute, the National Engineering School, the

National School of Public Administration, and the Medical School. Who can go ahead and who cannot is rigidly prescribed. For similar reasons of manpower need, most of the 1,000 students at the University of Mauritius take courses in some way connected with the production of sugar cane. The rationale for these choices is that manpower surveys have shown patterns of surpluses and shortages, and thus higher education has a responsibility to train people to bring supply in line with demand.

High-priority job training needs in a country also depend on the level of resources. The majority of developing countries need health and extension agents, rural administrators, and subprofessional technicians. More developed countries like Singapore, the Philippines, or Mexico may be ready for more top business executives as well as middle management personnel, but here, too, the numbers trained are often determined by specific manpower needs.

In Monterrey, the hub of industrial development in Mexico, for example, the Monterrey Institute of Technology and Advanced Studies (ITESM) trains technical and professional manpower for industrial growth. At a somewhat higher level, it provides research, technical, and extension assistance to manufacturing and service industries, including agriculture and mining, but the research and service contracts are used to improve teaching as well as to solve industrial and agriculture problems. The program is geared to manpower needs. The Institute considers that it contributes to development primarily by producing graduates with a solid background, a responsible attitude toward the country's problems, and the skills to solve them. The demand for Monterrey graduates exceeds the supply.

Developing countries often have found it difficult, however, to establish manpower requirements. Frequently they do not have the necessary statistical data on which to base manpower estimates, and even when they do, priorities and training requirements change. A Unesco report on two African education conferences states:

> An economic plan of five years' duration rests upon the formulation of an educational plan in which decisions about type of training must be taken approximately seven years before the trainee will graduate from a school of higher education. The education of the trainee will in turn depend upon decisions about the number and type of teacher training institutions that should have been taken seven years earlier still. So that, in order to service an economic plan of five years, it is necessary to formulate a corresponding educational plan for about 20 years. [5]

The Asian Regional Report in this study proposes that the answer, especially in Southeast Asia, is mass access to higher education, that is, postsecondary institutions should not be more selective but should open their doors wider. For developing countries that have satisfactory growth rates, argues the Asian Report, "the more trained people there are, the better the prospects of developing the society (not just the economy)." The Asian Report maintains that "in the economic development of those nations which today are considered advanced . . . the highest payoff . . . has been investment in education. . . . Modern society needs all the manpower it can get."

The Development Academy of the Philippines (DAP) points up the advantage of having a large reservoir of trained people. A semigovernmental institution, set up in 1973 to deal with urgent development problems, the Academy was able to put together a staff of almost a thousand specialists, trained in higher educational programs in the Philippines. It has developed a package of training and development-oriented research and action programs in which groups of engineers, architects, economists, urban planners, social scientists, systems analysts, and business management experts, working together, inform, advise, and plan and implement programs for government and industry. Its staff are products of an extensive higher education system, and the Academy thus depends on a previous generation of training.

The program of the Asian Institute of Management (AIM), also in the Philippines trains needed manpower but does not tie numbers closely to predictions of need. The Institute is the result of a cooperative effort of two leading graduate schools of business administration and created on the model of the Harvard Business School. However its main efforts are concentrated on adaptation to Asian needs. Using the case method to develop analytic and decision-making skills, the Institute trains executives in junior, middle, and upper management levels. The Institute has made vigorous efforts to build a bank of case studies from all over Asia, which are linked to development needs. It seeks an international faculty and student body, of which it hopes at least 40 percent will come from other Asian countries. Its long-range goal is to train a pool of management specialists for countries throughout Asia.

The Asian Report acknowledges that there are "imbalances and inefficiency in the educational effort as well as inadequate government policies to absorb the output of the educational system." It concludes, however, that "the educated unemployed in Southeast Asian developing countries represents a temporary stage in development. . . . Under these circumstances, it is certainly better for long-run development to have reserves of trained people rather than a shortage."

All this assumes a free market rather than a socialist economy. In a free market, supply and demand determine salary levels; as the supply of qualified manpower increases, salaries go down, reducing

the costs of manpower and attracting fewer expatriates. At the same
time, as the supply of unskilled workers shrinks, their wages go up,
narrowing the income gap.

Furthermore, the Asian Report maintains, higher education must
produce "groups and individuals who provide the nation with alternative
policy directions, management concepts and resource allocation/distri-
bution schemes." Making these people available, says the Asian Report
is "not a luxury but a necessity for development, for they contribute
not only to the efficiency of public and private management but also to
the openness of society."

Leading authorities differ sharply on the ideal relation of higher
education to employment. This report has tried to summarize the
sometimes conflicting conclusions of the qualified observers who have
made these studies. They represent different philosophies and different
national experiences. Most agree, however, that different circumstances require universities to play different roles, and manpower
policies must reflect, among other things, a country's stage of economic and social development. Educational priorities compete with
other needs, and mass higher education is not feasible if resources
are not available.

ASSISTING IN DEVELOPMENT PLANNING (CONSULTANCY CENTERS)

If institutions of higher education are to be agents of social development or instruments of change in society, they cannot limit their
role to community action programs, to manpower training, or even to
educational reform. Universities especially cannot give up their traditional role as centers of intellectual leadership without endangering
the very meaning and direction of development. A list of what needs
to be done by higher education, therefore, must include recognizing
and analyzing the most urgent national problems, planning their solutions, and educating people who can do both.

A number of institutions in the case studies have joined with government or sometimes with business to determine the nation's priorities, either as consultants or as coplanners. Many of these institutions
struggle to maintain enough autonomy to ensure an independent voice;
some try to attract apathetic or suspicious ministries to planning partnerships. Consultancy centers, some autonomous, appear in institutions in all three regions. They may offer specific technical expertise
and facilities or more general policy counsel.

The Technology Consultancy Centre at the University of Science
and Technology in Kumasi, Ghana, is an autonomous unit through which
the University makes available expertise and resources to assist in

development. It negotiates contracts with outside agencies and recruits
consultants from among staff and from outside. A pioneer in stimulating grass-roots rural industrialization, the Centre tries to find local
substitutes for imported products, to promote small-scale, labor-
intensive industries, and to develop products cheap enough to find a
local market. In one such effort it makes glue from starch and in
another manufactures simple scientific instruments for secondary
schools. Its research projects include producing fiber, hybridizing
pigs, testing local materials for low-cost housing, developing new dyes
and looms for village craftsmen, testing local clays, designing pumps,
and investigating the medicinal properties of local herbs.

In the Maeklong Integrated Rural Development Project in Thailand,
a major emphasis during the next year will be on how to identify and
solve problems of social development and rural welfare. Each research
leader in the field prepares a list of problems and ranks them in order
of difficulty, possibility of solution, and probable impact. An executive
committee screens these analyses and selects problems that seem to
offer the greatest chance of successful solutions. Once program priorities are set, research leaders study and discuss proposals and prepare work plans for an interrelated series of pilot projects. University
staff may take direct action or may intervene with government organizations and private agencies, coordinating activities and evaluating
their effectiveness.

Among other consultancy centers offering advice in special fields
are those in health and agriculture. The University Centre for Health
Sciences in Cameroon monitors health services in the country as a
whole, and PRIMOPS at the University of Valle in Colombia advises
the Maternal and Child Division of the Ministry of Health. In Peru,
the Ministry of Agriculture relays farmers' requests for consultation
or assistance to the National Agrarian University's Program for
Transferal of Technology, which sends out students and professors
to work with villagers in rural areas.

The Monterrey Institute of Technology and Advanced Studies receives consultant fees from business, industry, and government, under
contracts to study specific problems. Last year, its Division of Engineering and Architecture conducted 64 research projects under this
arrangement. For industry, the ITESM investigated and tested building
materials (fire-resistant paints, glass foam, and plastic reinforced
with bamboo), designed mathematical models for the construction industry, and analyzed problems of ventilation in low-cost housing.
Government agencies have sponsored studies of recycling solid waste
for construction filler and finding industrial uses for arid-zone plants.
The division developed in-service curricula, formulated regulations
for controlling contaminants in industrial and domestic wastes, designed a method for purifying industrial water for human consumption,

and measured contaminants in air and water to help the city meet environmental standards. When it has designed a solution, the Institute has finished its job; it leaves implementation to the contracting agency.

Like Monterrey, the Development Academy of the Philippines receives fees from its government and business clients for planning, training, and program implementation. It contributes by analyzing a wide range of development problems, from small irrigation systems to national land use and industry location. It has prepared ecological management schemes, advised some 135 corporations and factories, developed medium- and small-scale industry, and designed computer systems for improved decision making.

The DAP regards development as a multifaceted effort and training as linked with management, project monitoring, and financing. In its unusual training programs for government and business executives, officers of rural banks (about 900 have been trained to date), rural judges and land reform specialists, the DAP trains all the key executives of an agency or industry in a course tailored to the resources and goals of the clients. It seeks to foster, through a total program of academic courses and social interaction, a sense of team work, and it follows up the training with on-the-job evaluations and assistance to trainees.

NOTES

1. Higher Education and Social Change, Volume II: Case Studies, ed. Kenneth W. Thompson, Barbara R. Fogel and Helen E. Danner (New York: Praeger, 1976).

2. This survey of Nigerian postsecondary institutions was made by A. Babs Fafunwa, dean of the Faculty of Education, University of Ife, Nigeria, in a special report for this project. See Higher Education and Social Change, Volume II: Case Studies, ed. Kenneth W. Thompson, Barbara R. Fogel, and Helen E. Danner (New York: Praeger, 1976).

3. "Education Reform in Burundi," IIEE Bulletin (February 25, 1974).

4. August 1972, Convocation Address by Dr. Toh Chin Chye, Vice-Chancellor of the University of Singapore and Minister for Science and Technology.

5. Quoted in Choh-Ming Li, "Emerging Patterns of Higher Education in Asia," Institute of International Education Report, 1973, p. 7.

3

THE INSTITUTION: ORGANIZING FOR DEVELOPMENT

The emerging view of universities playing a more active role in society poses a series of challenges to universities and other post-secondary institutions. How can these institutions combine extension programs with training and research essential to the purpose of higher education? How, in institutions built on separation of disciplines and professions, can they mobilize the various disciplines into a concerted attack on complex problems? How can they cooperate with government, political parties, or private interests without giving up independence of thought and action? How can they attract community participation and cooperation? Can the institution offer a new, more comprehensive, more action-oriented program from within an old structure?

INSTITUTIONAL MODELS

There are a variety of ways in which institutions of higher education can be organized for development. Some institutions deal primarily with curriculum, some combine curriculum and training, some offer advice to government, and some delegate development problems to satellite organizations with varying degrees of autonomy. Different purposes seem to produce different organizational models, and each model has a different mixture of the ingredients that higher education contributes to development: understanding, training, advice, and methods of implementing theory through social action. It is important to know what mixture makes the most sense for a particular institution at a particular time.

In a tentative analysis of case studies and thoughtful opinion, four basic models have been identified, each of which emphasizes one way higher education contributes to development: by broad understanding, training, consultation, and community action. The models are neither pure nor exact and they tend to overlap. Nevertheless, they do suggest certain broad categories that give focus and order to thinking.

The first model is the traditional university in which teaching and research are directed largely toward understanding development needs rather than doing something specific about them; the institution expects its graduates to acquire a general knowledge of arts, sciences, and social studies and to bring this knowledge to bear indirectly on social problems. Building such understanding in a critical mass of individuals may be the step any country must take before any of its institutions can participate directly in development. (In the past decade, many graduates of this institutional model have returned to their own or other institutions, strengthening faculties and often paving the way for new approaches to development.) It may be that new nations seeking national identity strive first for the excellence of an outstanding traditional university. National leaders, moreover, who can bring about basic transformations in domestic and international policy require more than technical or specialist training. The more traditional university, strong in humanities and social sciences, may still be essential for this kind of broad development education. Soedjatmoko of Indonesia remarks that, "A sense of moral direction, cultural continuity, and a self-image and identity as a nation, but also the capacity to relate economic and social goals to moral purposes are crucial elements in any sustained development effort."[1]

A second model emphasizes training for development jobs, therefore starting with a need. Often institutions conforming to this model have a partly autonomous faculty or special institute inside the university structure in which research or training is closely connected to social needs. An example is the medical faculty at the University of Valle in Colombia, where public health centers set up to train medical students for practice in rural areas produced new research on medical treatment and fed back the results into the faculty's curriculum. In two Latin American national universities, La Molina in Peru and Bahia in Brazil, curriculum, teaching, and research meet the needs that its social action programs uncover. Ngee Ann Technical College in Singapore, the Monterrey Institute of Technology and Advanced Studies in Mexico, and the Maeklong Integrated Rural Development Project in Thailand are other examples of training tailored to meet special needs.

In a third model, the institution, usually through a separate development institute, furnishes advice to government and development planners. Development institutes, such as those at Addis Ababa University in Ethiopia, the University of Nairobi in Kenya, and Gadjah Mada University in Indonesia, generally operate with considerable autonomy and are attached to the institutions of higher education with varying degrees of interchange. Advisers and consultants may also come from faculties within the institution, as in the University of the Philippines at Los Baños.

A fourth model is geared to direct public policy training and action. A wholly independent institute, such as the Development Academy of the Philippines, with its own university-trained staff complemented by consultants drawn from a broad manpower pool, may devote itself entirely to research, training, and action required by specific development problems. The international agricultural institutes are outstanding examples of this kind of single-purpose model.* Set up to solve food production problems of the developing countries, they have continued to focus scientific research and training on developing food grains and livestock. Their aim is simple and unambiguous, and their means of evaluating success are also clear-cut. Their directors attribute much of their success to their ability to concentrate their efforts on a few clearly defined problems, and both training and research are geared to making available improved food technology.

Out of this still tentative analysis two general propositions emerge: (1) the more the activities within an institution of higher education are oriented to action, the more they are likely to be detached from the parent institution in an institute or special project; and (2) the price of such detachment may be the siphoning off of the more action-oriented people from the institution and the isolation of the students and remaining professors from the social problems handed over to the institute. Institute personnel also are increasingly separated from teaching and university work. There are cases, on the other hand, where the institute draws together a variety of disciplines to solve a development problem and this interdisciplinary approach is then carried back to teaching and research. How to find ways to relate curriculum, research, and action so that each enriches the other is a matter of importance in all models. In all models, too, the impact on development may be less the immediate or local benefits than the way the institution influences the whole philosophy of higher education in the country.

----

*Higher Education for Development questionnaires sent to the directors of international agricultural institutes brought replies from the International Rice Research Institute (Philippines), the International Maize and Wheat Improvement Center (Mexico), the Asian Vegetable Research and Development Center (Taiwan), the International Crops Research Institute for the Semi-Arid Tropics (India), the Centro Internacional de Agricultura Tropical (Colombia), and the International Institute for Tropical Agriculture (Nigeria). J. George Harrar and F. F. Hill, with other directors, met with HED staff and certain donor representatives to discuss what part of their experience was applicable to other higher education for development programs.

SERVICE, EXTENSION, TRAINING, RESEARCH

Over the past ten years, a number of service and study programs have been developed, designed to bring students in touch with community problems. Some programs have been voluntary and others have involved compulsory service mandated by government or university; some have been part of the curriculum and some have been added before or after academic terms. Most were instituted with a variety of hopes: that they would counteract student elitism, that they would motivate study and interest in social problems, that they might even contribute to constructive community change. In Ethiopia, students were sent to teach for a year in rural areas; in Peru, students at La Molina help farmers and farm groups to use new technology; and volunteer Thai students serve as teachers and community workers in rural villages. Students in Ghana's University of Science and Technology undertake, during term time, fieldwork in industry and agriculture in different parts of the country.

The emphasis on work-service-study is more than an educational frill in the developing countries. Most of the programs are efforts to influence student values as well as learning. In addition, both educators and students feel that a new form of training or experience is needed to make class work more meaningful. Even at the Ngee Ann Technical College in Singapore students find it difficult to apply what they have learned to practical situations or real-life problems. Philip Limb, Deputy Principal of Ngee Ann, suggests that for some, where education and learning are highly valued in their own right, applying what has been learned is of secondary importance. Choh-Ming Li, vice-chancellor of the Chinese University of Hong Kong wrote: "The Asian cultures have long produced the tradition of respect for book-learning and disdain for professionalism, not to mention manual labour."[2]

Institutions are also looking for ways other than training in which they can bring their resources to bear on specific development problems. African Regional Director Aklilu Habte has said: "The future of extension is a vital issue for higher education in Africa and Asia. Universities need guidance and help in developing service and continuing education systems."[3]

Case studies show that service activities are most effective, and serve teacher, researcher, and student best when they feed back into the formal educational program. The theoretical researcher hears about practical problems from the extension workers, and the teacher of practical skills draws on the researcher's findings and results. For the students, service activities can illuminate theory and link up with textbook study (although staff may be reluctant to revise courses to equip students for village work and to take into account practical experience). In only a few cases, such as Monterrey and the Technology Consultancy Centre in Ghana, is there more staff than student participation. While internship cannot substitute for theoretical training, professors can help students develop professional competence by combining theory and practice, by emphasizing problem-solving skills, and by evaluating service experience in terms of theory. At the University of Dar es Salaam, teaching through research programs give second-year students the chance to acquire the skills of data collection, collation, and analysis in local research projects, while at the same time deepening their knowledge of local problems and adding to the information available for teaching.

Ideally, student fieldwork should receive course credit, as it does in Ahmednagar's social work program, which recently achieved university M.A. and Ph.D. status. In this Indian college, work in nearby villages is evaluated by professors who work in shirtsleeves alongside students. (A major achievement of the international agricultural institutes and of national agricultural programs has been to wean their trainees away from their contempt for dirty hands.) Students also earn academic credit (and a salary) in Gadjah Mada's Kulia Kerga Niata Mahaseiswa Project in which students in three subregions near Jogjakarta, Indonesia, help villagers to implement such government programs as planting crops, raising poultry, and reforesting hillsides.

Although the Program for Transferal of Technology at the National Agrarian University in La Molina, Peru, involves only those who volunteer, many do volunteer, and participating students and staff combine service and research in rural areas that ask for assistance. Professors supervise student research and theses, and eventually the University plans to give academic credit for field activities. In turn, the quality of advice furnished to rural clients has improved. In the first year of the program, 1,200 students and 80 professors visited villages and farms, and 42 research projects were completed. (A cattle food industry was established as a result of one thesis.) According to the La Molina case study, "Work in the rural areas . . . creates an informal, close relationship between professors and students and begins to transform the teaching process, since it changes the impression that professors and students have of each other." Professors and students live together with community people during their work and share experiences and deprivations.

Designers of the Maeklong Project foresee long-term benefits to the universities themselves through faculty and student participation in development activities. Faculty teaching based on practical experience has proved more effective; students acquire a better understanding of rural development from a combination of such teaching and their own fieldwork. As noted in the Introduction, and it bears repetition, Puey Ungphakorn, HED Asian Regional Team Director and rector of

Thammasat University, said: "We have been taught that the primary duty of students is to study, in order to render service to society. But, in fact, service itself has become study par excellence, and the simple truth is that a circle exists—study for service for study."

Such new educational ideas, however, take root only when students and staff are well prepared and when faculty and community members, including local professionals, do not arouse antagonism and suspicion in one another. In Ethiopia, the Ethiopian University Service (EUS) work program was meant to provide students with both academic and service experience. The field experience, however, did not always reinforce classwork, and there has been mounting criticism of insufficient planning. In Ghana, as well as in Ethiopia, some students felt their fieldwork assignments were poorly designed to further their learning, and, in addition, professors had little understanding of how to relate experience to classroom work. It was hard to convince Cameroon medical faculty, too, that learning outside the university was good enough to receive credit. And in Ethiopia and elsewhere students sent to teach found only limited opportunities to do so.

In Colombia, another problem developed. Medical students at the University of Valle, each assigned to watch over the health needs of an individual family in the community of Siloé, became so emotionally involved with the family that they sometimes assumed father roles, thus weakening the building of more independent family units and affecting their own professional objectivity. Cameroon medical students in the University Centre for Health Sciences had another kind of psychological shock, that of returning to conditions of misery they thought they had escaped. Both the Colombian and Cameroon programs later tried to prepare students for their own reactions to community work by explaining the reasons for them. While these and similar difficulties have appeared in some experiments, service-study programs in many places have provided effective links between curriculum and understanding of social issues. At Thammasat University in Thailand, 65 percent of the graduates who went through the Graduate Volunteers Service Program returned to rural areas to live and work. Data of this type could be collected in future case and tracer studies elsewhere to determine the lasting effect on students of the new service programs.

THE INTERDISCIPLINARY APPROACH

It is often extraordinarily difficult to bring together different academic disciplines for work on a common problem, and yet all social problems require interdisciplinary skills and knowledge. Equally important, if graduates of higher education are to be society's leaders

and planners, they need a broad social and historical perspective that
is difficult to achieve in separate academic disciplines.

One way to unite the efforts of more than one faculty has been to
start a project or service activity in one faculty and bring others into
it as needed (for example, the health program at the University of
Valle and the urban development program at the Federal University of
Bahia). Another way has been to combine different universities. In
Thailand, when Kasetsart, primarily an agricultural university, could
not supply all the expertise needed for a large-scale development project, Thammasat University, oriented to the social sciences, and
Mahidol University, which emphasizes the medical sciences, agreed
to join forces with Kasetsart in the Maeklong Project.

Curriculum reorganization has been another vehicle for interdisciplinary cooperation. The Faculty of Arts and Social Sciences at
the University of Dar es Salaam was reorganized in 1971 to incorporate
problem solving as part of its overall philosophy. Traditional subject
divisions of the degree structure were replaced by multisubject streams
and interdisciplinary courses, such as "Development Studies" and
"East African Societies and Environment." One of the coordinators of
the latter course observed that it is one of the very few successful experiments in African universities "to create areas of knowledge, and
methods of acquiring knowledge, that are both indigenously relevant
and interdisciplinary."[4]

Teaching at the University Centre for Health Sciences in Cameroon
also uses themes rather than subjects, and brings medical, nursing,
and technical students together in common core courses. All students
have training in three technical units—biomedical sciences, clinical
sciences, and public health—representing groups of attitudes, skills,
and knowledge. In this umbrella university, organization reinforces
the integration of subject matter, unit heads merely facilitate staffing,
equipment, and space, while the overall director has responsibility for
teaching, service, and research and for harnessing all resources to
the objectives of the Centre.

Initially, both faculty and students opposed the Cameroon program.
Some staff members resisted the radical change in teaching and some
were disoriented by the new system. Students feared substandard
training that would prepare them only for "work in the bush." Like
work-study programs, new interdisciplinary approaches need careful
orientation and explanation in which staff, students, and public participate.

Another approach to multidisciplinary work has been to establish
semi-independent development institutes. The Institute of Development
Research at Addis Ababa University in Ethiopia and the Institute of
Rural and Regional Studies at Gadjah Mada University in Indonesia are
examples. A variation of the more usual development institute, the

Development Academy of the Philippines, is staffed by graduates of several universities, is independent, and is financed by both the government and private sources.

Autonomous institutes have several advantages. They can coordinate research and training on specific social and community problems without going through sometimes unwieldy university structure and channels. They bring together the requisite disciplines. They can offer such incentives as transportation, housing, or extra salary to staff participants; and they often provide faculty members with unusual opportunities for specialized research. (Too little time for research is a common complaint of faculties in most developing countries.) They concentrate the experience and intellectual powers of a group of outstanding scientists and scholars on a single set of problems.

They have disadvantages as well. Autonomous institutes may not provide for tenured faculty positions, presenting career obstacles to otherwise interested staff members. (Outside donor agencies can sometimes help by insisting that researchers whom they support have continuing appointments.) They may also be caught between dual loyalties, to government, on the one hand, and to an academic department, on the other—a problem not unknown in developed countries.

Although their independence is a spur to action programs, one further hazard of the autonomous institutes is that, in becoming separated from the parent institution, they may weaken rather than strengthen the educational training and research effort as a whole. To guard against this danger, the Research and Education Program at the Federal University of Bahia, Brazil, requires students in teacher training and medical programs to work within multidisciplinary action programs and to exchange information. At Ahmadu Bello University in Nigeria, according to a university publication, "All the Institutes work closely with their sister faculties, often sharing staff. This has produced an interesting blend of academic programmes and direct service to the community." African Regional Director Aklilu Habte says that the twin questions about development institutes are how to make them more relevant and how to combine them more effectively with other university efforts.

RELATIONS WITH GOVERNMENT

John Hannah, former administrator of USAID and now executive director of the World Food Council, has observed that the single most urgent factor affecting the contribution higher education makes to development in the developing countries is its relation to government and the nation's political and social leadership as a major consumer of its product. Many worthy experiments falter precisely in this area. The vice-chancellor of one of Nigeria's newest and most development-oriented universities, in discussing the problem of government-university communication in the placement of his university's graduates in government positions, has noted, that we did everything right from the standpoint of development, but the government has not wanted our product. "There is a serious need," said the African Regional Report, "to examine university-government relationships."

In providing up to 25 percent of their national budgets for education, governments understandably wish more voice in how the money is spent. In many countries "the university no longer stands apart from the government," says the African Report. Indeed, when a nation wishes to create a sense of national identity through higher education, it essentially takes over the system. Once the university and government are wed, their bonds can range from cooperation to domination. There is a similar variation in relations with private enterprise.

The Tanzania case provides an example of the most intimate university-government relations. An informed observer points out that "higher education in Tanzania gains strength from the fact that it is developing within a clear educational philosophy which assigns the university a central role in . . . development."[5] Government planners fix the intake of secondary students not only as to numbers but also as to specific fields of study.

The link between governments and service institutions, such as the Economic Research Bureau, the Bureau of Resource Allocation and Land Use, and the Institute of Kiswahili Research, is direct and continuous. The budget of the University of Dar es Salaam is presented to the parliament by a government ministry, and plans for university development are routed through the several government ministries. Certain staff at the University are on secondment from the ministries, and some University staff are posted to particular ministries; the two-way flow is intended to join the theoretical and the practical and to reduce status distinctions. Nearly all students hold government bursaries, and government representatives make up 38 percent of the University Council. The president of the republic, who is chancellor of the University, appoints the vice-chancellor, and the first vice-chancellor was formerly national executive secretary of the TANU political party. For one to two years after secondary school and before they are admitted to the University, students must demonstrate performance and commitment to community service, working alongside peasants and workers in rural and urban areas. They must be recommended for entry to the University by their employers and by the TANU branch in their workplace.

While Tanzanian education is perhaps most closely linked with government development planning, higher educational institutions in

other countries are moving in much the same direction. Political
considerations have taken precedence over all other university goals
at the University of Malaya. In order to stabilize a society torn by race
riots and give increased educational opportunities to the majority ethnic
group, government has taken more and more of a role in higher education, decreeing that Bahasa Malaysia should be the main language of
instruction in the universities and controlling enrollment ratios of ethnic groups, principally by requiring that three to four government jobs
out of five should go to Malays. In Mali, the various institutes of higher
education depend upon particular ministries, such as education, agriculture, and interior, and report directly to them. In Cameroon, the
University Centre for Health Sciences relates to a network of inter-
ministerial commissions, and the government health services fixes
the allowances of teachers.

In Nigeria, Ahmadu Bello's institutes—Education, Administration,
Health, and Agricultural Research—each has a governing board made
up of half government and half University members under the chairmanship of the vice-chancellor. In Singapore, the Ministry of Finance
carries on continuing manpower planning, and forecasts are sent for
comment and reaction to Singapore's three technical institutes, which
then negotiate for government funds for proposed programs. The governments' overall manpower development plans determine the training
level at both the Ngee Ann Technical College in Singapore and the University of Science and Technology in Ghana.

Indicative of the expanding role of governments in education, the
Latin American Report, summing up its case studies, says: "All of
the programs have been carried out in conjunction with the government,
either directly sponsored and financed by the government as in the Peru
case, through a decentralized (governmental) institute as in the Antioquia case, closely related in its planning and execution as in the Valle
and Bahia cases, or carrying out specific studies for the government
as in the Monterrey case."

Government, moreover, needs institutions of higher education
not only for manpower training but also for help in identifying problems and in bringing its resources to bear on them. The postsecondary
institution is well equipped to serve as consultant, researcher, evaluator, or designer of pilot studies that integrate agriculture, health,
credit, and marketing. It can test on a small scale the effectiveness
of any given package. Ideally, it can act as a seeing-eye dog for government planning. The three cooperating universities in Thailand are
performing such a function in the Maeklong Project, and the Institute
of Rural and Regional Studies at Gadjah Mada University in Indonesia
is doing the same.

Government's view of the university as an instrument of development is critical to the university's ability to conceive and practice a

new developmental role. The president of Tanzania has stated: "The role of a university in a developing nation is to contribute: to give ideas, manpower, and service for the furtherance of human equality, human dignity, and human development."[6] With such support, the university is able to break away from colonial educational patterns and to experiment with degree structure, course content, and organization, among other aspects of the educational system.

As higher education plays an increasingly important role in development, however, it must at the same time guard against direct government control. Alexander Kwapong, vice rector of the United Nations University, observed,

> . . . a university which is a mere tool of government and
> a mere department of government ceases to be a university
> as the term is accepted and understood. A university must
> not only serve but must also challenge through critical and
> independent thought the orthodoxies of the moment, dissent
> being a necessary feature of academic integrity.[7]

"A university's commitment to intellectual excellence is its primary and most significant contribution to a developing nation," says the Asian Report. "No government," it says, "has a monopoly of wisdom, inventiveness, and effectiveness in higher education, and governments should not deny the society the benefits of private sector initiative. We are impressed by the results forthcoming—the imagination, vigor and dedication—when government supervision and regulations are flexible. . . ."

Sometimes there are real tensions between the dominant values in the society and those that predominate in the university. There may be ideological, ethnic, or class differences between the university and the country's political leadership, or the university may succeed in becoming an oasis for liberal and humanistic values. It can also, though less often, become a center of critical social comment.[8]

Government must play an important role, says the Latin American report. "There is a danger, however, that the institution may become merely an arm of the government or turn into a simple service agency. The university . . . can design and test samples, but it is not in a position to . . . provide a direct, massive routine service." Although close relations with government are a sine qua non for higher education for development, educational institutions must also preserve a measure of independence and autonomy.

RELATIONS WITH PRIVATE ENTERPRISE

While institutions in the case studies have depended less often on private interests than they have on government, several have had programs designed to serve private business and industrial needs as well as government. A group of industrialists, bankers, and businessmen founded the Monterrey Institute of Technology and Advanced Study and has continued to contribute to its financial support, although student tuition covers about 65 percent of its budget. Business, industry, and government contract for the services of its Research and Extension Program, and demand for such services thus far has exceeded its capacity and resources.

The Center for Research and Communication (CRC) was established in the Philippines to provide modern economic research for private business firms. Like Monterrey a private, nonprofit institution, CRC receives fees for industrial research and for establishing practical business guidelines. At the same time it trains students for graduate degrees in industrial economics and in economic education. Similarly, the Ngee Ann Institute in Singapore is responsive to job requirements and has close ties with private business and industry, largely through its work-study program in which students work in private firms. While the Asian Institute of Management in the Philippines does not engage in consulting as such, its trained professionals do.

Private interests as well as government can threaten educational independence. When contributors to an institution are entitled to the use of its facilities (as they are in the CRC in the Philippines), does the institution's need for funds determine its educational program? Or does the fact that a large number and diversity of firms contribute fees to an institution mean that no single institution can dictate policy? No definitive answers are provided for all institutions, but leadership of those institutions studied insist they have preserved their independence.

Private funding has advantages as well as disadvantages. Private contributions can offset those of government, encouraging independence. They can build up an important counterweight to publicly supported programs. They can also create an important stake in higher education for private individuals, private businesses, and commerce and industry.

In each of these cases—Monterrey, CRC, and Ngee Ann—both business and government use consultation services and manpower. (The University of Science and Technology in Ghana hopes that its services, like those of Monterrey, will generate significant private contributions, although none are yet forthcoming.) The process of balancing pressures requires judgment and skill, especially when educational leaders move back and forth among institutions and government ministries and business as they often do.

NOTES

1. Soedjatmoko, "Some Thoughts on Higher Education" (Paper prepared for a seminar on Education, Employment and Equity, University of Indonesia, Jakarta, March 6, 1975) (New York: International Council for Educational Development, 1975.)

2. Choh-Ming Li, "Emerging Patterns of Higher Education in Asia and Their Effect on International Education," Institute of International Education Annual Report 1973, p. 6.

3. Aklilu Habte, in-house memo.

4. Yash Tandon, "1973/74 Status Report on Third Year Faculty Course, East African Society and Environment," University of Dar es Salaam, Faculty of Arts and Social Science, mimeo, 1974.

5. David Court, "The Experience of Higher Education in East Africa: Prospects for a Developmental Role," revision of the study prepared for the Institute of Development Studies, University of Nairobi, Kenya, p. 42.

6. Julius K. Nyerere, "The Role of Universities," in Freedom and Socialism (Nairobi: Oxford University Press, 1968), p. 183.

7. Alexander Kwapong, "University Autonomy, Accountability and Planning," in Higher Education: Crisis and Support (New York: International Council for Educational Development, 1974), p. 174.

8. R. Cranford Pratt, "Universities and Social Values in the Developing Areas: Some Reflections," in Higher Education and Social Change, Volume II: Case Studies, ed. Kenneth W. Thompson, Barbara R. Fogel, and Helen E. Danner (New York: Praeger, 1976).

4

LEADERS: HOW TO
GET THINGS GOING

The conventional approach for helping higher education seems to have focused largely on structure. In most of the case studies, however, it has been strong leaders who have most determined the success or failure of the projects. If the program has the necessary leadership, the structure of the program can vary. Leaders often come from professional schools—medicine, agriculture, architecture, engineering, or law—but they may also come from any discipline, any kind of postsecondary institution, new or old, or any level within the institution. Their effectiveness depends more on their commitment and on their status within the institutions than on their particular discipline.

Institutions need human catalysts who plan and organize development efforts, who assemble people from different disciplines, who cut through red tape, and who inspire students. But, in turn, innovative individuals need to the help and support of the institution, an institutional quality and structure capable of nurturing their plans. Institutions cannot move on their own, but they can help or hinder the ini initiative of individuals within them.

No one knows quite how leadership is bred. Leaders appear in rural villages as often as in universities, and developing developers is probably the most difficult task of education. But certain conditions seem to help them flourish: exposure to new ideas and to field experiences in areas of need; colleagues, administrators, and government leaders who receive new ideas sympathetically; an institutional system that encourages ideas to spread and take hold.

The Asian report says: "Foreigners, such as members of foreign aid agencies, can introduce innovation, based on their or others' experience abroad." Few foreign ideas take root, however, unless nationals are receptive and outsiders sensitive to their needs. "Among the nationals of the country, innovation comes often, though not by any means exclusively, from persons who have had international exposure through such experiences as fellowships for advanced study, international seminars, field trips, or work experience." But, again, the wrong kind of overseas training can also lead to cultural disorientation and harden resistance to new thinking at home. One way of countering these reactions is to allow the developing country fellow to do his research study on a problem relevant to his own country often within that country.

The Asian Report notes that students have had little direct effect on innovation or development orientation in higher education, but indirectly their drive for progress has brought about better teaching and faculty change. On the other hand, Africans report that students, especially those exposed to development needs in village or countryside, have been important sources of program ideas. As student groups become increasingly self-conscious of their roles, they may be expected to become increasingly important factors for change.

Individual faculty members and administrators or small groups of faculty and administrators can bring about change. At the University of Valle in Colombia the concept of a modern university was the work of two or three outstanding physicians who left private practice to build a more relevant medical school. On the other hand, organized faculty with a stake in maintaining the status quo can be resistant to change. Frank Bowles maintained that new and innovative programs must be launched without appearing to take anything away from such groups. What is needed is a continual dialectic between the individual and the institution. Innovation, whether within or outside a faculty, requires both the original thinker and a critical mass of development-oriented reformers to reinforce and multiply new thinking. Innovators must form a mutual protection society. When faculty members hold themselves apart from development problems or feel they endanger their careers by starting something new, the individual, no matter how imaginative, can make little headway.

Faculties within one institution, moreover, can be at different stages of development. "Staff development has been a prerequisite for educational development in every case we have studies," says the African team. Only where there has been a high level of faculty scholarship and training and social commitment on the part of educational planners have new educational directions been possible. The Development Academy of the Philippines, the University of Valle in Colombia, the Federal University of Bahia, and the three universities cooperating on the Maeklong Project in Thailand are all evidence that education for development does not start from scratch: it carries the legacy of past educational efforts and past individual training.

Unquestionably, the administrative and power structure of an institution has an effect on its hospitality to new educational ideas and on its role in development. "The new commitment," says the African report, "is social and ideological, expressed in a new arrangement of the policy-determining power." Strong autonomous faculties tend to erect barriers against ideas or methods from other faculties or administrators and even against the needs of the community. There must be some central planning and authority to encourage interdisciplinary programs and to spread new ways of doing things, including circulating information on innovative projects. The existence of an initiating nucleus within the institution, says the Latin American report, is of great importance since it "can radiate the spirit of community service throughout the entire institution. . . ."

The seed does not germinate, however, unless it finds good soil. Universities, such as the University of Botswana, Lesotho, and Swaziland, which inherited rigid traditional systems, found it difficult to be action-oriented or innovative (see Appendix A). There are at least as many examples of institutions that make promising starts but suffer setbacks as those that experience success. Unanswered is the question of how the lessons from more successful ventures can be transferred to problem-ridden centers, given the wide discrepancy in social, cultural, and political circumstances. The accomplishments of effective leaders in particular innovative efforts can at least furnish raw material for other educational experiments.

CHAPTER
5

ASSISTANCE

The main finding of the HED study is that the people and the leaders in developing countries are playing an increasingly important role in identifying urgent problems and in shaping national responses. If there was ever a time when external assistance agencies could call the tune, that day has passed. National leaders are coming forward, partly as a result of earlier assistance programs and partly because of the shifting world balance of forces, to assume leadership and to set priorities. Not only do their voices deserve attention, but to embark on technical assistance efforts of any significance without first recognizing local wishes is also to court failure. Nor will it do to pursue limited forms of consultation; partnerships in determining priorities require more, one study participant noted, than casual conversations over drinks or on the way to the airport.

As a corollary, national leaders have the responsibility to work out viable development plans and to seek the support of their governments and national agencies. The case studies supply evidence that unless national public and private agencies provide support, no amount of outside aid will be effective. Negative government policies can hamper educational development and international cooperation. For example, some governments tax incoming books and materials from external agencies, thus hindering institutional development and the full benefits of aid. Governments and businesses can thwart progressive and enlightened programs by refusing to accept trainees or graduates. Not only must higher educational institutions prepare development plans of their own but they must also coordinate these plans in concert with government policies and planning. It is encouraging, therefore, that the regional reports, particularly the African, direct their recommendations, first, to their own governments and only second to the donor agencies.

48

According to all three regional teams, it is in strengthening institutions and in building up a critical mass of scholars, faculty members, and development-oriented laymen that outside aid has played its most effective role. Such aid has laid the groundwork for present efforts to relate higher education to development. Study grants and funds to strengthen university departments have produced many of the leaders who are responsible for progress in the case studies.

"The highest payoff in the aid programs has been in training people," says the Asian report. The African report concurs: "The major positive and lasting contribution which assisting agencies and foundations have made to the universities appears to be the development of overall infrastructures, particularly in the field of human resource development." The Latin American team says that the guarantee for success of these projects is secured at the end by the human resources who are charged with their direction.

As nationally trained faculty members have replaced expatriates in many institutions of higher education, foreign aid has turned its attention from institution building to development programs and ways to support innovation. "All programs," says the Latin American report, "except the program of the National Agrarian University in La Molina, have received, directly or indirectly, substantial financial assistance from international agencies. All the institutions studied, including La Molina, have likewise received foreign collaboration. . . . Outside funds . . . served to promote community programs and have played an important role in their execution." The Asian report, too, found that "In almost all the successful programs studied here, foreign support . . . has been a crucial addition to local resources."

There has, however, been a growing change in donor-donee relationships. "Southeast Asian institutions of higher learning," says the Asian report, "have now progressed not only in the level of technological development and sophistication but also in their intellectual independence, their confidence, their ability, and their desire to make decisions for themselves." Institutions have come a long way in building indigenous staffs, and there may be less need for large-scale development programs, although the need for building local capacity is no less urgent as institutions reorient their programs to more direct development endeavors. Donor agencies may find they can be helpful by facilitating visits by national educators to neighboring institutions. External aid can assist first-generation institutions to help emerging second-generation centers and to spread ideas and successes more effectively.

Assistance agencies can also encourage new educational ideas and methods by helping institutions provide career security for staff members willing to experiment, and can help design new patterns and strategies to meet the problem of the brain drain. Support is most difficult to find at a project's conception, yet it is at the beginning that imaginative program leaders must have room to experiment and to try different approaches. Individuals showing strong and imaginative leadership and encouraged by donors to find their own way have often contributed the push that set a program in motion.

Another need is indigenous research. Many developing country educators see the importance of equipping students with a better understanding of the historical forces that shape growth and change in developing societies. There are few places at home or abroad where students can acquire such an understanding, and donor agencies can continue to support local research and teaching that foster such basic knowledge.

There is also a need to explore the questions of what forms of aid and assistance can best ensure ultimate financial self-sufficiency. For example, is aid most effective when it goes directly to an institution of higher education, through a government institute, through the central government, or through cooperative arrangements with developed country universities? Should it require a matching effort from local sources when possible? Kinds of aid vary from funds for planning, as in the Cameroon health center, the PRIMOPS health program in Colombia, and the Asian Institute of Management in the Philippines (which received professional advice and assistance from the Harvard Business School), to travel grants to innovative individuals studying and learning about other experiments. At the three Bangkok universities cooperating on the Maeklong Project, outside aid has stimulated and inspired volunteer service programs for students and younger faculty in rural areas. In the University Centre for Health Sciences in Cameroon, agencies (UNICEF, USAID, UNDP) have paid for transportation and laboratory facilities to help the University maintain its project without drawing funds from other ongoing programs.

Combined funding from both bilateral and multilateral agencies has particular promise in higher education. Because community development requires an interdisciplinary approach, it requires relatively large financial investments, not usually available at the institution of higher education or within the community. What is needed, then, is multiinstitutional support, including that of government, multinational, and private funding agencies, along with contributions from the community. Such broad-based support also integrates efforts to solve social problems at different levels of responsibility— local, regional, national, in the educational institution, and in the government.

Donor agencies may discover a natural division of labor for their assistance to higher education for development in the 1970s and 1980s. As two or three agencies join forces, they reinforce their strength. The World Bank and other banks may find they can make their greatest contribution through capital loans, with technical assistance and support tucked into the package. Unesco and UNICEF may continue to be most helpful with technical assistance. With their inherent flexibility, the foundations have less need to insist on detailed work plans before moving to give aid.

It is striking how often two or three donor agencies have ensured the success of a project by working harmoniously together as a team. By combining forces, they have been able to contribute the different building blocks a project needs, and by planning together, along with local project directors, they have helped provide an overall view. Officers of donor agencies who have participated in such cooperative actions have found that far from reducing their influence they have added to it in this way.

Because donor agencies have pooled resources, the Cameroon health center has been able to coordinate staff training and recruitment with curriculum revision, institutional reorganization, and a new concept of training health teams. The program is a good example of cooperation among different donors: France, Canada, the United States, UNDP, WHO, and the Cameroon national government. All agree on overall program objectives. The Program of Research and Education for Development at the Federal University at Bahia has been able to make both short- and long-term plans to deal with urban problems because three foundations (Rockefeller, Ford, and Kellogg) have guaranteed support for ten years. Outstanding examples of donor cooperation are, of course, the international agricultural institutes, which are developing new strains of rice, wheat, and maize, and providing crop and livestock research for farmers throughout the developing world. Ways should be found to encourage this dovetailing of efforts in other spheres of education.

Occasionally, however, donors contributing to the same project or institution have seen themselves as rivals, so concerned with protecting their own territories that they have refused even to confer with one another. When communication breaks down, plans and funding overlap and good intentions may cancel each other out. One agency can be played off against another, and the resulting tension among agencies becomes still another obstacle to the project's success.

HOW TO MAKE ASSISTANCE MORE USEFUL

The study's findings make clear that outside assistance has served and continues to serve as a catalytic agent and often a powerful force in getting an institution moving, that seed money can stimulate experimentation, and that innovation, at least in the beginning, requires special funding either from national governments or from outside agencies.

To make assistance more useful, donors might bear in mind some old and some new precepts.

1. Donor agencies should seek information from a wide spectrum of sources to discover innovative leaders and should provide seed money to give them room to experiment and plan new ways to relate higher education to development. Such innovators often assume responsibilities with too little security or tenure. Donor agencies may be able to encourage institutions to recognize the importance of bold initiatives and offer rewards and incentives and some form of security to these leaders.

2. Agencies should continue to help build a reservoir of scholars, faculty members, and development-oriented educators in developing countries. One way to do so might be to maintain and strengthen the present network of educators in developing countries responsible for this study.

3. Donor agencies must be represented by sensitive and expert staffs or cooperating university personnel. Professionals must communicate with emerging professionals, both in developed country agencies and universities and in developing country institutions. The International Health Division of the Rockefeller Foundation filled this need in the early decades of the century and the agricultural staffs of several international agencies have continued to do so. Patterns vary from country to country and agency to agency. Some build their own career services, while others, such as the Inter-University Council (IUC) in Great Britain, call on university resources. The sine qua non is first-class minds addressing themselves to first-class problems.

4. Assistance must have continuity. It has been said that many assistance programs try to meet 20-year development needs with two-year plans and one-year budgets. Staff development at most institutions requires an effort of 10 to 15 years. Fellowships are one way of preparing the ground for later projects, but here too, long periods of preparation and assistance are needed. Educational development is impossible if agencies give themselves over to fads and fashions.

5. Continuity is also essential in building mutual trust and confidence. Even the best agency staff members need time to lay the groundwork for understanding between themselves and local leaders. The short-term expert or visitor is understandably suspect, and when needed should be carefully prepared and briefed on the plans of ongoing leaders. In an era of heightened nationalism, moreover, the career professional from abroad should remain in the background, "on tap, not on top," a role that increases, not diminishes, the high requirements of ability and excellence.

6. Agencies, as well as institutions requesting help, should set forth their major goals and intentions. Both parties require well-thought-out plans with a beginning, a middle, and an end. Initiatives may come from either local leaders or outsiders, but the agreed set of plans must in the end be acceptable to those countries that must live with the consequences. Insiders and outsiders, therefore, should exchange and agree on plans and a timetable of assistance before making or accepting commitments for funds and personnel. While program flexibility is important, cooperation depends on a clear understanding, reached in the most serious and deliberate consultation.

7. Assistance programs should provide for mutual learning. People in developed countries can learn from developing countries about ways higher education can better serve society, and developing country institutions can learn from others in the same country or region. Donor agencies should support workshops and visits that encourage communication among people concerned with higher education for development, from both developing and developed countries. There has been all too little two-way flow in technical assistance, and yet in the end this mutual exchange may be the single most persuasive ground for cooperation.

8. Agencies should explore cooperative arrangements, combining bilateral and mutilateral assistance with local support. They should beware of donor rivalries and seek the most effective total pattern of financing. In a time of shrinking resources, the need for cooperation has never been greater. The experience of the present study has not been uniformly encouraging in this regard.

6

GUIDELINES

RECOGNIZING GOOD PROGRAMS IN HIGHER
EDUCATION FOR DEVELOPMENT

Higher education can contribute to development in at least five
ways. It can (1) define social needs and problems, (2) prepare effective
contributors to social development, (3) apply knowledge to the solution
of development problems, (4) strengthen education at other levels
(through teacher training, common language programs, curriculum
research, designing materials), and (5) help society define values and
purposes. Whatever its purpose, good higher education for development has certain common characteristics. Some of the elements that
have contributed to its success in the case studies have been sum-
marized and listed here as a guide. They might be converted to a
simple checklist for donors.

It Has Identified a Need

The first step in higher education for development is to identify
the most urgent problem or set of problems. The problem may be
social (health, agriculture, housing, employment), educational (more
effective learning, training for jobs and careers), or a combination of
both (such as the need for nurses and technicians, which, along with
the need for better rural health, led to the training program in
Cameroon). A problem can be identified by the university, the government, industry, or the community. The university or other postsecondary institution may analyze community needs through systematic

surveys or through student or faculty research. (The Maeklong Project
in Thailand ranks rural welfare priorities in order of difficulty, impact, and possible success.) The institution may also find that student
training is inadequate for problems students will face after graduation.
A faculty of medicine, for example, may discover that its students are
not being prepared for the term of rural practice requires by law.
Identification must be an ongoing process linked with the assessment
of manpower and resources.

A development problem, such as manpower need, can also be
identified by government or private industry. The Ngee Ann program
was established to fit Singapore's carefully prepared manpower development plans, and the Monterrey Institute's to fit business and industrial requirements.

The community may identify its own problems, to which the educational program responds. At the National Agrarian University in
Peru, the Transferal of Technology Program receives requests for
assistance directly from farmers and farm groups. The University
encourages such requests by continuing association between University
and community.

Whatever the identification process, it requires a vigorous attempt
to accumulate and analyze all necessary information and a conviction
that development is not only desirable but also possible and that the
institution of higher education has a role in meeting the need. The institution may be society's most effective tool in defining urgent needs
if it can bring to bear objectivity and intellectual resources to help
government determine development priorities.

It Has Formulated Objectives

Most of the case studies in this survey have combined several
development purposes. All, to some extent, have defined one or more
social needs, and most have sought to prepare contributors to development while applying knowledge to development problems. Within these
broad purposes, however, good higher education for development must
set specific and well-defined goals. Several directors of the international agricultural institutes, asked to prescribe for higher education for development, suggested that the more specific the goals the
more effective the program. Increasing food production or training
teachers, engineers, or sugar industry workers can be measured by
results; improving learning and changing attitudes and social values
may be equally important, but more difficult to plan or achieve. There
is a special need for higher education to define clearly more general
(and sometimes conflicting) social and educational ends—equity, mass

education, employment, the development of the individual, interracial harmony—and to devise direct and concrete means for reaching them.

It Has Sought and Secured Effective Support of Government, Community, Students, and Faculty

Government

Although institutions of higher education provide most valuable services to their societies if they are independent in thought and action, they need the interest and collaboration of government agencies and of key political leaders in programs for development. Many effective programs seek government support early in identifying problems, planning their solution, and setting priorities. The Transferal of Technology Program in Peru benefited, and some would say was propelled, by links between the University and the Ministry of Agriculture, encouraged by the Agrarian Reform Law. Some staff members at the University of Dar es Salaam are seconded from the Tanzanian government and many faculty members serve in government posts. In Brazil, the governor of Bahia, a former rector of the university, helped shape the philosophy of PROPED; the Ministry of Education and Culture offered funds; the Treasury Department facilitated duty-free import of equipment; and the secretary of agriculture is on PROPED's board of directors.

In a good example of university-government cooperation, the Extension Research Liaison Service at Ahmadu Bello University passes on to research workers the farmers' agricultural problems; research results are channeled back to agricultural ministries and their extension specialists. The service runs radio and TV programs in 14 local languages and sends its own teams of extension workers to tour farms and to answer farmers' questions. Signs of higher education's influence on government are how much government uses the institution's consulting and advisory services and research results and how effectively it reproduces model programs on a countrywide scale. On the other hand, an institution challenging social and political orthodoxies must often forego government support but may, nevertheless, as a vigorous and independent critic, play an essential role. Higher education must be a source of ferment as well as of manpower.

Community

Higher education programs that seek community change need understanding, participation, and support from community members.

In a number of good programs students and staff regularly hold group meetings and talk with community leaders to explain proposals; include community representatives on advisory boards; distribute information through press, pamphlets, or radio; and often live and work with local inhabitants. No matter how effective the agricultural technology, it is useless if farmers don't accept it; however good the health facilities, villagers or city dwellers must be willing to use them. Program participants must also understand farmers' and workers' attitudes. Ahmadu Bello uses its Rural Economic Research Unit to find out why the findings of agricultural research are not being used on farms.

Students

Students must be convinced of the value of their training and service. They are most likely to provide support for new programs if there are jobs waiting for graduates and if service-work-study programs are carefully planned to improve student learning. Students must be prepared for assigned jobs and for regions where they work. Program prestige attracts applicants for admission, and effectively designed program structure and methods may create new student attitudes. Students should participate in the programs. As the programs become more complex, however, they tend to eliminate students, who then receive only indirect benefits.

Faculty

Staff members accept new programs more readily if they are included in the planning, if they are clear on purposes and organization, and if they are provided with meaningful incentives, such as time for research, better salaries and benefits, travel funds, improved facilities, and better career opportunities. When staff members are too immersed in administration, they are likely to give up their teaching roles and thus reduce the educational effects of the program.

It Has Plans for Carrying Out Its Objectives

Structure and Organization

There are a number of possible models for organizing higher education for development. Objectives of the program should define the structure. Universities and other large institutions of higher education are often too cumbersome and unwieldy to develop innovative programs:

they may be hamstrung by a maze of committees and bureaucracy and
by a rigid administrative structure in which faculties and departments
compete for funds. Single-purpose institutions, such as Mauritius or
Ngee Ann, may be freer of these constraints. Despite their advantage
in producing needed manpower, however, such institutions may reinforce a one-crop economy or fail to look at broader needs.

An institute or center within rather than outside an institution of
higher education can have flexibility and also act as a clearinghouse
for the institution's expertise. At Monterrey, the Institute draws on
seven academic departments and three industrial research and extension activities. Autonomous centers or institutes make possible unorthodox programs, but must guard against total separation from the
resources and educational purposes of the parent body. Organizing
an appropriate structure for new programs and new ways of teaching
may be helped by affiliation with another educational institution, local
or foreign (as Ngee Ann's with the London Polytechnic Institute). Whatever the institutional structure for the program, it must have a full-
time, flexible, efficient, and forceful leader who can both delegate
decision making and bring people and disciplines together in joint efforts to solve development problems.

Staff Development

To carry out new objectives, an institution or faculty may need
new staff or special training for present faculty members. Four years
before Cameroon's University Centre for Health Sciences received its
first students, WHO and other donors financed postgraduate studies
abroad for Cameroon physicians. The Cameroon government's National Planning Commission helped identify people qualified to organize
and teach in a health center, and other staff members were recruited
and paid by various technical agencies. Effective programs plan training and orientation and provide staff incentives to attract the best faculty members to the program and to continue staff development. They
also consider the balance between staff trained at home and those
trained abroad to avoid the danger of institutional inbreeding.

Full Participation

The more students, staff, community members, government officials, and private agencies that take part in or are aware of higher
education for development programs, the better. PROPED at the
Federal University of Bahia included in its planning professors from
key faculties and schools, the vice-rectors, and a community council
(three religious leaders, two businessmen, two elementary school
directors, and a first lieutenant). Staff members defined priorities,

established objectives, and planned operations. Program planners set a firm launching platform for a program when they consult with outside experts, government and educational leaders, staff, students, and community. The Bahia case study points out that "all university sectors [must] verify the program's relevance and receive sufficient information . . . to overcome any uneasiness which may exist."

Communication and Orientation

Planning should include wide dissemination of information about a proposed program and its purposes; it is easier to recruit well-qualified and enthusiastic staff and students when there is a demand for admission to the program. Directors and participants should, if possible, visit similar programs.

It Integrates Teaching, Research, and Service

Service activities should feed back into curriculum and teaching, thus making theory more meaningful for student and teacher and providing opportunities for research. A sufficient volume of research on the nation and region is a necessary basis for teaching and for successful service programs. In all operational programs, there should be an easy flow among all three aspects of a project; each affects the other. Faculty members should be required to participate in field activities and have time to carry out field research; service activities should be planned on the basis of solid research and should enrich teaching. Students should have opportunities to see theory in action in the field and to bring service or work experience back into the classroom for analysis.

Service-study programs are promising means for relating these three educational purposes but, as the case studies show, they have had varying degrees of success depending on how they were carried out. They sometimes fail when (1) the student sees little connection between classroom and the community in which he works because student job assignments are badly planned and supervised; (2) faculty members neither participate in nor understand service activities; (3) service activities are voluntary rather than an integral and required part of course work (although programs such as the Voluntary Technology Group at the University of Science and Technology in Ghana, which begin by recruiting volunteers, may later integrate service and curriculum in a nonvoluntary structure).

Work-study differs from service-study in the nature of extracurricular jobs students do. Work-study jobs may be in business or

industry and may have no direct social impact. They may be valuable
if the institution of higher education and the employer cooperate to relate theory and practice. In Ghana, a vocational training organizer
arranges student placement and staff visits. The University releases
lecturers for practical experience in industry and also engages professionals as part-time lecturers so that students can benefit from their
practical knowledge. Singapore's firms actively support Ngee Ann's
vacation job program.

It Uses a Multidisciplinary Approach
to Solve Development Problems

Such problems as health, education, housing, and employment are
closely interrelated and require team efforts. Successful programs
have brought the disciplines together in different ways: they may design a curriculum that cuts across departmental specialties or combines professional and technical training, as does the Rural Polytechnic
Institute in Mali; they may coordinate various types of expertise as the
Maeklong Project in Thailand did by joining the forces of three specialized universities; or they may form a multidisciplinary group of
professors and specialists to exchange information and points of view,
as in Tanzania or at the Institute of Rural and Regional Studies at
Gadjah Mada University in Indonesia.

Such teamwork often requires restructuring faculty and administration and giving up departmental autonomy for common courses,
staffs, and facilities. While painful for many traditionally trained
faculty members, such restructuring may bring benefits not only to
community programs but also to teaching in general. An autonomous
institute or consultancy center attached to a university can, by its
flexibility and central purposes, facilitate interdisciplinary attacks on
development problems. The Technology Centre in Ghana coordinates
multidisciplinary projects, assesses departmental contributions, and
recruits staff and consultants from outside bodies. The international
agricultural institutes bring together scientists from various specialized fields in an intensive study of rice, corn, or wheat production
problems.

It Draws on a History of Educational Development
and of Concern for Social Issues

New institutional structures and programs do not appear full-
blown. They stem from antecedent institutions and educational tradi-

tion. For more than a decade, at both the Federal University of Bahia and the University of Valle, the faculties of medicine have had programs of preventive medicine that tied into teaching and research. The Voluntary Technology Group at the University of Science and Technology, Kumasi, Ghana, later became the Kumasi Consultancy Centre with formal ties to the University and to the government.

A number of institutions of higher education, particularly in Africa, have evolved from or absorbed a secondary-level institution, and these earlier institutions influence their successors in many ways (see Appendix I). The new upgraded postsecondary institution only slowly moves away from specialized or elite education toward mass education and education that is responsive to development needs. A university that undertakes development programs too early may founder; it may need first a period of internal integration. As an institution of higher education achieves maturity, it passes from a limited teaching role to the integration of teaching, research, and service, which it must have if it is to play its crucial role in development.

It Has a Means of Evaluation

Once a need is defined and goals are set, a program's effectiveness must be assessed in terms of its purposes and starting point. Institutions that seek primarily to fill manpower needs must look at the success of their graduates and at what industry and government still require. On the other hand, an institution whose goal is mass education uses a more general economic and social yardstick to measure results. The circumstances determine the purposes that are pursued.

Whether the goal is employment, mass education, or community development, training must be evaluated in terms of what trainees do later; the production and use of manpower are inseparable. (The Cameroon health center reinforces its training of health teams by seeking to ensure their willingness to serve in rural areas; young graduates begin their professional careers at the district level and, by the time they are married and have children of school age, they are posted to towns with adequate schools.)

A program's impact can and should be tested also for measurable social change: Is infant mortality decreasing? Are farms more productive? Do people have more to eat? Is there less illiteracy? The Maeklong Project found that differences in the conditions of different areas made it necessary to develop and test several development packages. Could those programs that benefited one group of villages be successfully extended to others? If methods for such evaluation are not built into programs, the programs are not useful pilots.

Relating costs to benefits is important but difficult. Education costs for training income-producing manpower can be established, but it is hard to determine a fair price for attitude changes or leadership. Government costs for higher education can be reduced by transferring some of the burden to the student, but how does such a change affect the numbers and kinds of students with access to higher education? Cost-benefit assessments, nevertheless, are indicators of efficiency and effectiveness. The Monterrey Institute of Technology and Advanced Studies has a cost accounting system that guarantees the sponsor and the institution efficient management of financial resources. Poor management and poor cost accounting are often roadblocks to success.

It Has a Capacity for Innovation, Adaptation, and Discovery

Institutions of higher education and the people in them must be open to new ideas if they are to respond to development needs. Such openness is encouraged by social attitudes, as well as by travel abroad, visiting faculty members, research opportunities, salaries, and other incentives that attract scholars and men and women of imagination. (In Mauritius, said a World Bank report, "The unique . . . blend of races which had to cohabit within a small area resulted in a population that is open to the external world, is receptive to outside ideas and can easily adapt to imported techniques."[1]) Institutional organization can permit easy contact between people in different disciplines or it can build barriers between competing faculties. The institution can provide a framework for development, bringing together disciplines in efforts to attack specific development problems. Semiautonomous development institutes that focus on solving development problems may generate new methods, new concepts, and a sense of common purpose, which, in turn, is hospitable to innovation.

Perhaps more than anything else it is the freedom to experiment, to take risks, and to adopt unpopular views that is higher education's intellectual yeast. The social innovator, like the Nobel scientist, is a rare animal, not easy to breed. He should be protected, supported, and encouraged. But, like the scientist, the imaginative program planner needs freedom and the opportunity to try various routes. Although institutions of higher education must seek government cooperation in their efforts to solve development problems, they must guard zealously against government domination or control. They must also guard against rigidity in thought and curriculum. Good higher education for development programs flourish where there is high academic quality, an interest in social well-being, and the freedom to experiment.

It is Linked to Other Parts of a System of Education

"Education is probably the most important activity and concern of Africa," according to the African report. Higher education must take responsibility for an overall view of systems of education: for identifying the needs in the rural classroom, for designing and producing teacher guides and student textbooks and for training primary teachers to use them, for strengthening teacher training schools, and for bringing secondary schoolteachers into the university for special training. Addis Ababa University of Ethiopia, the former University of Botswana, Lesotho, and Swaziland, the University of Antioquia in Colombia, the Federal University of Bahia in Brazil, and Ahmadu Bello University in Nigeria, among others, have been performing one or more of these functions.

If countries are to develop their own leaders locally, there must also be a variety of postsecondary institutions. The university is only one of them. The problems of a developing society cannot be solved without teachers, technicians, and extension workers, and postsecondary institutions must provide attractive alternatives to the universities for secondary school graduates. New approaches to development arise out of the polytechnics, agricultural institutes and business schools, as well as from the more traditional learning centers; new ways to blend theory and practice come often from institutions concerned primarily with training students for specific jobs. In Africa, particularly, there is a marked blurring of the distinction between universities and other postsecondary institutions, and several have admitted students with lower academic qualifications into technical courses that were previously considered to be outside its terms of reference. Such changes in the composition of student bodies (in terms of age, background, and courses needed) are likely to make profound changes in the institution, more important perhaps than changes in standards or curriculum.

Access to education at all levels must concern all higher education for development programs. The system as a whole must produce both specialists and a sufficient number of people with a reasonable degree of competence. It must narrow rather than widen the gap between the educated and the non- or less educated.

OVERCOMING OBSTACLES TO SUCCESS

Obstacles to the success of higher education for development programs were surprisingly similar. Whether the program was in Africa,

Asia, or Latin America, its leaders had to contend with the resistance of students, staff, government officials, and community members. They had to design a way to administer the program that was flexible enough to respond to changing needs and circumstances but that also made efficient use of funds. They had to find a modus vivendi with government in which they achieved government cooperation and support without its domination. They had to devise better ways to integrate teaching, research, and service.

The following is a brief list of some of the problems most often mentioned in the case studies and the means by which some of the programs managed to solve them. Some solutions have been suggested by program directors or regional teams; where a country is mentioned, the solution has been tried there. Both the problems and the ways programs have devised to overcome them are more fully discussed in the body of the report and in the case studies themselves.

OBSTACLES TO SUCCESS	HOW THEY HAVE BEEN (OR CAN BE) OVERCOME

1. Student Attitudes

Students do not participate in voluntary field activities (Peru).	Assign academic credit for student work in rural areas. Fourth- and fifth-year students were encouraged to participate by financing their theses (Peru). Students receive credit for community projects at Gadjah Mada (Indonesia) and Monterrey Institute (Mexico).
	Pay students to help villagers implement government programs (Indonesia).
	Require fieldwork. Students must work alongside farmers and factory workers before entering higher education (Tanzania). A compulsory service plan was proposed by a student-faculty committee appointed by the president of the university (Ethiopia).

OBSTACLES TO SUCCESS	HOW THEY HAVE BEEN (OR CAN BE) OVERCOME
Students complain about job assignments in service-study programs. They claim they are neglected and cut off from the university when assigned to a distant region; allowance is inadequate; they have trouble with local colleagues (Ethiopia).	Counsel and supervise student more carefully. Provide better job placement. Put student representatives on university governing body. Encourage and publicize student studies on reform (Tanzania).
Students in local jobs have conflicts with police and thus create antagonism to the institution they come from.	Establish better relations with local community through orientation of students and community members. Provide better counseling and supervision of students.
Students fear training is substandard, that they are being prepared only to work in the bush (Cameroon).	Include students in program planning and inform them of program's purposes and progress.
Professional students have trouble accepting technicians as coworkers in double-level training (Mali).	Same as above.
Students show little interest in or knowledge of local conditions.	Assign local research. In teaching through research programs, students learn local conditions and social science research processes (Tanzania).
Students are unwilling to work in rural areas after graduation.	Assign youngest graduates (at start of their careers) to rural jobs (health, teaching, and so on) and later post them to towns and cities. Disadvantage is that rural areas have least experienced workers (Cameroon).
Radical students say university is being used to implement unacceptable government policy (Peru).	

OBSTACLES TO SUCCESS | HOW THEY HAVE BEEN (OR CAN BE) OVERCOME

2. Staff Attitudes

OBSTACLES TO SUCCESS	HOW THEY HAVE BEEN (OR CAN BE) OVERCOME
Faculty does not participate in voluntary field activities (Peru, Brazil).	Provide more money for housing and transportation and compensate for extra salary faculty member could get outside the institution in his free time (Peru). Provide relief from teaching loads to participating faculty.
Professors oppose university-government program because they fear university will lose autonomy.	Make university responsible for the program (Peru).
Faculty does not support program and knows little about it (Brazil).	Inform faculties and departments of program's goals and achievements.
Professors identify education exclusively with classroom teaching. They avoid evaluation trips or use trips for other purposes. Staff does not reinforce in the classroom students' field learning (Ethiopia).	Include faculty in planning. CEDUR proposal was originally submitted to professors from different faculties. The group met for eight sessions to define priorities, establish aims, and develop a plan (Brazil).
Regular teaching staff resents and opposes development institute because it thinks it will conflict with its own consulting and research (Mexico).	Make use of regular staff in institute. Encourage teaching-research-consulting relationship. Professors receive additional pay for institute work (Mexico). Professors may regard program as opportunity for applied research (Peru).
In an institution geared to employment, staff feels it can no longer pursue legitimate interests in scholarship, research, and academic excellence (Singapore).	Provide opportunities for staff development in all institutions of higher education.

OBSTACLES TO SUCCESS	HOW THEY HAVE BEEN (OR CAN BE) OVERCOME
Staff feels threatened by new teaching approaches (Cameroon). Instructors not capable of providing new kind of instruction, for example, double-level training (Mali).	Orient and inform staff. Build secure, knowledgeable departments. Staff experience with other community programs is helpful (Brazil, Colombia, Cameroon).
	Cameroon health program is the result of several years planning and consultation among government, medical educators, staff, and outside agencies. Staff visited other programs.
	Students and professors work together in rural areas (Peru).
Faculty members complain they must work on traditional research problems to have papers published in international journals, a requirement for promotion.	Consider establishing prestigious national development academy (with national journal) that would elect to membership scholars who have made distinguished contributions.
Faculty members risk losing tenure by working as administrator of development institute.	University can give more security to academic staff working in social development.
Faculty with overseas training reinforces patterns of education unsuitable to local context.	Encourage prospective staff members to take shorter overseas programs in connection with Ph. D. program at home (Tanzania). Identify promising graduates as future staff members and pay them part of staff salary during overseas work (Tanzania).
	Carry on thesis research within own country on topic appropriate to that country.

OBSTACLES TO SUCCESS   HOW THEY HAVE BEEN (OR CAN
                                                    BE) OVERCOME

3. Community Attitudes

Community members are hostile. Determine carefully community
Community has experience of priorities. Program participants
past deceit on part of agencies hold meetings with community
and politicians (Peru). groups to tell them about program
(Peru, Thailand). Students and
farmers live and work together
(Peru).

Agricultural research and Find out why the local farmer does
service programs bring no what he does and how he does it be-
change in farming methods and fore advising him to change. Stu-
practices (Nigeria). dents and farmers living together
brought change of farmers' attitudes
(Peru). Rural Economic Research
Unit at Ahmadu Bello University
(Nigeria) was established to find
out why local farmers were resist-
ing change. Analysis has produced
more acceptable research.

Community is passive or dis- Help organize community members
interested. to seek solutions for their own problems (Brazil). Program created
community council (Brazil). Health
services program met with community leaders before the program
was instituted. Village chiefs do-
nated buildings for the program
(Cameroon).

Community makes few requests Inform the community of program's
for available services (Peru). services through meetings, radio,
posters. La Molina program met
requests in almost any technical
field or any region of country, created student, professor, and community enthusiasm (Peru).

OBSTACLES TO SUCCESS	HOW THEY HAVE BEEN (OR CAN BE) OVERCOME
	Extension Research Liaison Services unit at Ahmadu Bello University runs radio and TV programs in 14 languages. Teams tour farming regions answering farmers' questions (Nigeria). University health campaign reached 2 million people with booklets, radio, and discussion groups (Tanzania).
	Make changes in curriculum and academic calendar to allow for continuous rather than intermittent services.

4. Attitudes of Government
   Workers

Government officials sometimes feel programs intrude on their functions (Peru).	Include government officials in planning and implementation of program. Keep them informed of results.
Government technicians and extension workers in rural areas resist intrusion of students and professors, think radical students may create problem (Peru).	Students and professors seek to win them over.
Government underestimates need for support of higher education.	Collect data to show demand for higher education and effects of programs.

5. Management

Management of the institution is inflexible.	Set up partly autonomous and more flexible program administration.
The program has no place in the institution as a whole, and no impact on total system (Brazil).	Reorganize the institution to emphasize interdisciplinary approach (Cameroon). Harness resources to achieve teaching, service, and research goals. Adopt a more

OBSTACLES TO SUCCESS   HOW THEY HAVE BEEN (OR CAN
                              BE) OVERCOME

5. Management (continued)

                              interdisciplinary approach to re-
                              search (Ghana). Draw up a manual
                              of policies and procedures describ-
                              ing relation of program to institution
                              (Brazil). Integrate programs under
                              general development approach
                              (Brazil).

Director of program devotes only   Create full-time directorship with
part time to the program and   imaginative, enthusiastic, and able
does not have time for necessary   leader as director. Leaders need
activities (Nigeria). Director   flexibility, problem-solving skills,
serves also as promoter, pay-   ability to avoid collision between
master, professor, and public   protagonists of new and defenders
relations officer.   of old (Cameroon). Administrators
                                   of innovative program may have to
                                   be specially trained. Director
                                   should be able to delegate decision
                                   making to participants and recruit
                                   consultants (Peru, Ghana).

Difference between program and   Institute a well-organized system
ongoing institutional costs is   of cost accounting. Monterrey has
blurred. Costs of program are   exact cost accounting for each pro-
unclear.   gram (Mexico).

When programs are sponsored by   Give institution responsibility for
government, procedures tend to   program, with government coopera-
be rigid, controls excessive,   tion.
payments delayed, and hiring of
personnel difficult.

6. Relating Experience to
   Curriculum

Jobs or service activities are   Counsel and supervise students.
poorly related to classroom   Enlist government and/or employer
work. Students do not have   aid in job placement. Students use
chance to use special knowledge   social science skills to analyze
or skills (Ethiopia).   local problems (Tanzania).

OBSTACLES TO SUCCESS	HOW THEY HAVE BEEN (OR CAN BE) OVERCOME
Difficult to convince government agencies to use students in jobs.	Enlist aid of individual officials.
Staff reluctant or unable to relate student field experience to classroom work.	Staff members participate in service activities in rural areas (Thailand).
	Oblige teaching staff to participate regularly in ongoing research and experiments. Impose career penalties on teaching staff who do not regularly adjust syllabus and compulsory reading list. Encourage curriculum reform as continuous process.
Graduates have difficulties applying education to practical situations, possibly because of high cultural value on education and low value on application and inadequate equipment to practice on (Singapore).	Prepare for and follow up on jobs. Secure active support of vacation work program by commerce and industry (Singapore). Vacation training organizer at University of Science and Technology in Ghana arranged for student placement and staff visits.
Institution has poor relations with industry.	Lecturers spend varying periods in industry to get practical experience; university hires professionals as part-time lecturers so students can benefit from practical knowledge. University appoints professionals from industry as external examiners, especially in practical exams (Ghana).
	Mauritius ensures feedback between staff and employers through part-time teaching by working professionals and administrators.

OBSTACLES TO SUCCESS	HOW THEY HAVE BEEN (OR CAN BE) OVERCOME

7. Manpower Planning

Students increasingly adopt materialistic values, choose only courses that have bright employment prospects (Singapore).	
Manpower forecasts may be wrong. Even the most accurate can't foresee contingencies (Singapore).	Keep curriculum flexible, moving from more general to more specific courses. Ngee Ann requires basic disciplines in first two years and offers series of options in last year (Singapore). Ahmadu Bello changed training to provide more research workers (Nigeria).
There is an oversupply (or undersupply) of graduates.	Regulate student intake to reflect manpower needs (Mexico, Mauritius, Singapore).
There is an undersupply of middle-level personnel.	Train professionals and subprofessionals jointly. The University Centre for Health Sciences trains technicians and nurses along with physicians, bringing into the university students with lower academic qualifications (Cameroon). Rural Polytechnic Institute trains professional and technical agricultural personnel in a similar double-level program (Mali).
	Reinforce career structure by providing opportunities for technicians to move to university for either undergraduate or later advanced training.
System of higher education lacks coordination; functions of various schools overlap (Mali).	Prepare overall manpower plans into which individual institutions fit (Singapore).

OBSTACLES TO SUCCESS	HOW THEY HAVE BEEN (OR CAN BE) OVERCOME
Graduates refuse jobs in rural areas or in needed technical but less prestigious occupations.	Provide more training opportunities for part-time students (including adults) presently working in needed fields.
	Help student to see entrepreneurial opportunities in villages. Scholarships at University of Malaya carry condition that grantee serve government for five years (Malaysia).
Graduates are not qualified for available jobs.	Have university share responsibility for suitable placement of graduates; consumer needs and weaknesses in preparation would thus show up.

8. Program Evaluation

Programs are difficult to evaluate.	An outside agency may assist and finance an evaluation. AID with technical assistance from Tulane University is starting an evaluation of PRIMOPS at Valle (Colombia).
The decision maker needs evaluation at each phase of the program.	A good mix of administrators, operators, and evaluators should work together at the planning stage and thereafter (Unesco).

9. Relationship with Government

There is little government cooperation.	Look for influential help. Group of alumni and former professors at La Molina sought to break down barriers between government and the university (Peru).
	Enlist support of high-level leadership. Top ministry official participated in and had commitment to the program at La Molina (Peru). Outstanding advantage at CEDUR

OBSTACLES TO SUCCESS	HOW THEY HAVE BEEN (OR CAN BE) OVERCOME
9. Relationship with Government (continued)	(Brazil) is relationship with the governor of Bahia, former rector of the University. Program in Brazil also has cooperation of the mayor, Treasury Department, Ministry of Education and Culture, and the Ministry of Agriculture.
	Set up joint university–government governing boards. The state secretary of agriculture is a member of the program's board of directors at PROPED (Brazil). Ahmadu Bello's two institutes (Administration and Agricultural Research) have joint boards, emphasize problem solving, and have good cooperative relationships (Nigeria).
	Invite government professionals to serve on academic faculties. At Ahmadu Bello, this helped university staff orient teaching and research to practical problems (Nigeria).
	Include government representatives when considering community priorities.
	Create liaison unit. Extension Research Liaison Services at Ahmadu Bello acts as a channel through which farmers' problems are passed on to research workers at the University and results are passed to the Ministry of Agriculture, which is responsible for extension to the farmer (Nigeria).

OBSTACLES TO SUCCESS	HOW THEY HAVE BEEN (OR CAN BE) OVERCOME
The government has too much control; is the source of too many pressures to conform.	Satisfy government by orienting program to practical problems and at same time keep university autonomy in managing program (Peru).
	Establish nongovernmental body to channel government funds to higher education. Institutions of higher education in Nigeria receive financial support through the National Universities Commission.

10. Lack of Agents of Change

There are not enough leaders with new ideas on education for development nor enough committed participants in or workers for such education.	Encourage contact with development-oriented scholars who have experience or insights to share. Visiting professors of high academic quality contributed new ideas of development of PROPED (Brazil). Professors who had worked directly with the community (in the Department of Preventive Medicine at Bahia) were interested in the program.
	Support a buildup of a critical group of development-oriented scholars and administrators. It is important to keep this critical mass intact against the lure of higher pay (Asia).
	Promote a dialogue between communities of scholars (Asia) and leaders of successful programs.
	Investigate the kinds of institutional organization that most encourage innovation. Are people with creative ideas most likely to come from an institution that has an interdisciplinary structure or one that has

OBSTACLES TO SUCCESS	HOW THEY HAVE BEEN (OR CAN BE) OVERCOME
10. <u>Lack of Agents of Change</u> (continued)	
	separate faculties or departments? From centralized or decentralized institutions?
	Identify 20 innovative people in the country, whatever their field or job, and enlist their thinking on education for development programs.
	Encourage the university to act as leader in society.
11. <u>Financing</u>	
Programs are hard to start.	Seek grants for initial planning. Donors should provide seed money when people or ideas seem promising. Rural development projects need money for first research visits to villages. Three foundations (Rockefeller, Ford, and Kellogg) guaranteed ten-year support for basic operations of PROPED (Brazil).
A large financial investment is needed for an interdisciplinary approach to community development.	Seek collaboration among donor agencies, including governmental, multinational, and private agencies (Brazil). WHO, UNICEF, CIDA, USAID, FAC, and UNDP helped in planning and providing a variety of necessary resources for Cameroon's health program.
Too many strings are attached to funds.	Donors must recognize the growing sophistication of institutions of higher education in developing countries and their right to determine their own requirements (Asia).

OBSTACLES TO SUCCESS	HOW THEY HAVE BEEN (OR CAN BE) OVERCOME

11. Financing (continued)

	Governments must recognize the importance of maintaining an independent source of ideas, critical judgment, and knowledge.
Donors feel institutions and programs can be transferred uncritically from one place to another.	Donors must be aware of differences between countries. Program leaders and potential program leaders should be encouraged by grants to visit programs and institutions in other countries and to decide what and how they can adapt.
Institutions within a country compete for government funds.	A National Universities Commission acts as a channel for government financial support to the universities (Nigeria).

NOTE

1. Memorandum on Recent Economic Development and Prospects of Mauritius, IBRD, Washington, D.C., February 1974, p. 1.

APPENDIX A

PATTERNS OF EDUCATIONAL DEVELOPMENT

Frank Bowles, author of Access to Higher Education, who served as a consultant to the study, said that educational systems must go through certain stages of growth before they are ready for new ideas and methods. Mr. Bowles, in a special study for this project, pointed out that patterns of educational development in developing nations can be classified into five stages, which he described as follows:

Stage 1: Formation of a basic national educational system including primary schools and vocational, teacher training, and preuniversity secondary schools, which may be extended into short cycle (two- to three-year nondegree) postsecondary programs. Ordinarily, this system provides for more than 10 percent of the potential student body.

Stage 2: Formation of a university offering undergraduate studies leading to first professional and/or liberal arts degrees. In most cases, there are no graduate studies and research programs at this stage. Parallel programs in higher technical training may be offered outside the university.

Stage 3: Political movement to generalize the basic national educational system, as described in Stage 1, to reach up to 50 percent of the 6 to 12 age group.

Stage 4: Maturation of the university, with emerging graduate studies and research programs that relate the university to national problems. At this stage, the university can offer full faculty training in some fields.

Stage 5: Extension of the university's role. The university can now reach out to communities, develop new methods of educational delivery, and adjust to the political necessities of national service programs.

Mr. Bowles points out that Stage 3 is the crucial stage in development, since it involves what is essentially a change of course from the elitist educational system subsumed in Stages 1 and 2 toward a mass educational system that will ultimately include mass higher education. He points out that the postwar educational history of the developed nations shows that steps toward mass education are politically irreversible, and raises the question as to whether the major international donor agencies have considered the educational, political, and financial consequences for the developing nations, particularly those afflicted with apparently incurable poverty, of programs leading directly and rapidly toward mass education.

APPENDIX B

DONOR AGENCIES

Canadian International Development Agency

Ford Foundation

French Ministry of Foreign Affairs

Inter-American Development Bank

International Bank for Reconstruction and Development

International Development Research Centre (Canada)

Ministry of Overseas Development (United Kingdom)

Rockefeller Foundation

United Nations Children's Fund

United Nations Development Programme

United Nations Educational, Scientific and Cultural Organization

U. S. Agency for International Development

APPENDIX C

CASE STUDIES

Place	Project	Prior Financing by HED Donor Agencies
AFRICA		
Botswana, Lesotho, and Swaziland		
University of Botswana, Lesotho, and Swaziland	Prospects for Regional Universities in Africa	British government Ford Foundation AID IBRD
Cameroon		
University of Yaoundé, Yaoundé	The Role of the University in the Medical and Health Services: The University Centre for Health Sciences	UNDP UNICEF French government CIDA British government AID Ford Foundation Rockefeller Foundation IBRD
	Functional Bilingualism: An Emergent Issue of the African University	British government
Ethiopia		
Addis Ababa University, Addis Ababa	The Public Service Role of the University.	IUC AID Ford Foundation IBRD Unesco
Ghana		
University of Science and Technology, Kumasi	Technology at the Service of Rural and Industrial Development	CIDA

APPENDIX C (continued)

Place	Project	Prior Financing by HED Donor Agencies
Mali		
Higher Education System	Higher Education in Mali	Unesco
Mauritius		
University of Mauritius, Reduit	Developing a University in a Small Country	IUC CIDA
Nigeria		
Ahmadu Bello University, Zaria	Agricultural and Educational Development Roles of the University	IUC CIDA AID UNICEF Unesco Ford Foundation
Sudan		
University of Khartoum, Khartoum	Staff Development in an African University	Ford Foundation
Sudan Higher Education System	Higher Education for Development in Sudan	
Tanzania		
University of Dar es Salaam, Dar es Salaam	The University's Response to Manpower Needs	Rockefeller Foundation British government IBRD AID CIDA

ASIA

India		
Ahmednagar College, Ahmednagar (Maharashtra)	Center for Studies in Rural Development (documentary case study)	
Indonesia		
Gadjah Mada University, Jogjakarta	The University's Role in Rural Development	Rockefeller Foundation Ford Foundation AID

Place	Project	Prior Financing by HED Donor Agencies
Malaysia		
University of Malaya, Kuala Lumpur	Development of Cultural Unity	CIDA IUC
Philippines		
Development Academy of the Philippines, Tagaytay	Training Developers	
Asian Institute of Management, Manila	Training Managers for Asian Countries	Ford Foundation AID
Center for Research and Communications, Manila	Management Economics for Industry	
Singapore		
Ngee Ann Technical College, Singapore	Training Technicians through Nondegree Polytechnic Programs	
Thailand		
Thammasat University, Mahidol University, Kasetsart	Maeklong Integrated Rural Development Project	Rockefeller Foundation Ford Foundation IBRD

LATIN AMERICA

Brazil		
Federal University of Bahía, Salvador	Center for Urban Development (CEDUR)	Rockefeller Foundation CIDA Unesco IDB
Colombia		
University of Antioquia, Medellín	Education for Rural Areas	Ford Foundation AID
University of Valle, Cali	The Research Program for Systems of Health Services Delivery (PRIMOPS)	Rockefeller Foundation Ford Foundation

APPENDIX C (continued)

Place	Project	Prior Financing by HED Donor Agencies
Colombian Higher Education System	Structure of Higher Education for Development of Colombia	
Mexico		
Monterrey Institute of Technology and Advanced Studies, Monterrey	Research and Extension Program for Industrial Development	Ford Foundation
Peru		
National Agrarian University, La Molina	Program for Transferal of Technology	Ford Foundation AID Rockefeller Foundation

SUMMARIES OF
CASE STUDIES
CONDUCTED BY
REGIONAL TEAMS

The Complete Studies will appear in Volume 2.

PROSPECTS FOR REGIONAL UNIVERSITIES IN AFRICA

University of Botswana, Lesotho, and Swaziland

The University of Botswana, Lesotho, and Swaziland (UBLS) was established in 1964 to serve three countries with a combined population of under 2.5 million. All three poor countries, they joined forces for reasons of economy and size to answer a common need for skilled and high-level manpower. Nevertheless, after 11 years of unified adminis-tration, the University came to an end in November 1975 after bitter dissension.

The nucleus of the three-nation university was a Catholic college established in 1945 to prepare black secondary school graduates for a University of South Africa external degree. Black students were not admitted to the all-white colleges in southern Africa and had few alter-natives. Pius XII Catholic College started with four priests and five students in an abandoned primary school in Roma, near the capital of Lesotho (then Basutoland). The College entered into a special relation-ship with the University of South Africa in 1955 and grew to include 188 students and 32 academic staff members. Beset by financial difficul-ties, it was transferred in 1963 from the Catholic Church to the three High Commission territories, which were seeking a way to start a co-operative institution of higher education. Funds required for the trans-fer were provided in part by the British government and the Ford Foundation.

When the three territories became independent nations, each cre-ated its own political and economic link with the outside world. Only the Customs Union and the University drew them together, and, until recently, the three governments appeared eager to preserve the University link. All three were represented on the University Council and on its important standing committees. The University also consulted regularly with the three governments on major policies, and the governments, in turn, drew on University resources for expert advice and assistance. A University study on local government, for example, was designed to help the three governments formulate local government policy.

As a trinational university, UBLS maintained headquarters in Lesotho but tried to avoid identification with any one country. The College of Agriculture, a postsecondary institution before it was incorporated into the University, is in Swaziland; the Faculty of Education provided in-service teacher training in Lesotho and Botswana. The perennial and most controversial issue at the University, however, was how to apportion resources fairly. In 1974-75, the main campus in Lesotho had 535 students, Swaziland had 387, and Botswana had 300. For a number of years, Swaziland and especially Botswana exerted pressure to increase their respective shares in student places and to establish a larger University presence in their respective countries.

The question of decentralization was the most widely and heatedly discussed issue within the University. Several University commissions over a period of years recommended that UBLS consider ways in which it could devote more of its resources to activities in Botswana and Lesotho. In 1970, a commission set up by the University and the three governments, with members from the United Kingdom, the United States, Canada, and the West Indies, recommended that courses in Botswana and in Swaziland should provide the first two years of the four-year UBLS degree course. The University, said the commission, should have a single council and senate, a common board of studies, and one president, registrar, and bursar to ensure unified administration. Each campus, however, would have its own vice-president and its own academic board with authority on local campus academic matters.

Although the University implemented most of the recommendations, the controversy continued. In 1974, another commission, presided over by the dean of the Faculty of Education and including representatives of the three governments, was asked to produce detailed plans for "a balanced University presence on the three campuses," at the same time bearing in mind "the need to minimize duplication of staff and facilities and the capital and recurrent costs of the University." The commission again recommended modifying university structure and governance, but its plans raised more issues than they resolved. The task of satisfying three governments apparently was impossible.

The final blow to UBLS was occasioned by a dispute between the government of Lesotho and the vice-chancellor; as a result, the

Lesotho government unilaterally declared the Roma campus in Lesotho the new National University of Lesotho. In decentralizing courses, Lesotho claimed, among other things, that the vice-chancellor gave too many advantages to the other two countries.

Botswana and Swaziland are expected to create another university made up of the two remaining campuses. The UBLS study underscores two questions: (1) Can independent nations collaborate in running one educational institution? (2) Can traditional university mechanisms adapt to new university roles in developing countries?

THE UNIVERSITY CENTRE FOR HEALTH SCIENCES

University of Yaoundé, Cameroon

The University Centre for Health Sciences at the University of Yaoundé was set up in 1969 to meet chronic shortages in all categories of health personnel, to improve the training of medical students, to improve rural health services by creating integrated medical teams, and to change fundamental attitudes toward health practice, medical education, and work in rural areas.

A long period of investigation and planning preceded the Centre's founding. Cameroon physicians and educators visited other medical and health science faculties. They conferred with teachers of medicine from other parts of Africa, with the government, with WHO, and with the UNDP. A special government planning commission, assisted for three years by a medical educator assigned to WHO, culled information and advice and finally decided to create a center with a pioneering concept of health education.

Unlike a traditional faculty of medicine, the Centre trains physicians, nurses, and technicians to combine their skills and to work together to deliver health services. Students with different academic qualifications pursue different programs but share the same teachers and buildings and common core courses. Teaching is integrated by themes, rather than by subjects or disciplines. Three technical units—biomedical sciences, community hospital or clinical sciences, and public health or epidemiological sciences—represent the principal groups of attitudes, skills, and knowledge each student must acquire. Medical students, nurses, and technicians must have basic training in all three units. Activities focus on a combination of teaching, service, and research.

All students participate in practical team training in clinical and rural health. A group or team of students helps run an assigned health center for a village or group of villages. A pilot health service project has been started in one of the six health demonstration zones created by the government. Students and staff undergo field training here and, during the next ten years, will extend their activities into other parts of the country.

Four years before it received its first students, UCHS launched a staff development program. The Cameroon government's National Planning Commission identified people qualified to teach in and organize the Centre and chose Cameroon physicians to receive fellowships for advanced study abroad. Various technical assistance agencies (UNDP, WHO, FAC, and USAID) recruited and paid for additional staff and have since financed advanced training for more Cameroonians.

Most full-time staff are medical graduates of universities in Britain and France and of African medical schools (especially Ibadan in Nigeria and Dakar in Senegal). Teaching, service, and administration are conducted in both English and French; each teacher uses the language in which he or she is most competent and students must be bilingual.

The government of Cameroon and UNDP provide the principal financing, with WHO serving as executing agency for UNDP. Other financing agencies that have pooled their resources are UNICEF, FAC, CIDA, USAID, and the United Kingdom Ministry of Overseas Development.

The program already has had an influence on students, teaching staff, and the university, and a number of other African countries recently have decided to create similar centers. Most students accept the new philosophy of integrated learning and health care, and most are willing to begin their professional lives in the provinces. Teaching staff, brought together from a large number of countries and disciplines, has learned to train health workers rather than to teach isolated subjects.

In accepting the health team concept, the University has changed. It has admitted students with "lower" academic qualifications into courses previously considered below university level. The first two African vice-chancellors of the University, moreover, were both selected from among UCHS's medical professors. UCHS teachers receive government health services allowances, challenging professors in other faculties to participate in community development in their own fields.

Despite its general success, the new program has encountered certain difficulties. Some students fear being used as guinea pigs; staff is sometimes disoriented, unable to grasp the new system or resistant to change; traditional methods of administration do not work; integrated teaching requires staff cooperation rather than faculty autonomy; and project directors must be specially trained, flexible, and good at problem solving.

Program leaders cite three lessons learned: higher educational institutions should adapt themselves to local conditions; manpower production and use are inseparable; and attitudes can be changed but the change cannot be hurried. A UNDP/WHO evaluation in 1974 reported that most objectives for 1970-73 were attained.

FUNCTIONAL BILINGUALISM: AN EMERGENT ISSUE OF THE
AFRICAN UNIVERSITY

University of Yaoundé, Cameroon

Since 1472, six languages have been used officially at one time or another in Cameroon—Portuguese, Spanish, Dutch, French, English, and German. In addition, Cameroon has at least ten indigenous language groups, which break up into about 285 language or dialect variants.

Today Cameroon has two official languages, English and French, and bilingualism has been strongly supported by the government and head of state. The University, founded in 1961, thus became bilingual. Because it was started with the help of the French government, however, most administrators and teaching staff, since its founding, have been French-speaking and/or French nationals. (In 1973-74, 292 members of the academic staff were French-speaking and 52 English-speaking; 4,456 students spoke French and 493 spoke English.) English-speaking students had to learn French for most degrees. This imbalance of language groups and the pressure to use only French in the University became a matter of official concern.

To break the linguistic divide between English-speaking and French-speaking Cameroonians and to defuse the mounting hostility between them, the University of Yaoundé took steps to give all students bilingual skills. It encouraged the British government to accept responsibility for a chair of English and to send English-language teaching staff to the University to develop English-language courses for French-speaking students. It required every student in the University to spend at least two hours a week in learning the second official language and to pass a test in it.

Language training presented a curious administrative problem. Under the French teaching tradition, bilingual training fell into the category of secondary school teaching and therefore beneath the academic dignity of university teaching staff. The English Department, therefore, took over the teaching of both English and French. Recently, language teachers have been posted to the various faculties where they train the student not only in language but also in the special vocabulary

of the field. (Some faculties, including the University Centre for
Health Sciences, require the second language for admission.)

The University has also tried to promote bilingualism by allowing
each teacher to lecture in his own language. In the law faculty, French
law is taught in French and British law in English; Cameroon law is
taught in English or French depending on the language of the teacher.
A bilingual course in the Faculty of Arts requires students to do half
the course in English in the English Department and the other half in
French in the French Department. Students have an incentive to become proficient in a second language; those who pass their examination
in this course are sent abroad for intensive study, English-speaking
students to France and French-speaking students to England.

Cameroon feels there are great advantages in bilingualism. As
part of its heritage, it helps to define a national personality; it speeds
communication between French-speaking and English-speaking faculty
members and their students; and it unites the nation by reducing conflict between the two language groups. With more bilingual scholars
and professors, the University also feels it will have less need to rely
on foreign academic personnel.

THE PUBLIC SERVICE ROLE OF THE UNIVERSITY

Addis Ababa University,* Ethiopia

The Ethiopian University Service, a work-study program in which
all students served for one academic year in rural areas, was established in 1964 to expose students to rural Ethiopia, to supplement the
inadequate supply of teachers and other skilled workers, and to provide a practical ingredient to higher education. It lasted until 1974.

The University's six constitutent colleges earlier had involved
students in community activities: the Public Health College included
fieldwork in its curriculum, students in the Institute of Building Technology helped to identify and improve local materials, and mobile
staff-student teams from the University College taught shepherds
literacy.

The University statute establishing the Service for the University
as a whole made the year's work a graduation requirement. Students
were expected to meet the standards of government agencies with
whom they served, but the University was to administer the program

---

*Formerly Haile Selassie I University. The formal programs of
the University have been suspended since the 1974 change in Ethiopia's
government.

in accordance with the premise that the University Service "is a part
of the university's basic education program."

While the program expected to assign students to work related to
their fields of study, almost three quarters of the 3,759 students who
participated between 1964 and 1973 served as teachers. The 25 percent
who did not served in rural hospitals, community development centers,
the courts, construction works, geological explorations, and agricultural research stations.

The program had its own budget and was attached to the School of
Social Work because of the School's expertise in community and rural
development. A full-time administrative staff was responsible for
student orientation, assignments, liaison with the employing agencies,
and evaluation of the program.

In their third year, before their fieldwork, students took a one-
credit-hour orientation course on problems of Ethiopian society.
Course topics included administration of education, methods of teaching, community development, health practices, problems of change,
and the ways in which agriculture, education, and law enforeement
were related to development. On their rural jobs, students received
an allowance and a basic living kit, including first-aid equipment, a
folding bed, chair and table, and, in some cases, a water filter and
a kerosene lamp.

The program encountered a number of difficulties. Some staff
members thought fieldwork unrelated to higher education and either
avoided evaluation or supervisory trips altogether or used them for
other purposes. Government agencies offered few service opportunities to students other than teaching. The program lacked funds to
employ enough student counselors, supervisors, and staff; and students complained of feeling neglected and cut off from the University,
of inadequate allowances, and of conflicts with colleagues, administrators, and government and police authorities. Local communities
sometimes had no forewarning or plans to use students prepared to
teach.

The program has four major achievements. (1) It enriched student education. Faculty agreed that students returned from their jobs
more mature and more practical, and students felt that they had ac-
quired insight into the nation's problems. (2) It improved primary
and secondary schools. An estimated 120,000 elementary and junior
high school students throughout the country received instruction from
University students. (3) It contributed to Ethiopian development.
Many services would not have been performed if students had not been
available for them. (4) It set an example of a feasible and potentially
valuable student service program.

The University also linked academic work to national problems
in three other ways: part-time extension courses, summer in-service

training, and use of University staff in a comprehensive national Education Sector Review.

The extension division in 1973-74 offered 140 part-time courses for adults, ranging from remedial language and mathematics to law. It graduated 2,831 students: about 9 percent with degrees, about 70 percent with diplomas, and about 20 percent with certificates. Most students had government and business jobs. Staff came from regular university faculties, as well as from government, industry, and business. A correspondence school was begun to widen the clientele to rural areas.

The in-service summer training in the education faculty upgraded elementary schoolteachers in subject matter and teaching methods; a few were later admitted to degree-level programs. The program included special training for elementary school principals, supervisors, and district education officers; two out of three school principals and almost all supervisors are graduates of the course. Education ministry officials taught some courses and worked closely with faculty in evaluating, criticizing, and improving the program.

The Education Sector Review, completed in 1972, brought together representatives of ministries, professions, and international and bilateral agencies to gather information on national education and to recommend ways to improve it. About 40 percent of the participants were University staff.

TECHNOLOGY AT THE SERVICE OF RURAL AND INDUSTRIAL DEVELOPMENT

University of Science and Technology, Ghana

Designed primarily to meet national development needs, the University of Science and Technology, established in 1961, combines training, research, service, and consultancy. It trains both high- and middle-level manpower under the University umbrella, offering four-year degree courses as well as one- and two-year courses leading to diplomas and certificates. As part of its research, the University develops new products for local use and export and promotes small-scale industries. A pioneer in stimulating grass-roots rural industrialization, it makes its expertise available to government, industry, and local farmers.

The University has seven faculties: agriculture, architecture, art, engineering, pharmacy, science, and social studies. All focus on practical problems and involve fieldwork and on-the-job training. Students are expected to spend a minimum of eight weeks during their long vacations in jobs related to their courses. During term time, most students work on farms or in agencies in various parts of the country, and all four-year courses require projects in the final year that coordinate practice and theory.

The practical aspects of the program have involved some difficulties. Students are sometimes assigned vacation jobs unrelated to their course work or employers may be uncooperative or disinterested. Staff sometimes provides inadequate supervision of work periods and some students are indifferent to their job experiences. To bolster the practical point of view, the University helps faculty members gain industrial experience by arranging for them to spend periods in industry, engages outside professionals as part-time lecturers, and appoints experts from industry as external examiners.

Research, too, is directed to practical needs. Recent projects include studying the conditions for cultivating kenaf, a local fiber plant; hybridizing pigs to produce better meat; testing local materials for low-cost housing; investigating local clays and dyes for use by village craftsmen; developing a standard for testing cement; designing a bore hole pump and a soil block press; and investigating local herbs for medicinal properties. Efforts have been made to adopt a more interdisciplinary approach to research problems.

The University contributes its technical expertise to solving national problems in other ways. University staff members serve on management advisory boards of national and international organizations. Some faculties as well as individual staff members participate in national projects. The Faculty of Agriculture gives short demonstration courses for farmers. As long as faculty consulting activities do not interfere with normal teaching and research, they are encouraged by the University as a means to enhance the quality of teaching.

In 1968, about 20 staff members created the Voluntary Technology Group to solve specific technical problems referred to them by small businessmen, manufacturers, and farmers. They charged fees just large enough to cover expenses. The success of six years of volunteer service led the University to establish in 1972 the Technology Consultancy Centre, which gave a more formal structure to University consulting work. An autonomous unit within the University, the Centre acts as a clearinghouse through which the University makes available its expertise and resources. It negotiates consultancy contracts with outside organizations and submits proposals to Government for research development. The Centre's director coordinates the multidisciplinary projects and recruits consultants from among staff members or outsiders.

The Centre seeks to upgrade existing craft industries, such as textiles, pottery, and woodwork, by introducing new products and new techniques; to generate new small-scale industries; and to assist the entrepreneur. It encourages small businesses by training craftsmen and managers, developing products, testing the markets, and demonstrating operations. (A small manufacturer of cassava starch, for example, learned to make glue from the starch and sell it profitably.) After it has set up a production unit, the University hopes entrepreneurs or craftsmen's cooperatives will take over. The Centre has designed and started plants that produce nuts and bolts, caustic soda, fabrics, tableware, concrete blocks, traffic lights, well pumps, pharmaceutical products, and scientific instruments for school use.

The Centre depends for financing on the government and outside sources, since the small businessmen and farmers it serves can afford only modest fees. The Centre hopes eventually to be self-supporting, offsetting free services with income from industrial contracts. It provides not only a clearinghouse for industrial and agricultural problem solving but also an important point of contact between the University and the community.

HIGHER EDUCATION IN MALI

In 1962, two years after gaining its independence, Mali reorganized its former colonial educational system under an educational reform law. The new law was designed to increase literacy, to establish more primary schools in rural areas with a program "rooted in the environment," and to train, on the secondary and postsecondary levels, the technicians, specialists, and professionals the country needed.

In 1970, 23 percent of the 6 to 13 age group were in the nine-year primary or basic schools, a growth of 250 percent in 11 years, but students were leaving rural areas for the cities where most secondary schools were located. To halt urban immigration, the Malian government, with help from Unesco and UNICEF, tried to link basic education more firmly to rural life through work programs in industry and crafts. Teachers, however, were unwilling to change their methods, and basic education is still seen as an "escape route from bush." The 70 percent who do not pass the entrance examination to the seventh year in the basic schools have no vocational or educational alternatives, and many do not return to the land.

The 11 secondary schools accept about 20 percent of those who finish primary education. Most secondary school graduates receive arts diplomas, but authorities hope that eventually 70 percent of secondary students will receive scientific and technical education.

Higher education has developed as a series of specialized schools and institutes, not yet organized into a university, although a university appears to be an official goal. While there is little overall plan-

ning and coordination among schools to bring training in line with
national needs, the five institutions, each linked with a government
ministry, generally have responded to the requirements of the market-
place and to a desire for social and economic usefulness. Until recently, most students seeking higher education were trained abroad;
in 1963, only 30 percent were trained locally. In 1972, however,
nearly 80 percent of all Malian B.A.s received their education at one
of Mali's five postsecondary institutions.

The system of higher education began with the Higher Teacher
Training School, or ENS (Ecole Normale Supérieure), which now trains
80 percent of Mali's teachers of general secondary education. (Teachers of basic education classes receive their training in Regional Teaching Centers or, for second-level basic education teachers, at the
Secondary Teacher Training School.) Applicants to ENS must have
passed the baccalaureat. The three-year ENS training includes only
six months of practice teaching, which students consider inadequate,
and suffers from several other handicaps: too few methodology courses,
too many graduates in arts and too few in sciences, and inadequate
training for ENS's own teaching staff.

The Rural Polytechnic Institute trains professional engineers and
middle-level technicians in a double-level system in the various departments of agricultural development. In a common course at the
beginning and in practical work, students are encouraged to work together and to see the two levels as complementary, although instruc-
tors are not always capable of this kind of teaching, and upper-level
students sometimes have trouble accepting technicians as coworkers.
Employers for whom students work during eight months in the field
sit on examining juries that evaluate student work. The only one of
the five institutions of higher education to link professional and technical training, the Institute seeks to break away from traditional
teaching methods and to provide more connection between training and
job. The Production Ministry helps design the programs and the minister sits on the Institute's board of directors.

The National Engineering School was strengthened in 1970 to train
the additional 110 engineers that planners estimated would be needed
in three years at Mali's current economic growth rate. Applicants
must have received the baccalaureat. The four-year training assigns
little time for practical work, but the school has made efforts to include businesses and government in seminars on current problems
and in research and consultation activities.

Created in 1963, the National School of Public Administration was
intended to train both upper- and middle-level personnel for Mali's
civil service. Since 1969, it has provided only higher level training.
Entrants must hold the baccalaureat, but officials already in service
may take a professional course. The program includes only three

months of fieldwork in the government department in which the student
will serve after graduation. (An offshoot of this school is the Institute
of Production Management Forecasting, which trains management
personnel in 15 months and retrains personnel already in business.)

The Medical School, opened in 1969, emphasizes public health and
tropical medicine. Its program differs from medical studies in most
African countries in that physicians are trained in five and half years
rather than in seven, clinical training begins in the first year, students act as interns in the fourth and fifth years without taking exams
and thus learn medical administration and preventive medicine early,
and students specialize after only two years of practice. The Medical
School has 155 students, including 15 women in the first year. As in
all the other schools, students receive full scholarships from the state.

DEVELOPING A UNIVERSITY IN A SMALL COUNTRY

University of Mauritius

The University of Mauritius, created in 1965, devotes almost all
its activities to training middle-level manpower for the sugar economy, which accounts for 40 percent of the island's gross national
product and 90 percent of its export earnings. Most of the 1,000 students work for a certificate or diploma; only about 10 percent pursue
degree-level courses. The University has three faculties or schools:
agriculture, administration, and industrial technology. There is no
faculty of science or arts. A number of students take short intensive
courses to upgrade their job skills without seeking a diploma, certificate, or degree. Committed to relate its training to the immediate
needs of the country, the institution is a good example of a development-
oriented university.

The University's constitutent units have grown out of special manpower needs. The School of Agriculture has trained sugar industry
technicians, managers, and extension workers for 40 years, as the
College of Agriculture, before it was incorporated into the University.
Established by the Ministry of Agriculture, and formerly the only
postsecondary institution in a country with a population of 850,000
people, it retained many of its staff and administrators and much of
its character when it became part of the new university. Its core program is still a joint diploma course in agriculture and sugar technology.
A number of professional staff from the Ministry of Agriculture and
the sugar estates teach part time at the School, helping to maintain
the practical nature of the course. Student intake is carefully regu-
lated to reflect manpower needs, and those who complete the course

are readily absorbed by the sugar industry. The School also runs diploma and certificate courses for medical laboratory technicians and for tea agronomy.

The newly created School of Administration, after an unsuccessful attempt to launch a degree program, also decided to offer subdegree courses. Students, as well as jobholders released by their government or industrial employers for training, study such subjects as cooperatives, accounting, and banking.

The School of Industrial Technology, like the other two schools, concentrates its offerings on diploma programs in physical and health sciences, mechanical and electrical engineering, building, and sanitary science. It also has part-time courses at the certificate level (in subjects such as refrigeration and air-conditioning technology and road construction), one degree course with limited enrollment, and an honors degree program in sugar technology.

The government of Mauritius spends almost three quarters of its education budget on primary education, and 86 percent of primary age children attend school. The government has little control, however, over secondary schools, which supply the University and enroll 31 percent of the secondary school age population. Almost all secondary schools are privately owned and operated. They are poorly equipped and housed, studies are overly theoretical and dominated by examinations, and science and technical subjects are poorly taught. Students speak Creole, French, or Asian languages at home and have trouble passing the English-language examinations.

The University's strength has been its pragmatic and realistic approach; it has tried to compensate for poor secondary school training and has concentrated on middle-level training as the area of greatest national impact. Two factors, however, may make it difficult to continue this strategy. First, while Mauritius is likely to remain heavily dependent on sugar for at least the next few years, the market for middle-level manpower is decreasing. Second, there is an increasing demand for degree qualifications.

Social stratification in Mauritius generally follows ethnic lines. Most whites and Chinese can afford to send their children abroad for university degrees; Indo-Pakistanis, the middle group, have been the beneficiaries of the middle-level manpower training of the University but may not remain content with subdegree qualifications. The lowest socioeconomic group, the blacks, has rising aspirations to which the University may have to respond. While for the past 40 years the University has defined its role with enviable precision, it may be forced to redefine its objectives and its mission.

AGRICULTURAL AND EDUCATIONAL DEVELOPMENT
ROLES OF THE UNIVERSITY

Ahmadu Bello University, Nigeria

Ahmadu Bello University was established in 1962, shortly after
Nigerian independence, to serve the needs of about 50 million people
in the northern two thirds of Nigeria. Its student body has grown from
519 to 9,750 in 12 years. On its main campus at Zaria, it has degree
programs in arts, social sciences, science, environmental design,
education, engineering, medicine, and veterinary medicine. At Abdullahi Bayero College, 110 miles north of the main campus, it has a
Faculty of Arabic and Islamic Studies; and at its agricultural complex
at Samaru, it has faculties of agriculture and of veterinary medicine,
the Extension Research Liaison Service, the Rural Economic Research
Unit, and four schools in the Division for Agricultural and Livestock
Services Training for middle-level extension workers.

In response to government concern that university research be
practical and oriented to problem solving, the University set up four
semiautonomous institutes designed to blend academic programs and
direct service to the community. Each of these institutes—Education,
Agricultural Research and Special Services, Administration, and
Health—has its own governing board with substantial government rep-
resentation. (Several University faculties also have invited ministry
officers to serve on their academic boards.) All work closely with
their sister faculties, often sharing staff. The institutes operate under
the general control of the University but, unlike the faculties, are not
governed directly by the senate except in regard to degree programs.
Each institute provides research, advisory and consultancy services,
and in-service training to the six states of the region.

The Institute of Education advises the ministries on any education
matters and collaborates with the ministries in planning and extending
educational facilities and courses of study and instruction. It coordinates all educational research, collects educational statistics, and
evaluates programs. It also establishes and maintains professional
libraries.

The Institute's Division of Primary Education develops primary
school curricula in all subjects, largely through teacher-specialist
10- to 14-day workshops. It also produces teaching materials, using
as much as possible local materials and concepts. Under a technical
assistance agreement with Unesco-UNICEF, the Institute tests equipment, materials, and curricula in more than 60 model schools and
trains teachers to use them.

The Division of Teacher Education encourages the 80 or so Grade II teacher training colleges throughout the states to apply for what has become prestigious membership in the Institute and sets minimum standards for affiliation. In return, the Institute organizes among teachers of the affiliated colleges boards of study to develop and improve curriculum. This division also provides subject area specialists, coordinates syllabi, and moderates examinations. It sends a mobile teacher training group from one teacher training college to another to advise, assist, and train as required. The division also provides vacation refresher courses for teachers and a one-year certificate training in educational administration.

In addition, the Institute of Education runs two three-year advanced teachers colleges that, between them, graduate each year 1,000 Certificate of Education holders qualified to teach at lower levels of secondary schools or to serve as primary school principals. In a one-year postgraduate course, practicing teachers alternate two summer school periods at the Institute with teaching under professional supervision and guidance.

The Institute for Agricultural Research and Special Services has over 250 research staff members and five research substations with which it conducts all crop research for the six state governments in the 250,000 square mile area. The Institute also undertakes contract research for the Federal Ministry of Agriculture and for the International Institute of Tropical Agriculture in Ibadan. Extension services include plant pathology diagnosis, pest control, production of new improved seed, and recommendations for fertilizer and pesticides. It prepared the draft for the government's 15-year plan for agricultural development in Nigeria.

To find out why research was bringing so little change in farming methods, the University set up the Rural Economic Research Unit, funded originally by the Ford Foundation and later by the Nigerian government. Using social science research tools, the unit discovered that research based on monocropping had run afoul of multicropping tradition, and the Institute adjusted research and extension services accordingly. In a Guided Introduction to Change program, the unit plans to work with farmers, introducing simple technology and arranging credit.

The Extension Research Liaison Service channels problems of agriculture in the field to University research workers and passes the resultant research back to the farmers through extension from the ministries. The service also runs radio and television programs in 14 local languages and sends teams of extension workers to farming regions to answer farmers' questions on the spot.

There are three other institutes at Ahmadu Bello. The Institute of Administration provides undergraduate and postgraduate diplomas in public administration, largely as in-service training programs, and also offers diplomas in accounting, banking, insurance, local government, and law. The Institute of Health maintains facilities for training medical students and runs hospital services for the community. It is trying to develop team training to include physicians, nurses, midwives, and technicians, and to better rural health programs. The Center for Nigerian Cultural Studies conducts research on the culture of Nigeria, particularly in the six northern states that Ahmadu Bello University serves. The Center concentrates on archeology, dance, drama, and musicology, and seeks both to preserve and present cultural traditions in these fields。

STAFF DEVELOPMENT IN AN AFRICAN UNIVERSITY

University of Khartoum, Sudan

When Sudan became independent in 1956, the University of Khartoum attained independent status, awarding its own degrees rather than those of the University of London. Both the University administration and faculty had been recruited largely from Britain or from Egypt; the vice-chancellor, the registrar, the librarian, the bursar, and all the deans were expatriates. The newly independent University's first effort, therefore, was to replace them with qualified Sudanese.

The University began staff development with a search for Sudanese to fill senior administrative posts. There were special shortages of financial managers and accountants, engineers, and building managers. Although, at first, the University depended on retired government employees rather than on qualified graduates for these positions, by 1958 it had appointed Sudanese to its major executive positions. Administrators were trained by short visits to universities outside the country, by long-term courses abroad, and by on-the-job training.

Academic administrators (deans of faculties and heads of teaching and research units and departments) were still more difficult to find. Sudanese university graduates eligible for training or appointment were attracted instead to the civil service because of its status and better conditions of service. The academic seniority system of the University, moreover, excluded Sudanese academic staff members from administrative appointments. The solution, rotating administrative posts, avoided seniority requirements, although it sacrificed continuity.

To replace expatriate teaching staff with Sudanese, the University instituted the Senior Scholars and Research Fellowship Scheme,

financed by a special University fund and by outside agency assistance.
Under the scheme, University departments selected outstanding Suda
nese graduates each year, appointed them as teaching and research
assistants, and sent them to universities outside the country for postgraduate degrees while paying them salaries at home. Upon successful
completion of their training, Fellows were expected to join the University's academic staff. The University also sent abroad a number of
undergraduates and some young Sudanese members of the academic
staff to strengthen their qualifications for university teaching. A special committee of faculty representatives, chaired by the vice-
chancellor, made final decisions on selections and established the
delicate balance between academic standards and the demand for
trained faculty.

It took three to four years to train one graduate at an average cost
of $1,000 a year, excluding salaries paid at home. (Training in the
United States and in the United Kingdom costs about three times as
much.) Although a few failed to return to the Sudan after their training,
most joined the University's faculty. When the University became independent, Sudanese academic staff on the level of lecturer and above
was less than 5 percent of the total. Two years later, when the first
Sudanese vice-chancellor was appointed, it had reached 10 percent.
By 1975, Sudanese made up 80 percent of the total staff, the highest
percentage of local staff in Africa. From 1960 to 1974, 300 Sudanese
were prepared to fill the academic and teaching posts of the University.

The fellowship plan was extended to graduates of other Sudanese
universities and later included laboratory technicians as well as teaching faculty. Neither the selection method nor the University salary
structure, however, attracted the best technician candidates. Candidates were selected only from among secondary school graduates who
had failed to get a place in a university, and of those qualified for
training, a number stayed abroad for more money or joined other local
institutions that paid higher salaries. The number of qualified technicians available increased only when the University established an internal training program and offered better salaries for laboratory
technicians.

Case study investigators drew the following conclusions: (1) the
training scheme has been a useful and valuable policy; (2) crucial to
the program is the trainees' willingness to serve the university when
they return from study abroad; (3) since university enrollment in most
developing countries has increased beyond what was predicted, as
many candidates as possible should be trained; and (4) training nationals is only one part of successful staff development. To fulfill its
teaching, research, and national development responsibilities, a university must continuously provide its staff with access to and links
with colleagues inside and outside the country through such methods

as exchange programs and sabbatical leaves. These principles may be helpful in staff development programs at other developing universities.

HIGHER EDUCATION AND DEVELOPMENT IN SUDAN

If Sudan carries out its present development plans, 75,000 to 85,000 jobs per year will be created over the next ten years. Of these, 10,000 to 12,000 per year will require secondary education or higher, and 1,000 will require university training.

Two thirds of Sudan's 21,500 university students are enrolled in foreign universities, including the University of Cairo branch in Khartoum with 9,500 students. The other third is in Sudan at the University of Khartoum (6,783 students) and the Islamic University of Omdurman (600 students). Additional postsecondary training colleges in Sudan enroll about 2,400 students, of whom 800 are in teacher training. There are, in all, 39 postsecondary training institutions, including universities.

High-level staffing needs for new development could be met in two years if Sudanese graduates from overseas universities were included. Present postsecondary technical training programs, however, even if doubled, cannot meet projected development needs, and there has been no overall development policy that includes manpower planning.

Sudan combines unemployment and underemployment of higher education graduates in some areas with crucial manpower shortages in other areas. There has been an overproduction of graduates in the nonscientific fields, aggravated by an earlier government policy of employing all postsecondary and university graduates, whether or not there were jobs for them, and an underproduction of technicians.

The shortage of technicians results primarily from the low status of technical education. Students who pass ninth-grade leaving examinations with the lowest scores are directed into secondary-level teacher training and technical education. Similarly, at the postsecondary level, only those who do not get into a university apply for technical and teacher training. Without prestige, technical training cannot even ensure jobs; private employers prefer more expensive but better trained expatriate technicians. Sudanese technicians fit no career structure, receive poor salaries, and have little chance for further schooling. As a result, while they are no competitive threat to professionals, professional skill and achievement suffer.

Besides its manpower training imbalance, the higher educational system has two other problems: its failure to train women (only 13 percent of the students in postsecondary institutions) and its overemphasis on foreign university training. Such training carries with it a number of hazards. In the first place, the University of Cairo branch at Khartoum and other foreign universities offer alternatives for applicants who might otherwise press for expansion of enrollment at home. The two Sudanese universities are thus relieved of the pressure to take in more students, to establish evening programs and large extramural centers, or to introduce vocational and technical programs. Second, undergraduates who study abroad often return with foreign outlooks, modes of life, and work patterns, and are not attuned to local conditions. Sudan can now provide undergraduate training in most fields; its needs abroad are for postgraduate and professional training.

Sudan's economy has suffered in the past few years from political instability, lack of foreign aid, a poor export market for cotton (over 60 percent of Sudan's foreign exchange), and inadequate and costly transportation. It has, however, a large potential for growth, and some consider that its development is at a takeoff point. If so, its higher educational system must be able to adjust.

To make this adjustment, several reforms have been recommended:

1. To establish firm government regulation and control of all higher education. Only government can deal with the relationships with Egypt, the countries of Eastern Europe, Muslim leaders in Sudan, and militant secondary school students—all of which affect higher education.

2. To establish a new Sudanese umbrella university, carefully planned to meet specific educational and development needs and to ensure close ties between training and jobs and between professional and technical education. It should include a medical center oriented toward preventive medicine; an agricultural education center with supporting technical programs; a faculty of engineering, also supported by technical programs at diploma level, and engineering research laboratories; and a community college offering basic science courses in preparation for professional programs. It would not include the conventional university faculties of arts, law, commerce, and social science.

3. To establish specialized postsecondary training in the south on which a university can be based later. This war-torn region has an immediate need for practical, technical training at secondary and postsecondary levels in animal husbandry, agriculture, fisheries, forestry, and wild life; for supervised work experience; and for an education college to upgrade the untrained teachers now presiding over rural schools.

THE UNIVERSITY'S RESPONSE TO MANPOWER NEEDS

University of Dar es Salaam, Tanzania

The College of Dar es Salaam opened in 1961 with 13 students. In 1963, it became one of the three constituent colleges of the federal University of East Africa (Makerere in Uganda and Nairobi in Kenya were the other two), and in 1970, it was established as the University of Dar es Salaam, an autonomous national institution.

As a national university, Dar es Salaam set out to achieve four goals: to provide a center for higher learning, to further economic and human development, to contribute to Tanzania's economic and political revolution, and to train high-level manpower needed by the nation. To reach these goals, the University has been changing its program, its organization, its research priorities, and its relationship to government.

Modeled on the traditional British university, Dar es Salaam now seeks to make course material and learning methods more relevant and more interdisciplinary. The Faculty of Arts and Social Sciences has supplemented the traditional curriculum with multisubject streams and courses, such as "Developmental Studies" and "East African Societies and Environment." In teaching through research programs, second-year students do research on local conditions, becoming familiar with social science research processes and adding to available information.

In addition, students now spend almost half of the three-month vacation, which comes after each three academic terms, in factories, offices, and ujamaa villages.* It is hoped that in this way students will be brought closer to the needs of the people and the ways in which their knowledge can be applied.

There is intense competition for entry to the University. The government determines manpower needs and then specifies the number of students to be admitted into each professional program. (Government controls the flow of students even at the secondary school level by deciding how many shall learn various subjects.) Male students from areas with the most developed primary and secondary schools are most heavily represented. (The proportion of women in higher education is small.) Although Tanzania concentrates new educational resources in poorer regions, the imbalance is difficult to correct.

----

*Ujamaa villages are new, communal villages designed to bring residents of the countryside together, principally for easier access to services such as hospitals and schools.

A new element now helps determine access, however. Before
going to the University, prospective students must spend no less than
a year on farms or in factories. To be accepted for a University place,
they must be recommended by their coworkers and the TANU (the national political party) branch on the basis of character, work performance, and commitment. The University also admits some older
students under two programs, the "mature age entry" and the "special
entry" schemes, giving a second chance to those who have had less
conventional educational preparation.

To develop a Tanzanian staff, the University identifies prospective
staff members and pays them while they train briefly in an overseas
university and for a longer period of postgraduate work in Tanzania.
Although the University continues to depend on foreign sources for both
staff and research funds, this program is a move to counteract what
are considered the most harmful influences of overseas training. The
staff, however, has little formal organization, and, since members
are often promoted for reasons other than merit, it is difficult to attract and keep competent faculty.

Government and University are closely linked. The civil service
employs most holders of postgraduate degrees in economics, political
science, and education. In addition, two applied social science research bureaus and three education and research institutes provide
advice, information, and personnel to government planning units. Staff
members are encouraged to participate in the TANU Youth League and
the public militia, and TANU is represented on University committees.
Some University staff are seconded from government, and a number
of faculty members serve in government posts. The University budget
is approved by government ministries, and most Tanzanian students
hold government bursaries. Party and government represent at least
38 percent of the University council.

Some observers fear that these close government-University ties
may lead to an unthinking conformity and a lack of flexibility on the
part of the University. Like other African universities, Dar es Salaam
must balance the needs of independence against those of national responsiveness.

8

CENTER FOR STUDIES IN RURAL DEVELOPMENT

Ahmednagar College, India*

Ahmednagar College, established in 1947 to educate rural youth and provide leadership to the villages, found that its students were, in fact, seeking education to escape the villages. To prevent this brain drain from the countryside, the College started the Rural Life Development and Research Project in 1961 to fulfill what it described as its social mission. It hoped that students who studied the problems of the rural area surrounding the college and who took part in their solution would be more likely to become responsible citizens and leaders and to act as a yeast for rural progress.

The program, combining research and service and focusing on the village rather than on the campus, ran into initial opposition. Faculty members saw no academic benefits, disapproved of students and faculty working alongside villagers, and believed that giving credit for such work would disrupt the examination system. Government officials were unenthusiastic, and villagers resisted collegiate meddling.

---

*This case study, unlike the others, which were made at the institutions themselves, is based on written material obtained from S. K. Hulbe, the project's director, and from John Peters, president of World Neighbors. Project staff also interviewed Mr. Hulbe, Mr. Peters, and Telfer Mook of the United Church Board of World Ministries, which has helped fund Ahmednagar.

To win the confidence of these groups, a small core of interested planners invited faculty and student body to attend discussion groups and lectures, talked with government officials, established friendships with village elders, and brought movies, plays, and children's programs to the villages. As understanding grew, the project selected a tribal community 6 miles from the College. Students and faculty visited it daily to discuss problems, help villagers decide priorities, and help organize classes in literacy and public health. They looked for ways to encourage village initiative and leadership.

Fourteen years later the program had expanded to 29 villages surrounding Ahmednagar and had made an impact on more than 100 villages and 15,000 people. The Rural Project, now the Center for Studies in Rural Development, has initiated soil conservation, health and literacy, and adult education programs, food projects, and family planning. Students have helped farmers start cooperatives, form inter-village associations, build an oil mill to process peanuts, and set up a medical facility. Villagers take active roles in the programs and district officials cooperate.

Although originally the College gave no credit for the course, it now offers the only master's degree in Rural Social Work given in India and a Ph.D., both granted by Poona University. The one- and two-year interdisciplinary programs of study and research combined with participation in community affairs have three times as many applicants as the Center can accept. Along with specialized courses, students have special assignments in rural work in which they learn research methodology, channels of communication, and processes of decision making. Teaching staff is drawn from the regular social science faculty of the College, and technical specialists are invited to lecture.

Undergraduates at Ahmednagar College (about 80 percent of them come from rural areas) may volunteer for fieldwork in the villages under Center auspices. Although they receive no credit, about half of each class of 200 students spends up to 60 days a year in field activities. About 90 percent of the rural students go back to rural areas after graduation.

The Center also provides training for groups outside the College. The government's National Service Scheme, modeled on Ahmednagar's project and designed to encourage students to study firsthand rural and urban poverty, sends professors and student leaders from other colleges for training at the Center. They receive a two- to three-week orientation course, sponsored by the Indian government, so they can set up similar programs in their own colleges. The University of Bombay and the Catholic Seminary in Poona send students to the Center for training in rural village work. The Center also helps organize one- or two-day programs for government workers in family planning, public health, agriculture, and small-scale industries.

According to its director, the Center has affected the educational program of the College as a whole. Teaching and learning, he said, have been improved by the involvement of both faculty and students in the problems of the surrounding society. The College, "while endeavoring to serve the community will in the process be enriching its own academic life."

Fourteen years after the project was launched, farm production in the region had quadrupled. It is expected to increase tenfold in the coming years. Poona University, with which Ahmednagar is affiliated, has incorporated the program into its regional outreach, and 41 colleges have adopted some or all of its aspects.

THE UNIVERSITY'S ROLE IN RURAL DEVELOPMENT

Gadjah Mada University, Indonesia

Gadjah Mada, a state university, was established in 1946, and in 1974 had 15,000 students. When it recently sought ways to make teaching more meaningful and to serve better its region and country, it had a number of problems to overcome. First, 18 separate and independent faculties had little or no contact with one another; each had its own program of classes. Second, an Indonesian oral tradition of instruction gave little emphasis to either independent research or practical problem solving. Third, faculties, generally inbred and, in most cases, not exposed to education abroad, resisted change; faculty members were suspicious of infringement by other faculties, were oriented to delivering lectures, and had little commitment to public service.

Nevertheless, Gadjah Mada, assisted by foreign financing, recently established programs in rural development that have not only contributed to meeting community needs but also have instituted changes in teaching and university structure. The programs are the responsibilities of two different university organizations: the Institute of Rural and Regional Studies and the Council of Social Development.

The Institute of Rural and Regional Studies draws its staff from various faculties. (Many donor agencies require joint institute programs as a condition of assistance.) The Institute's director manages and coordinates research projects, looking for researchers best qualified for a given project. Staff members, recruited for a year at a time, are paid basic salaries by their home faculties but receive an honorarium from the Institute for the project.

The Institute's projects include a survey of rural patterns in communication, irrigation, and systems of landholding, marketing, and credit that seeks to help define the most effective regional units of

development, starting with the simplest at the local level; an inventory
and evaluation of government and nongovernment development programs; and field projects defined and initiated by local village leadership.

The Council of Social Development had several projects in 1974
that involved students and faculty members. One, the project at
Girirejo Mangunan, sought to develop methods of increasing agricultural production by improving soil fertility and preventing erosion. In
another, Merapi Slope, members of the project, including three lecturers, ten students from the faculties of engineering, agriculture,
and animal husbandry, and a number of villagers, are laying water
pipes to help the people of three villages (a combined population of
12,000) reach natural springs and wells. In the Kulia Kerga Niata
(KKN) Mahaseiswa Project, 30 students teach or help villagers to implement government programs, such as planting rice, raising poultry,
and reforesting hillsides. They also help with local programs, such
as dam construction or improvement of rural roads. Students are paid
a monthly salary and also earn academic credits for their work. The
project receives government financial support.

Rural extension or public service projects have also been carried
out for some time by the Agricultural Complex, which includes agriculture, animal science, veterinary science, biology, agricultural
technology, and forestry. The Ford Foundation, the Rockefeller Foundation, USAID, the Midwest Universities Consortium for International
Activities (MUCIA), the Agricultural Development Council, and others
provided visiting professors and fellowships for advanced staff training
to help build strong faculties in the agricultural complex. As training
and multidisciplinary programs progressed, related faculties in the
complex began to share facilities and to coordinate matters of common
concern.

In 1972, President Suharto suggested that all students of higher
education should spend at least six months working in village-level
development activities as a part of their curriculum. In 1973-74, 15
universities ran pilot projects in the KKN study-service plan, one of
which was Gadjah Mada's Kulia Kerga Niata Mahaseiswa Project,
already described. The 15 projects involved about 1,200 students.
The government plans eventually to include in the program all higher
education students during their third or fourth year, a total of 23,000
students per year.

The plan is likely to encourage university rural development
efforts. Gadjah Mada, along with other institutions, will be expected
to run its own KKN projects, based on common government guidelines
but tailored to local needs and conditions. It can provide national
leadership through an effective and innovative program at the Institute
for Rural and Regional Studies.

DEVELOPMENT OF CULTURAL UNITY

University of Malaya, Malaysia

Higher education in peninsular Malaysia is geared to training civil servants and professionals to meet expanding demand and to replace expatriates in public and private employment. Since Malaysia gained its independence in 1957, the nation has also looked to higher education to contribute to national unity and to give greater educational opportunity to Malays, one of the nation's three population groups.

The country has been increasingly torn by racial conflict. Malays make up about half the population, more than 70 percent of them farming at subsistence levels. The Chinese, about 36 percent of the population, are generally more prosperous; in rural areas they are involved in tin mining, growing rubber on small plantations, and vegetable gardening, and in the cities they hold skilled and semiskilled jobs in commerce, construction, and manufacturing. The Indians, the remaining population group, work mainly as laborers on plantations, most of which are owned and managed by Europeans. The Chinese and Malays compete, sometimes bitterly, for economic and political power within the country.

Under British rule, different racial and religious communities tended to run separate educational systems with different languages of instruction. When Malaysia became an independent state, however, the government saw education as a tool that could be used to restructure Malaysian society and to redress the imbalance between the haves and the have-nots. A common language and a unified system of education seemed a necessary condition of national identity and a way to reinforce the majority culture.

In higher education, the government, which gradually has taken over most of the system, directed that Bahasa Malaysia (Malay) should become the main language of instruction and that more Malay students should be admitted to the universities. Coming largely from the rural elementary and secondary school system, Malays have been at a disadvantage in competitions with the urban Chinese or English-language school graduates. Chinese students, well trained in science and mathematics at the secondary school level, dominate medicine, science, and engineering faculties at the universities, while Malay and Indian students are underrepresented.

The University of Malaya, the oldest, largest, and most prestigious of the five universities in the country, was modeled on the British provincial university and, until recently, taught in two official languages: Bahasa Malaysia and English. Under the government edict, it is making efforts to spread the use of the Malay language and to add

more Malay students and staff. It requires all students to take a course
in Bahasa Malaysia and it has directed all faculties to draw up plans
for replacing English, Chinese, and Tamil language courses. By 1983,
when students admitted to the University will have had their entire primary and secondary education in Bahasa Malaysia, all University
courses are expected to be taught in the Malay language.

The change in the language of instruction has encountered resistance on a number of accounts. Because Bahasa Malaysia does not have
an adequate independent technical vocabulary and literature, some educators argue that its use may hamper new research, weaken links with
the international scientific community, and raise new difficulties in
modernizing the country. Efforts to replace expatriate staff with Ma-
laysians have encountered some of the same arguments. The University has had to weigh the advantage of nationalizing the staff against
maintaining the University as an internationally recognized center for
higher learning.

The University also has expanded its enrollment and changed its
admissions policy. Racial quotas as well as examination scores determine student admission. Since the government requires that three
quarters of all government jobs and 40 percent of private jobs go to
Malays, the University has been under additional pressure to train
more Malays.

Malaysia is still in the process of coming to grips with its problems of racial integration and national unification. University dormi-
tories, for example, are integrated to promote interracial harmony,
but Chinese, Malay, and Indian studies programs tend to polarize students according to their ethnic origins. A need is seen for an integrated course covering different national cultures. In addition, some
feel that the attempt to unify the country within the politically dominant
Malay culture and language will not necessarily achieve national unity;
rather it substitutes one dominant group for another. More important
may be the University's contribution to solving the basic economic
problems of poverty and underprivilege.

MANPOWER TRAINING PROGRAMS IN
THE PHILIPPINES

The Philippines considers manpower its biggest resource. More
than 19 percent of its 20- to 24-year olds are enrolled in one of its
600 postsecondary institutions. It has the largest pool of trained technical, managerial, and entrepreneurial manpower of any country in
Southeast Asia.

The three institutions described here train middle- and high-level
manpower for both the public and private sectors. The Development

Academy of the Philippines is a semigovernmental institution seeking
to train large groups of key personnel; the other two, the Asian Institute of Management and the Center for Research and Communication,
are privately endowed and are mainly, although not exclusively, directed at the needs of private business and industry. Each has responded to a national need. All three are outside the universities and
the traditional tertiary education system.

Training Developers: Development Academy
of the Philippines

The Development Academy of the Philippines recruited almost a
thousand specialists to plan and implement programs for government
and industry and to train groups of essential personnel. It was established in 1973 by the National Economic and Development Authority
and five government financial institutions that agreed to support it for
five years with annual contributions of $71,500 each. By 1974-75,
however, its operations totaled $4.14 million, all of which it raised
itself by operating as a business and collecting for its services. Its
surpluses have been spent during the year they were earned to defray
costs of its nonrevenue projects, about $14,000 in its first 18 months
of operations.

DAP programs include not only training but also research and
policy studies, urban industry assistance, and consultancies to government and some 135 business and industrial firms. It has developed a
medium- and small-scale industry program, designed and executed
small irrigation systems, and prepared a national land-use plan, regional studies, and ecological management schemes. It designs systems (mostly computer based) for improved decision making,
programming, resource allocation, and monitoring. It has more than
1,000 staff members, including engineers, architects, urban planners,
social scientists, and technicians.

While it trains some farmer-irrigators and other lower or middle-
level technicians, most of the DAP training programs are in management and organizational development. During its first six months of
operation, it trained rural bankers (900 of them so far) to support
credit facilities for rural development. Because of the size and diversity of new national development programs, however, the DAP
decided to concentrate on retooling the higher bureaucracy of government.

Some critics of the DAP believe its training duplicates that of the
Philippines Executive Academy, an outgrowth of the University of the
Philippines' Institute of Public Administration, which has graduated,

since 1962, about 400 government and private executives with up-to-
date skills and a high promotion rate. Unlike the Executive Academy,
however, the DAP does not accept applications from individuals. It
regards training as part of an overall development program, and all
key executives in an organization must take part. The DAP first identifies agency resources, goals, and future plans and looks at the back-
grounds and assignments of the company's executives. The final plan
is tailored to fit the special objectives and needs of its client. The
DAP also conducts posttraining, on-the-job evaluations, and helps
work out individual problems within the agency or company.

The DAP draws on a wide range of faculty: engineers, economists,
political theorists, behaviorists, systems analysts, psychologists,
and ecologists. It encourages informal as well as formal relations between faculty and participants, and blends study, sports, and social
functions into a total experience designed to foster teamwork within
an organization.

The head of the management training programs, a former vice-
president of a private development bank, has recruited his staff from
the church, government, universities, private industry, and business.
Staff members are young and well paid. (DAP salaries are not subject
to government scales since it receives no direct appropriations from
government as payment for services.)

In its two years of operation, DAP prestige has attracted even
cabinet planning sessions to its facilities. DAP problems—too many
activities, size, suspicion from government agencies—stem from its
success. It claims it creates markets that other institutions do not
serve and supports development projects otherwise neglected.

The DAP is a second-generation institution, that is, its officers
and staff are products of a higher educational system without which it
couldn't exist; many of its specialists were trained at the Executive
Academy, the University of the Philippines, and other Philippine universities. Its founding board is made up of bankers and financiers
who see DAP as an investment in development.

Training Managers: Asian Institute of Management

In 1963, the Ford Foundation made a grant of $250,000 to
strengthen business education in three leading graduate schools of
business. The institutions—the University of the Philippines, De La
Salle College, and the Atenéo de Manila—were to decide among themselves on individual specializations—financial or production management or marketing—and would then build competent faculties (through
overseas fellowships and visiting professors) and design case studies

for classroom use. The three institutions eventually realized that they could not each develop a first-class business school, and De La Salle and Atenéo therefore agreed to coordinate their efforts. Together, in an unprecedented mobilization of private funds for an educational project, they attracted support from international agencies, government, and Philippine and foreign business firms, and organized the Asian Institute of Management as an affiliate of both Atenéo de Manila University and De La Salle College.

The Asian Institute of Management is a graduate school of business administration based on a model of the Harvard Business School. Using the case method to develop analytic and decision-making skills, it trains people to fill junior, middle, and upper management positions. It has built a bank of case studies from various parts of Asia and seeks a student body representing a large number of other Asian countries. An advisory board of government and business leaders from eight Asian countries ensures the Institute's relevance to Asian needs.

All 30 faculty members are now Filipinos, and most have advanced degrees, largely earned in the United States. The original Ford Foundation grant for AIM provided for training a Filipino staff through a Southeast Asian Faculty Development Fellowship that put 15 fellows through AIM's master of business course. The fellows, who must have business experience and come from Southeast Asian countries, are encouraged to teach at AIM after their training by a scheme of loan repayment. The fellowships can be repaid in the form of teaching either at AIM or at an acceptable institution in their home countries. Four years of teaching at AIM or six years in a home institution pays for two years of study.

In the seven years since it was founded, AIM has expanded its manpower training from its original two-year, full-time master of business management program to include shorter courses for junior-, middle-, and upper-level managers, who are released by their firms for intensive training, ranging from two weeks to a year and a half. All programs seek to upgrade management skills, prepare participants for greater responsibility, and provide an Asian and developmental perspective. AIM receives five times more applications for its programs than it can accept.

To meet financial problems, AIM has raised tuition and contracted for more short-term training programs, such as one for airline executives, to meet specific business needs. Local financial support has been rising: 32 donors maintain student scholarships and six individuals and corporations have given general-purpose funds. AIM also has received support from corporations in Japan and Malaysia and from businessmen in Taiwan and Singapore.

In answering a charge of elitism, AIM maintains that the Institute has sought to widen the circle of management experts to serve better the businesses and economic development of Asian nations. It reaches out to many areas in its search for students and makes available scholarships and loans. It also reviews case material continually to keep itself relevant to Asian problems.

Several conclusions have been drawn from AIM's history: its position outside a traditional university setting has given it autonomy and freedom to develop; a good faculty was attracted by the objectives of the institution, its prestige, high salaries, and good publicity; developing a predominantly Filipino staff has made the program more stable, relevant, flexible, and less costly; and a delicate balance has been maintained between service to the community and overextended activities.

Management Economics: The Center for Research and Communication

The smallest of the three Philippine training institutions discussed, the Center for Research and Communication was established in 1967 to conduct business and economic research for private business and industry, and it set up a training program as a by-product of that research. It was conceived by two young economists, just returned from advanced study in the United States, who saw that government economic planning could not succeed unless private business understood, cooperated with, and contributed to development plans. They joined in setting up the new center, now operated by the Southeast Asian Science Foundation, an organization of industrial, educational, and other professional leaders in the Philippines.

CRC derives its income from foundation grants and fees for special research projects, private firms, and government agencies. Over 400 "friends of CRC," including large and small firms, also contribute varying amounts and, in turn, are entitled to use CRC facilities. No single firm contributes a significant percentage of CRC's total income, and thus the Center is able to maintain academic freedom and independence of research.

At first devoted primarily to research commissioned by private businesses, the CRC discovered that young staff researchers needed on-the-job training. Accordingly, it designed a two-year work-study program for staff members, divided among classroom work, research, and on-the-job experience. In 1969, it received authorization from the Bureau of Private Schools to award participants a master's degree in industrial economics and later granted similar degrees in economic education and business economics.

While CRC runs the industrial economics program primarily for its own staff members, companies may send one or two promising young professionals to participate as well. The program stresses communication and team work and relates academic theory to current issues. Participating staff members spend some time in internship programs in business firms between periods of classroom work. The course focuses primarily on five fields: economic forecasting, inter-industry relations, specific industry analysis, economic planning, and specialized research. Participants must have a bachelor's degree and two to five years experience in business or government. Of the 62 participants between 1969 and 1974, 11 were sent by private firms and 51 granted scholarships by CRC. Of the 51, six are now the CRC's faculty and eight are studying abroad to offset faculty inbreeding.

The master's program in economics education was originally funded by the Ford Foundation to provide competent economics teachers at the secondary and postsecondary levels. Participants, economics or social studies teachers in high school or college who have taught for at least one year, alternate study at CRC with teaching and research in their own schools.

CRC has only eight full-time faculty members, two with Ph. D. s and the others with M. S. degrees in industrial economics from CRC itself. They and the research staff, who are also in large part the students of the Center, conduct the individual research projects, occasionally assisted by economists from other institutions.

Besides research for individual firms, CRC activities include professional conferences, a three-day live-in program for company executives, a nine-month program in which company managers and planners study the requirements of corporate strategy making, and a program designed to train research analysts. CRC also issues research papers, monographs, and monthly bulletins.

＊   ＊   ＊   ＊   ＊   ＊

The three Philippine manpower programs have several common characteristics: (1) They all rely on a supply of competent manpower, produced in the Philippines by a mass higher education system whose history goes back more than 60 years. (2) Outside the postsecondary educational system, they are not bound by government or university bureaucratic regulations. (3) The programs all started with one person or a small group of individuals with foreign training who saw a problem and sought ways to solve it. (4) All three programs were able to involve private interests as well as government, local as well as foreign donors, and were able to raise the funds necessary for their success. (5) Each program has catered to a special clientele and a demand for trained people. (6) All three have local rather than expatriate staffs, although AIM originally was staffed largely by professors from the Harvard Business School.

TRAINING TECHNICIANS THROUGH NONDEGREE
POLYTECHNIC PROGRAMS

Ngee Ann Technical College, Singapore

Singapore's higher education system is closely coordinated in order to limit duplication. National manpower needs determine its programs, and its planning is guided by a philosophy of selective as opposed to mass access. It is perhaps the only country in the region that, for reasons of demand, has demoted an institution from university to technical college status.

Ngee Ann College was established in 1963 as a private institution to prepare Chinese-speaking students to enter the job market. It awarded a bachelor's degree and offered four-year degree courses in arts, sciences, and commerce, largely in Mandarin, although it taught English as a valuable job qualification. Its graduates, however, did not command as high a salary in either civil service or in private employment as did graduates of Singapore's two universities, and the Ngee Ann clan, which founded the college, appointed a committee in 1966 to review its future.

At the same time, to meet the increased demand for technical personnel, the government began to reorganize Singapore's educational system to focus on technical education. It recommended changing Ngee Ann into a technical college offering diploma courses in engineering and commerce below the degree level.

The College and its founders agreed to the change as a way to meet both the problems of finance and the problems of its graduates. In 1967, therefore, Ngee Ann was converted into a public institution, and in 1968 it was transformed into a technical college. A number of student demonstrations protested the downgrading of the institution from degree to diploma level, but students applied no subsequent pressure. In 1970, the language of instruction was changed from Mandarin to English in accordance with a government bilingual policy.

In 1974-75, Ngee Ann Technical College had 1,400 full-time students (there were no part-time students), about a quarter of whom were women and a third from other countries. All students paid fees, but various scholarships were available. The staff was new (only one teacher remained after the College's change in status) and included 70 full-time and eight part-time faculty. Half the academic staff were expatriates.

The College graduates about 160 students a year in engineering and 60 to 70 in business. The number is largely determined by Ministry of Finance forecasts of manpower needs and is coordinated with the other postsecondary institutions through the budget process. The manpower forecasts go to Singapore's universities and three technical institutes for comment, and the institutions then negotiate for funds on the basis of demand for graduates.

Present manpower predictions foresee a lessening demand for university graduates, but more demand for middle- or technical-level graduates. Ngee Ann, accordingly, plans a five-year expansion program, three quarters of which will be financed by a loan (U.S. $3,870,700) from the Asian Development Bank and the rest by the Singapore government. Such expansion, along with the efforts of Singapore's other postsecondary institutions, is expected to eliminate the shortage of technicians by 1980.

The Asian Development Bank loan in 1970 included technical assistance, which Ngee Ann received through affiliation with the Polytechnic of Central London. The Polytechnic consultant, sent to Singapore on a British government grant to advise on what the Polytechnic could provide, is now chief operating official of the College. The two institutions are further linked through an external examiner scheme; on graduation, diplomas are awarded jointly by Ngee Ann and by the Polytechnic of Central London. Polytechnic advisers in each department have helped to upgrade staff and instruction, and the staff-student ratio has improved (in 1975, it was about 1 to 20). The College has made continuous efforts to improve courses and reduce the number of examinations. Some second-year students and all third-year students take part in a summer work program where they are placed in business firms and government agencies.

The job market for Ngee Ann graduates is good; most graduates find employment within one month after final examinations. A technician in electronics or mechanical engineering gets a starting salary higher than that of a university graduate in arts. Because of this demand, the number of applicants has increased, and the College has been able to raise entrance requirements: only about 20 percent of applicants are admitted.

MAEKLONG INTEGRATED RURAL DEVELOPMENT PROJECT

Kasetsart, Mahidol, and Thammasat Universities, Thailand

The Maeklong Integrated Rural Development Project, for the first time in Asia, brings together three major national universities, each with its own expertise, in a pilot project to improve rural conditions. Each of the three Thai universities, over the years, has developed programs designed to relate its teaching and research to the solution of rural community problems. Kasetsart had a number of agricultural

extension projects; Mahidol had community health projects; and at
Thammasat, the Graduate Volunteer Service Program, open to graduates from any Thai university, has been sending young men and women
to rural areas since 1969 to serve as teachers and community workers.
The Maeklong Project is thus an extension of their public service interests.

The project was conceived when Kasetsart, an agricultural university, created in 1943 by the Ministry of Agriculture, sought to improve
land- and water-use technology in the rural area surrounding its new
campus and experiment station near Bangkok. Because the rural problems were complex and interrelated, it invited two other universities—
Thammasat, oriented to the social sciences, and Mahidol, which
emphasizes medical sciences—to join with it in finding solutions to the
problems.

The three universities chose the Maeklong River Basin area because it was close to Bangkok and to the universities. Its varied to-
pography, soil conditions, and climate also make the region a good
laboratory. The area includes 1,466,700 hectares and, in 1972, had
a population of about 2,000,000, 70 percent of whom depend on agriculture for their livelihood.

In 1974, the project set out to gain as much knowledge as possible
about the area and to outline an interdisciplinary and interuniversity
approach to improving the production, income, health, education, and
other aspects of life in the area. Teams of four people each—a university teacher-researcher and students in agriculture, medicine, and/or
social sciences—were sent to six different parts of the region to enlist
the support of local people while living among them, to determine the
needs of the locality, and to collect firsthand information about village
life.

The investigations of these faculty-student teams confirmed the
original conviction that the area would be a good place to test development methodology and to improve rural conditions. Villagers appeared
willing to accept change. Faculty and students from all three institutions demonstrated ability to work together, responded enthusiastically
to the call for volunteers, and got along with both rural people and
government officials.

Eventually, each research leader will prepare a list of problems
in one zone of the Maeklong area and will rank the problems in order
of difficulty and possibility of solution. An executive committee will
screen these analyses and will outline an interdisciplinary program
for action in each zone. Research leaders and specialists will discuss
and modify these work plans, and pilot projects will then be established.

Planned projects include courses to train village health leaders
to handle first-aid problems, to recognize common health problems

requiring more expert attention, and to advise villagers on sanitation and diet; drives for functional literacy and vocational training in which team members will first serve as teachers and will then be replaced by villagers; improvement of crop and animal production by introducing new crop varieties, better husbandry practices, improved methods of irrigation, more efficient fertilizers and insecticides, and credit and marketing arrangements.

The project is backed by a seed money grant of $125,000 from the Rockefeller Foundation. It is administered by a policy board of four persons representing Kasetsart, Mahidol, Thammasat, and the Rockefeller Foundation, with the Kasetsart representative serving as chairman. A project director, appointed by the board, is responsible for the overall administration of the project and coordinates the researchers assigned by each university. The project involves cooperation with both government and private agencies.

The Maeklong Project seeks to test several development "packages" for impact and for evidence that programs that benefit one group of villages can provide similar benefits elsewhere. In addition, the project foresees long-rang benefits to the universities themselves through faculty and student participation in development activities. Project planners hope learning experiences will be introduced into classroom teaching and that the combination of better teaching and fieldwork will give students a better understanding of rural development.

9

LATIN AMERICA

CENTER FOR URBAN DEVELOPMENT

Federal University of Bahia, Brazil

On the basis of three previous programs in community health, preventive medicine, and urban planning, the Federal University of Bahia created, in 1973, an interdisciplinary Center for Urban Development (CEDUR) under the administrative and financial aegis of its Program of Research and Education for Development (PROPED). CEDUR was designed to create and test models of community development that could be adapted to poor urban areas in other parts of the country. The program was to encourage interdisciplinary research in health, education, architecture, and socioanthropology on which government could base better economic and social policies; it was to facilitate cooperation among university professors and students and professionals and government officials; and it was also to provide advisory services for public and private institutions. It was financed by the University, the secretary of public health, and the Rockefeller and Ford foundations.

The Salvador district of Northeastern Amaralina was chosen as the program's base because of its well-defined geographic boundaries, dense population, high birthrate, and urgent housing, education, health, and sanitation needs. It had also been the site of a previous three-year University community health program. In the fall of 1973, volunteer students collected preliminary data on the district's characteristics and made initial surveys of health, housing and educational problems.

Since then, CEDUR projects in Northeastern Amaralina have included:

1. A study of why so many students repeat first grade. Seven psychology students, two psychologists, and a supervising professor are looking at the way 650 first-graders learn in public, state, and municipal schools.

2. An analysis of social awareness in children and preadolescents from low-income groups, based on observation of status, role, and self-respect of members of 20 families.

3. A survey of urban architectural problems: housing, electricity, water supply, and sanitation.

4. Eight health projects that seek to develop systems of health services delivery, one of which is training 16 health promoters to work in the community.

5. A research project in nutrition that measures the effects of diet on the health of children in the area and compares it with diets in other areas.

Program successes have been attributed to strong leadership support from PROPED's director, who is also vice-rector of the University, and from the governor of Bahia, former rector of the Federal University of Bahia; faculty interest, especially among professors in the Department of Preventive Medicine; community acceptance, assisted by a community council; financial support; visiting professors who contributed new ideas; good relationships with government agencies; student participation and support; and an emphasis on practical learning.

The program has been aware of the following drawbacks: an initial lack of a well-defined overall strategy to determine priorities of community needs; reliance on faculty volunteers; too little group cohesion among CEDUR participants; and apathy or hostility among the faculties, owing in some cases to ignorance about the program's activities.

Project directors cited the following lessons learned:

1. Once community needs are identified through systematic studies, government agencies should be consulted on priorities and operational approaches for meeting these needs, although the process of working with government is slow and involves delay.

2. Both professors and students must be convinced of the importance of the program and the advantages of participating in it. How well the program is incorporated into academic course work depends on the participating professor and, to a lesser degree, on the curriculum's flexibility.

3. The community must participate in establishing its own needs and in planning action to meet them.

4. A multidisciplinary approach requires special motivation and interest, encouraged by time and opportunities for exchanges of information and points of view. It may take some time before a group is ready to act together.

5. The administration of an interdisciplinary, multi-institutional group such as CEDUR requires full-time professionals with decision-making powers.

6. Program directors and participants should observe and learn from similar programs.

7. There is a special need for flexible financial support in the early planning stages of such programs.

Suggestions for improving the program include:

1. Maintain enough autonomy to be innovative and to use unorthodox methods. (The program would benefit from a manual of policies and procedures, including a description of its relation to PROPED.)

2. Strengthen interdisciplinary teams by relieving team members of administrative responsibilities and by continuing a systematic search for outstanding team members.

3. Encourage scientific research in which community, university (professors and students), government, and private agencies cooperate.

4. Define more clearly relationships with government and private agencies at top levels.

5. Seek ways to secure more information about similar projects, including observation trips and workshops or seminars where experiences and opinions can be exchanged.

6. Integrate all programs under a more general development approach.

EDUCATION FOR RURAL AREAS

University of Antioquia, Columbia

The Faculty of Education at the University of Antioquia has developed two programs to deal with the problems of primary schooling in rural areas. These problems are essentially low enrollment, poor quality education, isolation, and lack of teacher training.

Three quarters of the rural schools in Colombia have only one classroom and one teacher. In the One-Teacher School Program, started in 1968 with the collaboration of the secretary of education of the State of Antioquia, teachers in these schools receive special training and specially designed teaching materials. The program trains them in group dynamics, psychology of learning, and evaluation, helps them to organize their own teaching schedules, and instructs them in using new teaching techniques and programmed material.

So far, the program has published materials for the first four years of elementary school and hopes to complete others for the fifth grade by 1976. These materials were designed by nine programmers and four illustrators and were supervised and reviewed by members of several University faculties. They have been used by more than 70 rural schools in Antioquia and Sucre.

The One-Teacher School Program has been financed by the University of Antioquia, the secretary of education of Antioquia (SEDA), the National Ministry of Education, and the Colombian Institute for the Development of Higher Education (ICFES). It has been supported in part by local towns where pilot schools are located, by parents, by the National Federation of Coffee Growers, and by National Community Action. It has received no foreign assistance, and its funds have not been adequate for long-range planning or for substantial expansion.

The One-Teacher School Program has had to contend with other difficulties as well. It has lacked specialists in primary education and people trained to structure and carry out the program. There has been no clear definition of the roles to be played by the various participants and contributors, and it has not had the financial resources for an objective assessment. Among the most difficult problems is the unwillingness of trained teachers to remain in rural areas. Neither methods of selection nor financial incentives have prevented teachers trained for one-teacher rural schools from moving to the cities. While the National Ministry of Education has shown interest in the program, the University believes the program should not be extended on a large scale until it has been more carefully evaluated, until students, teachers, and parents are better prepared, and until costs have been more accurately determined.

The Program on Individualized Instruction and Flexible Schooling, another University-designed experiment in programmed instruction for rural schools, seeks a way of meeting the problem of low school attendance. It has set up a rural school model that requires children to attend class only three days a week and to do some work at home on the remaining two days. The days on which children will attend school are chosen in consultation with their parents, according to when they will be needed at home or to help on the farm. Teachers are trained to use individualized instruction techniques and to use specially prepared materials, including teaching cards, which allow the child to work independently. Thirty-four rural schools have used the materials and techniques, and 25 teachers have received special training.

Teachers, supervisors, students, and parents have responded well to the program. Financial support has come from the University, the state secretaries of education in Antioquia and in Sucre, the Colombian Institute of Pedagogy, the Ford Foundation, and USAID. Despite this support, however, the program has had a number of problems. Like the One-Teacher School Program, it needs better assessments of methods and materials and has suffered from a lack of trained professionals qualified to conduct training courses on primary school curriculum and method. The link between the program and University curriculum needs to be strengthened and reinforced.

Nevertheless, the Individualized Instruction and Flexible Schooling Program has established and validated a model for the delivery of educational service in rural areas. It has focused on how to make rural education more effective and has succeeded because its working group was small, because it had several years of experience with the One-Teacher School Program to build on, and because it had state government cooperation.

Both programs have potential value for solving the serious problems of rural schooling, and materials and training should be extended to other areas. Such extension requires long-range financial assistance, close cooperation between government and university, and stable direction. It has been suggested that these needs might be fulfilled by a national center for rural education with its own budget and with enough independence to ensure autonomous direction without political interference. Such a center should publish tested and approved material for all regions and should have facilities for evaluation. It should preserve the already established and valuable relationships between an official agency and a faculty of education.

THE RESEARCH PROGRAM FOR SYSTEMS OF HEALTH SERVICES DELIVERY

University of Valle, Colombia

The Research Program for Systems of Health Services Delivery (PRIMOPS) grew out of more than 15 years of community and social medicine programs at the Division of Health of the University of Valle. Beginning with the urban district of Siloé in 1955, the division sought to tie teaching and research to specific efforts to solve community health problems. In 1958, building on its experience in Siloé, it set up a health center in urban Candelaria, where, for ten years, it made medical, sociological, economic, and demographic studies, developed health teams, and brought in other University disciplines to meet the related problems of housing, sanitation, nutrition, and education.

The program in Candelaria significantly lowered the death rate and the incidence of malnutrition in the community and has increased the availability of medical services. Its success encouraged the division to design PRIMOPS, a new program to deliver maternal and child health care to the 90,000 residents of six districts of Cali. The initial planning was financed by the University and by the Family Health Foundation of Tulane University.

The program got under way in 1973 with additional support from the Municipal Health Service and the Ministry of Health. For several months it conducted a campaign to explain the program to the community and to obtain community support and participation.

PRIMOPS has three objectives: to design and operate a model system of health care delivery that offers good care, high coverage, and low operating costs to low-income families in an urban area; to deliver maternal and child health care that decreases maternal and infant mortality, improves nutrition, and prevents infections and disease; and to prepare better qualified health professionals and para-professionals.

Under an agreement with the Municipal Health Service of Cali (SMS), already providing health care in the Cali area, the University's Division of Health designs changes in the existing health services delivery system and advises SMS on personnel recruitment and training, community relations, and other aspects of its operation. It also evaluates the program. SMS, in turn, has sole authority over operating the system.

PRIMOPS health services are delivered to the community on five levels: (1) the home, where families are visited by a health promoter, a midwife, and a nurse's auxiliary, all of whom live in the community and receive special training; (2) the health post, which gives primary health care to a population of 10,000 to 20,000 and refers those who need more treatment to the next level; (3) the health center, responsible for 90,000 inhabitants, which supervises the first two levels, treats patients referred from these levels, and refers cases to the urban hospital; (4) the urban hospital, which provides short periods of hospitalization, surgery with postoperative care at home, deliveries, and emergency room treatment; and (5) the university hospital, which has the most complete resources and treats pregnancies and illnesses requiring specialized methods of diagnosis and treatment.

PRIMOPS has shown results in primary care training, medical education, and expansion to other areas. So far, it has trained 30 health promoters, 40 midwives, and 11 nurse's auxiliaries, and has prepared 11 training manuals and 14 instruction booklets for promoters and nurse's auxiliaries and two manuals for supervisors. Other agencies have used these materials to train approximately 500 health promoters and nurse's auxiliaries throughout Colombia, and the Division of Health proposes to use the materials for training students in primary care. The Ministry of Health plans to expand PRIMOPS within Cali and to start similar programs in four other cities. The Pan American Federation of Faculties of Medicine has sponsored courses for doctors from other Latin American countries to encourage them to start similar projects. The program has fed back into the classroom through curricular changes.

Program directors say the following factors have contributed to the program's success: preliminary community studies; support from University and government administrators; experience in Siloé and Candelaria; acceptance by the community; good relations with government agencies; willingness to seek new approaches to health services delivery; and the presence of Division of Health graduates in government offices.

Initial obstacles to the program's success were skepticism about adapting Candelaria methods to other areas; government agencies' fear of university dominance; lack of finances; lack of community materials on health; and opposition to "foreign imperialism" as represented by foreign technical assistance.

Program directors point to the following lessons learned: (1) health programs should both meet community needs and fit into the priorities of government agencies responsible for services; (2) a program must be based on substantial knowledge of the community; (3) teaching staff must be persuaded of the program's importance to teaching and curriculum; (4) university and agency roles in the program should be clearly established from the beginning; (5) community support and participation must be enlisted; (6) a good program requires multidisciplinary efforts; and (7) a program model is not transferable unless information about the program and its results is widely publicized.

Suggestions for the program include further testing and evaluation; better communication with the community; more efforts to relate the program to classroom teaching; training interdisciplinary professional groups to assume leadership of the program and help adapt it elsewhere; and continuing cooperation with government agencies.

The program has given rise to two recommendations for donors: education for development programs should have long-range support since both programs and institutions take time to develop; and the planning and evaluation phase needs more financial assistance.

STRUCTURE OF HIGHER EDUCATION FOR DEVELOPMENT IN COLOMBIA

As student demand for higher education has increased dramatically in Colombia, the quality of higher education seems to have dropped. Each state has wanted the prestige of its own university, and new institutions, many with low academic standards, have sprung up throughout the country. Student-professor ratios have increased, especially in private universities where rising costs have had a special impact. (In 1970, the ratio of students to professor at public universities was 13 to 1; at private universities it was 28 to 1.) Many Colombian educators believe that higher education faces a dilemma: increase enrollment and impair teaching quality or improve quality and cut down enrollment.

Seeking to improve quality, some universities look to two kinds of efforts: increasing full-time teaching staff and decreasing the number of part-time professors; and developing the university's research capacity. A few also feel that both program and research should be made more responsive to community needs through more extension programs.

In 1970, slightly more than half the teaching staff in public universities were full-time professors, while in private universities only about 17 percent were considered full time. Costs have made changing the ratios difficult.

Colombian universities, although varying widely in quality, financing, and course offerings, almost all lack research programs or extension services. National research is done largely by institutes annexed to the various ministries rather than by either universities or industry, but no procedure or unified national budget coordinates research activities. While government supplies most of the funds for research, Colombia invests only 2 percent of its gross national product in research. The research, moreover, tends to have little relation to the problems of either industry or national development.

Within the universities, funds are allocated almost entirely to teaching, although the universities have tried in the last few years to increase the number of research projects. Social sciences find it difficult to obtain either funds or trained researchers, since disciplines, such as sociology, anthropology, demography, and history, are relatively new in Colombia and are still viewed with some suspicion. Government and private industry rather than the university conduct agricultural and livestock research, and no one does much basic science research of any kind. Only health science research receives institutional support from the universities, and departments of health science are virtually alone in relating research to community needs.

Strengthening postgraduate programs is considered one step in developing university research capacity, since postgraduate science programs, first established in Colombia in the 1960s, appear to have a close correlation with university research. Universities that emphasize postgraduate study also have relatively large numbers of research programs. Out of a total of 86 postgraduate programs in Colombia, 77 of them are concentrated in five universities. Of the 665 research projects underway in the country, 388 are in the same five universities.

The extension program is a recent development in Colombian higher education. Although in theory it allows the university to establish contact with the community and confront course theory with field

practice, few extension programs have genuine community or teaching
ties. University extension programs may be sponsored solely by the
university or carried out in conjunction with other educational institutions or with government or industry. The university applies research
results largely through agencies established for the purpose. At the
National University in Bogotá, the Industrial University of Santander,
and the Universities of Los Andes and Antioquia, centers of research
promote, coordinate, and carry out research projects. At Javeriana
University, a faculty of interdisciplinary studies coordinates and promotes interdisciplinary research and teaching. Faculties of medicine
or divisions of health traditionally have applied research through their
university hospitals.

Although most extension programs are based on research, research does not therefore receive priority within the structure of
higher education. Even within extension, the emphasis is on teaching
rather than on research. A number of universities offer traditionally
taught extension courses in engineering, medicine, education, architecture, and fine arts, almost all given during the day. A few extension programs test innovative educational techniques, such as the
projects on Individualized Instruction and Flexible Schooling at the
University of Antioquia, the Open University Program at the Technological University of Pereira, design and production of educational
materials at Cauca University, and Education at a Distance at Javeriana University。

to revolve around teaching and lacks the research necessary to reinforce academic standards. Until research becomes more important
and more closely linked to national problems, the university cannot
reform its product or become an agency for development.

RESEARCH AND EXTENSION PROGRAM FOR INDUSTRIAL DEVELOPMENT

Monterrey Institute of Technology and Advanced Studies, Mexico

The Monterrey Institute of Technology and Advanced Studies
(ITESM), a private, nonprofit institution for higher education, was
established in 1943 by a group of Monterrey businessmen as a center
for technical education, designed to train competent professionals. It
continues to receive support from the business community, depending
on tuition for about 65 percent of its funds and on gifts from business
and industry for most of the rest.

In 1951, ITESM created the Institute for Industrial Research to
apply technological research to specific industrial and government

problems. The Institute was dependent on ITESM but separate from its academic program. In 1970, to establish better ties with the academic program of ITESM and to make better use of ITESM's faculty, the Institute was merged with the Division of Engineering and Architecture and became the Research and Extension Program for Industrial Development.

The Research and Extension Program offers two types of services: services to industry and government in the form of applied research, studies, and consultation; and services to professionals in the form of short courses, seminars, and practice schools of engineering. In its 23 years of operation (first as the Institute for Industrial Research), the Research and Extension Program has carried out almost 600 research and development projects. It has provided more than 6,000 tests and analyses of minerals, fuels, paints, and food, and has conducted studies in chemistry, chemical engineering, economics, agriculture, and demography.

Research is focused on four interrelated areas: systems, materials, resources, and housing. Projects include studies of housing materials such as fire-resistant paints and plastic reinforced with bamboo; design of a natural ventilation system for low-cost housing; measurement of industrial noise levels; development of industrial uses for arid-zone plants; perfecting equipment for transmitting heartbeats and identifying brain waves via telephone; and planning a civic center for an industrial suburb.

Research projects pay for themselves through contracts with a sponsoring agency—business, industry, or government. The greatest demand for services comes from industry, although government has contracted for projects, such as designing waste-processing and water-purification plants and drawing up regulations for control of city air and water pollution.

The research and extension projects are viewed as activities that primarily improve teaching and indirectly contribute to development by producing sound professionals and well-trained graduates. They draw on faculty members from seven academic departments and a small number of graduate students. Undergraduates do not generally participate in research projects and are expected to benefit principally from improved staff knowledge and skills. While both teaching and research are concerned with practical problems, their primary goals are staff development and student training rather than direct service to the community.

Because most sponsors insist that projects be confidential, there is no adequate analysis of project results other than the contractor's satisfaction. Almost all projects, however, have been successfully completed and implemented. Of the 64 projects initiated during 1973-74, only two were abandoned.

The director of the program attributes its overall success to the
support of Monterrey's business and industrial community, to the dynamic way in which ITESM's president, division directors, and department heads promote research and service, to outside foundation
support, to the increasing number of ITESM's graduates who hold
positions in business and industry, and to the program's efforts to
maintain continuing contact with sponsors of projects.

The program contributes to general economic and social development largely through defining industrial and some government needs
and problems and by preparing contributors to development through
its emphasis on improved teaching and problem-solving skills. The
program has also created jobs for the unskilled and semiskilled through
its projects and has raised the level of manpower skills by providing
in-service training programs.

Social development, however, is a secondary and sometimes in-
cidental part of the Research and Extension Program. While some
faculty members are interested in working on community development
projects, such projects lack sponsors and therefore funds. The program has other problems as well. Research does not always reinforce
the quality and content of teaching as it should, and faculty members
often do not have enough time after teaching to engage in research at
all.

It is suggested, therefore, that program directors seek financial
aid for projects designed to meet community needs from agencies interested in broad economic and social problems; that more students
be encouraged to participate in research projects by granting course
credit for such activities; and that faculty members who participate
in research projects have some relief from teaching loads.

The program has made both a national and an international impact
through the quality of its services and its training. Its excellent administration, competent professionals, and efficient financial management could be used increasingly for solving problems not only of
industrial productivity but also of community well-being.

PROGRAM FOR TRANSFERAL OF TECHNOLOGY

National Agrarian University, Peru

To help implement the Agrarian Reform Act of 1969 the National
Agrarian University at La Molina signed an agreement with the Peruvian Ministry of Agriculture in 1972 to assist in the transferal of technology to rural areas. The University Program for Transferal of
Technology, which began in 1973, seeks to bring the University's

specialized knowledge to bear on national problems and to acquaint students and professors with these problems by bringing them into contact with rural agricultural workers.

Under the program, students and professors volunteer on their weekends and vacations to give direct technical help to farm communities. Requests for assistance come from farm groups and cooperatives, individual farmers, the Ministry of Agriculture, and professors who travel to such communities and determine their most urgent needs.

In preparation for fieldwork, students receive briefings on the structure of land tenancy, on the process of change, and on plans for tapping resources and credit. They also receive 15 days of special training. They may combine the fieldwork with a thesis topic, and research may be carried out jointly by two or more students. At the end of each trimester, professors and area coordinators visit agrarian districts to evaluate student activities and identify new assistance needs. Reports of professors, students, and area heads are compiled into a general report that is presented at a meeting attended by principal ministry and University officials.

To reach rural clients and encourage requests for technical help, the program offers extension courses within farm communities and distributes pamphlets on such subjects as management techniques, sanitation, and the use of technology in growing crops and raising animals. The courses, along with individual associations between University and community people, have given rise to a large demand for services. Program directors are investigating possibilities of cooperation with other universities and hope for a national technical assistance system coordinated by the National Agrarian University.

The program is financed by the Ministry of Agriculture. Farm clients, however, furnish room and board for visiting groups. It is hoped the budget may be doubled in the next two-year period.

Program successes have been attributed to a combination of factors: support and interest on the part of top leaders of both the ministry and the University; general acceptance by students and professors; University autonomy; program flexibility; concern with practical problems; and the goodwill of the beneficiaries, achieved at least partly by students and farmers living and working together.

Program obstacles have included initial suspicion on the part of local community residents (largely overcome); the need to rely on volunteers; and some opposition from students, ministry officials, and government extension personnel already working in rural areas. (Radical students claimed the government was using the University to support its policies, and ministry officials and extension workers feared intrusion on their functions and trouble from students.)

The program claims to contribute to the social and economic development of the country in a number of ways: (1) it establishes a communications link between the University and the low-income agrarian population; (2) it encourages students to investigate urgent development problems; (3) professors see it as an opportunity to do applied research; (4) there are plans for modifying curriculum on the basis of student and professor work in rural areas; and (5) the complexity of practical problems has encouraged the coordination of a number of disciplines in solving them.

Program directors cite the following lessons learned:

1. To receive government support for the program, the university should consider government priorities and cooperate with government agencies.

2. Professor and student participation is essential to the program. It encourages practical problem research, it creates an informal and close relationship between professors and students, and work in the villages affords new opportunities to students and professors to develop leadership qualities.

3. Both high-level government officials and community members must take part in the program. The number of community requests for assistance is central to the program's success.

4. The program should be flexibly administered and autonomous (largely independent of both university and ministry). Effective administration requires university leadership and the ability to delegate decision making.

Suggestions for improving the program are to (1) make changes in the curriculum and academic calendar to allow for continuous rather than intermittent services; (2) provide formal recognition for student fieldwork through academic credit and thesis subsidies; (3) provide additional financial aid for participating professors; and (4) provide more administrative help to the program's coordinator.

Recommendations to donors are to (1) support efforts to coordinate similar programs, possibly through a national technical assistance system; (2) support evaluations of existing programs; (3) use flexible criteria for supporting promising programs at institutions that lack research resources; and (4) provide assistance for facilities, equipment, and planning not now supported by the Ministry of Agriculture. Such needs include transportation, communication, technical equipment, and financial incentives for faculty and students.

PART

III

REGIONAL
TEAM REPORTS

Each of the following Regional reports was written by one of the three regional teams—African, Asian, Latin American—that conducted the case studies for this project, and expresses the views and observations of a group of educators from that region. Team members are listed on pages 209-216.

10

BACKGROUND

This report is part of a worldwide study of higher education for development initiated by the heads of donor organizations meeting at Bellagio, Italy, in November 1973. It deals with the institutions of higher education functioning in what is sometimes referred to as sub-Saharan Africa, or Africa south of the Sahara. The study does not deal directly with the northern countries of Africa, which comprise an area of some 8.5 million square kilometers and have a university student population of well over 300,000 in over 15 universities. Nor, except for the study of the University of Botswana, Lesotho, and Swaziland, does it cover southern Africa, south of the Tropic of Capricorn, which comprises some 2.7 million square kilometers.

The area this study covers is approximately 19 million square kilometers, and includes eastern, central, and western Africa. These are some 44 independent African countries, most of which (excluding Rhodesia and the Republic of South Africa) are members of the Organization of African Unity. Some of these 44 countries, use English and some French as the language of instruction in their institutions of higher learning. Two countries are officially bilingual (Cameroon and Mauritius), three use Portuguese, and one (Equatorial Guinea) uses Spanish.

Of the 25 "least developed countries" in the world, most are in this region. Some of the most serious problems—illiteracy, ignorance, hunger, disease, lack of shelter, and drought, for instance—are rampant here, challenging the determination and capability of nationals and calling for the solidarity of mankind. In terms of the availability of land suitable for agriculture, the potential for cattle raising and fisheries, forestry resources, mineral deposits, energy resources, and other wealth, the region is relatively wealthy. It was perhaps this wealth that invited outsiders to interfere with and retard the process of its growth and development during the colonial era, however important their contributions may have been in other areas.

Although it is the second largest continent, Africa has only 9 percent of the world's population, with close to 80 percent of its population living in rural areas. It is growing at a rate of about 2.5 percent per year. (The figures include the whole continent, since breakdown figures dealing with the specific regions of the study are not readily available.)

Most of the countries only attained independence in the late 1950s and early 1960s. Between 1960 and 1970 the school population increased from 18,931,000 to 32,389,000 at the first level and from 2,115,000 to 5,075,000 at the second level. Despite this notable increase in enrollment, however, the following 1970 figures, showing the proportion of first-level school enrollment as compared with the relevant age group of 6-7 to 11-12, indicates how much is still to be done and how much divergence there is among countries. The situation is similar at the second level of education.

Enrollment-Age Group Ratio (in percents)	Number of Countries
Less than 13	8
Less than 28 but more than 13	9
Less than 55 but more than 28	10
Less than 80 but more than 55	8

Although the rate of adult illiteracy decreased between 1960 and 1970 from 81 to 74 percent, the highest rate of illiteracy is still found in Africa, the rate being much higher for the female than for the male population (see Table 1). These and other pertinent economic and social background and situational factors need to be remembered when considering the development of higher education in Africa.

MAJOR PROBLEMS OF HIGHER EDUCATION IN AFRICA

Quantitative Aspects

Although there were traditional centers of higher learning in Timbuktu, Mali, in several places in Ethiopia, and in other countries

TABLE 1

Percentage of Girls in Total Enrollment
in Higher Education in Africa
(selected countries)

Country	1960	1965	1970
Algeria*	21	20	21
Benin (Dahomey)	—	3	7
Burundi	7	5	6
Cameroon	—	4	8
Central African Republic	—	—	3
Congo	—	14	5
Egypt	17	21	27
Ethiopia	4	7	8
Gabon	—	—	—
Ghana	11	11	14
Guinea	—	4	8
Ivory Coast	11	16	14
Kenya	—	19	—
Lesotho	22	21	34
Liberia	21	21	22
Libyan Arab Republic	3	8	11
Madagascar	23	25	32
Malawi	—	7	18
Mali	—	12	11
Mauritius	—	1	5
Morocco	14	12	17
Nigeria	7	12	14
Rwanda	—	3	9
Senegal	17	18	17
Sierra Leone	11	17	16
Somalia	13	10	13
Sudan	5	7	13
Swaziland	—	—	40
Tanzania	—	13	17
Togo	—	19	12
Tunisia	17	18	23
Uganda	12	14	18
Upper Volta	—	21	15
Zaire	—	5	6
Zambia	—	—	15

*Algeria: 1962 instead of 1960.
Source: Statistical Reports and Series, No. 19, Unesco.

TABLE 2

Enrollment of Students in Higher Education: Number
of Postsecondary Students per 10,000 Inhabitants
(selected countries)

Country	1960	1965	1970
Algeria*	2.5	6.8	13.9
Benin (Dahomey)	—	0.2	1.2
Burundi	0.1	0.6	1.3
Cameroon	0.8	2.4	4.6
Central African Republic	—	—	0.6
Congo	4.8	12.1	13.1
Egypt	41.4	59.2	64.4
Ethiopia	0.4	1.0	1.2
Gabon	—	0.5	1.4
Ghana	2.2	6.2	6.0
Guinea	—	1.1	5.0
Ivory Coast	1.0	4.2	10.2
Kenya	1.5	3.3	8.5
Lesotho	1.9	2.5	3.9
Liberia	4.8	6.4	9.5
Libyan Arab Republic	5.4	11.9	21.8
Madagascar	1.4	5.2	8.3
Malawi	—	0.2	2.2
Mali	—	0.3	1.4
Mauritius	1.2	1.3	22.9
Morocco	4.0	6.8	10.2
Nigeria	0.9	1.9	2.6
Rwanda	—	0.4	1.1
Senegal	4.5	8.0	12.7
Sierra Leone	1.4	3.0	4.4
Somalia	0.2	0.2	3.5
Sudan	3.4	6.0	9.1
Swaziland	—	—	3.3
Tanzania	—	0.5	1.5
Togo	—	0.4	4.8
Tunisia	5.4	12.9	18.9
Uganda	1.9	2.0	4.9
Upper Volta	—	0.1	0.3
Zaire	0.9	2.4	7.1
Zambia	—	—	3.9

*Algeria: 1962 instead of 1960.

Source: Statistical Reports and Series, No. 19, Unesco.

long before modern universities were established, their impact has not been studied. Modern higher education in Africa is largely a post-1950 importation from Europe and North America. According to information supplied by the Association of African Universities, there were 4 institutions of higher education prior to 1950, 8 were created between 1950 and 1960, 19 between 1960 and 1970, and 8 since 1970. Thus, in two decades, there was almost a tenfold increase, and today there are over 36 universities in the region.

The situation is even more impressive if one looks at the growth of enrollment. The figures increased from 135,055 students in 1960 to 247,098 in 1965 and to over 375,884 in 1970—an increase of 12.9 percent per year between 1960 and 1965, 8.6 percent between 1965 and 1970, and 10.7 percent between 1960 and 1970. (See Tables 2 and 4 for comparison by country.)

Nevertheless, even this rapid and impressive growth shows a distinct degree of backwardness when compared with that in the rest of the world, in general, and with that in other developing regions, in particular. Note the following figures, which compare, by major world regions, the number of students per 10,000 inhabitants.

Regions	1960	1970
Africa	7	12
Asia	27	48
Latin America	27	57
Europe	73	135
Oceania	98	159
North America	190	402
World average	55	97

Source: Statistical Reports and Series, No. 19, Unesco.

The number of students in Africa in the 1970s was one quarter that of Asia, about one fifth that of Latin America, and less than one eleventh that of Europe.

If one looks at the proportion of students enrolled in postsecondary education as compared with the corresponding age group of between 20 and 24 years in Africa and compares these figures with the rest of the developing world, the problem can be seen to be still further accentuated (see Table 3). The African percentages for 1960 and 1970 were 0.8 and 1.4, respectively, while they were 2.8 and 5.7 for Asia and 3.2 and 6.7 for Latin America. The corresponding figures (percentages of age group enrolled in postsecondary education) are 8.8 in 1960 and 17.8 for Europe in 1970 and 30.6 and 48.0 for North America. Here again the African region is at the bottom (see Table 2).

TABLE 3

Ratio of Student Numbers to Total 20- to 24-Year-Old Group:
Enrollment Ratio in Higher Education
(as percentages)
(selected countries)

Country	1960	1965	1970
Algeria*	0.30	0.82	1.69
Benin (Dahomey)	—	0.02	0.13
Burundi	0.01	0.07	0.15
Cameroon	0.10	0.28	0.54
Central African Republic	—	—	0.07
Congo	0.54	1.37	2.15
Egypt	4.70	6.77	7.41
Ethiopia	0.05	0.11	0.21
Gabon	—	0.05	0.16
Ghana	0.24	0.73	0.72
Guinea	—	0.12	0.58
Ivory Coast	0.11	0.47	1.18
Kenya	0.17	0.38	0.97
Lesotho	0.22	0.29	0.45
Liberia	0.56	0.73	1.09
Libyan Arab Republic	0.62	1.40	3.39
Madagascar	0.16	0.59	0.95
Malawi	—	0.03	0.25
Mali	—	0.04	0.16
Mauritius	0.15	0.18	2.53
Morocco	0.46	0.77	1.19
Nigeria	0.10	0.24	0.30
Rwanda	—	0.04	0.13
Senegal	0.50	0.90	1.46
Sierra Leone	0.16	0.35	0.50
Somalia	0.03	0.03	0.38
Sudan	0.38	0.68	1.04
Swaziland	—	—	0.37
Tanzania	—	0.05	0.19
Togo	—	0.05	0.54
Tunisia	0.65	1.56	2.24
Uganda	0.21	0.22	0.57
Upper Volta	—	0.01	0.04
Zaire	0.10	0.28	0.81
Zambia	—	—	0.44

*Algeria: 1962 instead of 1960.

Source: Statistical Reports and Series, No. 19, Unesco.

A statistical report on research and experimental development in
African countries, prepared for the 1974 CASTAFRICA conference,
discusses the proportion of scientific and technical manpower per
million inhabitants. It asserts: "Number of scientists, engineers and
technicians related to million of total population in African countries
is two to three times smaller when compared with Asia and almost 30
times smaller than in Europe."[1] "The Conference recommended that
Member States take the measures needed to attain, if possible before
1980, the targets set out in the table below, having regard to the fact
that the target of 200 scientists and engineers engaged in R & D activities per million inhabitants is that adopted for Africa by UNACAST in
its 'World Plan of Action' and that it is barely half of those established
for Asia and Latin America:"[2]

Economic development level (per capita GDP) $	Number of scientists and engineers per million inhabitants	Number of scientists and engineers engaged in R & D per million inhabitants (10% of the figure in Column Two (2).
(1)	(2)	(3)
200 or over	2,000	200
100 to 200	1,400	140
Under 100	1,000	100

There is no question, therefore, that despite the increase of the last
decade (see Table 4), the position of Africa is still extremely weak
and needs much encouragement and expansion.

Criticisms

Despite the limitations of physical facilities and the unavailability
of qualified human resources to increase the number of students in
African universities, several grave and persistent allegations and
criticisms are directed at these universities' performance by students,
governments, national and international organizations, and observers
both within and outside Africa. Some of these allegations are serious
and genuine, while others are merely frivolous or faddish.

The criticisms that recur and have received much attention include
the following:

1. That the philosophy, curricula, and structure of African universities are still predominately importations, ill-adapted to the

TABLE 4

Average Annual Student Enrollment: Growth Rate
of Higher Education in Africa
(selected countries)

Country	1960-70	1960-65	1965-70
Algeria*	27.5	42.0	19.4
Benin (Dahomey)	37.5	17.6	51.5
Burundi	32.5	46.3	19.9
Cameroon	23.0	33.0	16.1
Congo	17.1	22.4	12.0
Egypt	7.4	10.3	4.6
Ethiopia	17.8	20.6	15.0
Gabon	—	—	25.3
Ghana	13.7	26.4	2.3
Guinea	—	—	39.3
Ivory Coast	29.2	36.8	22.0
Kenya	25.3	26.3	24.4
Lesotho	9.2	7.3	11.2
Liberia	8.7	7.2	10.1
Libyan Arab Republic	21.8	21.5	22.1
Madagascar	22.6	33.2	12.8
Malawi	—	—	60.5
Mali	28.7	12.7	39.4
Morocco	13.2	14.0	12.3
Nigeria	18.6	25.3	13.5
Rwanda	—	—	27.7
Senegal	13.6	14.9	12.2
Sierra Leone	14.4	18.9	9.9
Sudan	13.7	15.3	12.0
Tanzania	—	—	30.3
Togo	—	—	64.7
Tunisia	16.8	22.7	11.3
Uganda	10.2	3.3	17.6
Upper Volta	—	—	45.6
Zaire	29.0	31.8	26.6
Zambia	—	—	50.0

*Algeria: 1962 instead of 1960.
Source: Statistical Reports and Series, No. 19, Unesco.

socioeconomic realities of Africa and, therefore, manifestly irrelevant to the needs and problems of the people.

2. That universities undertake research on topics and problems that are esoteric and of little or no assistance to the immediate problems of their societies.

3. That university methods of teaching and programs of study are abstract and theoretical, tending to alienate students from the real world, their cultures, and their people.

4. That university teaching, being narrow and discipline-oriented, neglects the problems of the real world, which often defy the scope of a single discipline, and that, consequently, graduates are ill-prepared after society has invested heavily in them.

5. That, compared with the other levels of education, universities are unduly and excessively costly to their governments.

6. That universities are extemely elitist in their orientation, with little or no concern for or commitment to the underprivileged masses of their country.

These and other criticisms are being heard and written about more and more. The purpose of this study has not been to discredit or to support such allegations, but rather to show that, while there may be institutions in Africa that merit in part these criticisms, there are a number of others that have broken from the imported traditional practices and have introduced innovations with a view to serving (directly and indirectly) their people, solving their problems through research, teaching them in a variety of ways, and being committed to their society through service.

OBJECTIVES, APPROACH, AND LIMITATIONS OF THIS STUDY

Objectives

This study has been set up to make a preliminary exploration of how certain African universities have related themselves to their societies and brought their expertise and know-how to bear upon the problems and needs of their people. In what manner have they done this? And how successful have they been? Could these departures, innovations, or activities serve as useful examples to the others. What can higher education do to further its contributions to development?

Approach and Procedure

Our point of departure was not the institutions but the problems faced by the region, which are many and varied. We agreed to concentrate on problems in the following areas:

1. Improvement of medical and health services.
2. Improvement of agricultural practices and food production.
3. Improvement and expansion of educational services.
4. Application, use, and transfer of technology.
5. Extension, extramural, and continuing education activities of universities.
6. Adaptation of curricula to African realities, especially through the exposure of students to practical work experiences, so that students can both augment their education and, at the same time, render useful productive work to their societies.

Along with the regional problems, we also considered questions dealing with the university: its development (how it can improve and increase its local staff, for example), its future, and the prospects and limitations of regional universities.

By looking around, consulting with people knowledgeable about higher education in Africa, and using personal experiences, we found it possible to select two or more institutions to illustrate each of several of the problems listed above. Because of time and other limitations, these areas were illustrated by developing cases from the University of Dar es Salaam in Tanzania, the University of Khartoum in Sudan, Addis Ababa University in Ethiopia (formerly known as the Haile Selassie I University), the University of Yaoundé in Cameroon, Ahmadu Bello University in Nigeria, the University of Science and Technology at Kumasi, Ghana, the higher education system of Mali, the University of Mauritius, and the University of Botswana, Lesotho, and Swaziland. In addition, brief visits were made to the universities of Nairobi (Kenya), Dakar (Senegal), Accra (Ghana), and Bujumbura (Burundi) by one or two members of the team. Recent pertinent studies and reports on African higher education were also reviewed.

The African team, in its first meeting held in Dakar, Senegal, decided that it would be better and more prudent if the first draft of each case were written by a national of that country who is both knowledgeable and respected. (This was done, with the exception of the case studies in Mali, Mauritius, and the University of Botswana, Lesotho, and Swaziland, which were written by nonnationals.) Each study was later read, criticized, and revised by an independent outside reader. Furthermore, most of the institutions were visited either by the regional director or codirector or by both. Last, in its second meeting at the University of Yaoundé, * the African regional team, together with a few select outsiders, assessed the case studies, provided suggestions for their improvement, and approved the general theme of the regional report.

Limitations

As stated at the outset, this study is not intended to be a comprehensive survey of African universities but rather an exploratory and descriptive development of cases illustrating the involvement of universities in different parts of the continent with different systems of education in the major developmental activities. It is an open-ended inquiry, presenting a picture of African universities from the point of view of the universities themselves. For lack of time and resources, it was not possible to include more cases nor to treat the selected cases more deeply, but a series of lessons has been drawn from individual cases and from combinations of cases in fields such as health, agriculture, and so forth.

It is also important to bear in mind that the picture of higher education all across the continent is not as bright and as successful as it appears from most of the cases. It is hoped, however, that all institutions of higher learning in Africa will have the opportunity to read the studies as useful examples and to improve and adapt them for their own institutions.

HIGHER EDUCATION AND NATION BUILDING

Higher education within the structures of African nations has been formed, by both circumstance and intention, along two distinct lines in nearly all developing nations, namely, the university proper and other institutions of higher education.

---

*We would like to express our gratitude to the chancellor and vice-chancellor of the University of Yaoundé, as well as to Dr. Monekosso, the director of the University Centre for Health Sciences, for their interest and cooperation, as well as for providing facilities for the meeting.

The University

For the purposes of this report, the university is defined as the institution (or institutions) producing high-level manpower in professional fields and in the arts and sciences, and conducting research and advanced study in those fields in order to further the intellectual and professional development of the nation.

Under this definition, universities were formed in many African nations under the auspices of national and international agencies, supported by the industrialized nations. These universities were established in traditional patterns, with a degree of institutional self-government and autonomy (with respect to government) on the premise that such self-government and autonomy were essential to effective learning and the advancement of knowledge. This premise was reinforced by the fact that most of the initial teaching faculties were recruited from the industrial nations, which gave the institutions a marked external orientation. The study has found that autonomy and external orientation have, to a considerable degree, been replaced by internal political controls and national orientation. This has been accomplished by several discrete steps.

Administration by Nationals

With a few exceptions in small, recently formed institutions, such as UBLS and Malawi, and in a few specialized technical areas in other institutions, African universities are now administered almost entirely by experienced, well-trained nationals.

National Faculty

The training of nationals for faculty positions has proceeded rapidly, and most African universities are at or beyond the 50 percent mark in national staff. When the proportion is not this high, the rapid expansion in total numbers of staff, as at Ahmadu Bello University, has been one of the reasons. The case study of the University of Khartoum illustrates how this level was attained.

National Program Needs

As the case studies show, national needs have brought curriculum adjustment and frequently curriculum innovation to most African universities. Universities have been, and are, vigorously redefining their mission in order to be more useful to their respective societies. It is significant that, as far as the studies indicate, these changes have taken place without loss of intellectual content or reduction of academic standards.

National Commitment

The new commitment is social and ideological, expressed in a new arrangement of the policy-determining power. Basically, the policy direction of the institution has shifted in many places from the autonomous faculty with its policy committees to the ideological control center of the government (the political party in the case of the one-party structure, which has become characteristic of the African polity). Under this organization, the university no longer stands apart from the government but is now one component of a triangle, with the party and its planning and policy committee as another, and the government, as the administrative arm, forming the third.

The new arrangements deserve more study and exposition than they can have in this report, but it is obvious, even in the briefest statement, that they give the university a much more direct role in nation building than was contemplated in their original planning.

Self-Reliance in Setting Standards

Among African societies, there has been, and to some degree there still is, an excessive preoccupation with "international standards" at the expense of what is relevant and useful to local social needs. This attitude now seems to have fallen under question and, at times, has been openly and vehemently criticized. It is noticeable that in different universities, there is a budding self-confidence in regard to internal standards and an openness toward creative adaptation. The era of seeking one's "certificate of respectability" from others seems to be giving way as academicians and educational and political leaders genuinely encourage their staff and their institutions to be self-reliant by undertaking activities that are better adapted and more appropriate to local conditions.[3]

Other Higher Education

The phrase "other higher education" is defined as programs of instruction in methodology, technical practice, and fieldwork in areas not covered by university education, notably pedagogy, paraprofessional areas, and vocational-technical training. Courses take from two to four years in duration, including work training under supervision. They are based on secondary education, hence their classification as a form of higher education.

Generally, in African nations, other higher education had its beginnings in the colonial period as postprimary education. During the first postcolonial years, this education was slowly upgraded and much enlarged until it took the form of postsecondary education.

Most institutions in this category have had deplorably little support from government, particularly in terms of legislation that would define career structure and establish salaries at levels that would attract competent and ambitious students. As a result, most developing nations have suffered a severe shortage of students and of graduates in teacher training and in technical fields. In turn, this shortage has affected both the standards of the educational system because of the lack of trained teachers and the performance of university-trained professionals and civil servants because of the lack of competent clerical and technical staff.

The present study indicates that there is strong evidence that these problems now have been confronted and that productive programs are now operating in many countries, with clear prospects for continued improvement and the direct participation of this level of higher education in nation building. The results of this change are discussed next.

Blurring the Distinction Between the University and Other
Higher Education

Traditionally, particularly in European countries, the two forms of higher education have been separated by a presumed intellectual gap and an actual educational gap. This separation was transmitted to Africa in the development of its various forms of higher education. The result, until recent years, has been a frustrating shortage of technicians and teachers, combined with a growing surplus of secondary school leavers who refuse nonuniversity forms of higher education because of their low prestige and the consequent poor prospects for their graduates. Instead, secondary school leavers have swarmed to the universities as applicants, and, when unsuccessful, have swelled the ranks of the militant unemployed.

The economic, social, and intellectual problems created by this imbalance were perennial, with little promise of solution. What was needed was a change in attitude or a new concept to replace the outmoded distinctions that separated these two areas. The new concept that has indeed come into being is, in historical perspective, a direct attack on the imposed colonial standards of the 1950s.

The colonial system demanded separate institutions and separate standards. Technicians and schoolteachers were subjected to a narrow curriculum that emphasized methodology without reference to purpose, thus implicitly reducing their status to that of a mere part of the machinery. At the same time, the professional became a man who ordered actions that often he himself could not perform and that he had no way of verifying or improving. The schoolteachers trained in teachers' institutes had an even crueler fate, for they could never hope to move from the schools to which their training assigned them, could never cross the barrier and enter the university to increase their stock of knowledge or their competence.

The standard was reinforced by educational and social differences, both at the secondary and postsecondary levels. Professional performance was hampered by the limitations of technicians, and the university suffered because of the restricted skills and knowledge of the teachers lower down in the education system.

The relatively simple step taken in several African universities, notably Kumasi, Yaoundé, Ethiopia (Gondar), and Dar es Salaam, has been to develop combined, or comprehensive, courses, that train both technicians and professionals. The combination means that, for the first time in Africa (not to mention Europe, Asia, and Latin America), technicians are taught professional subjects by professionals, in classes with professionals, while the professional students learn technical procedures under experienced technicians, in company with technicians with whom they will work during their later careers. It is important to add that these and other universities have struck down the barriers that kept schoolteachers out of the university. The resulting benefits include improvement in teacher morale.

What is evolving, and this evolution still has far to go, is a new type of institution that may be called the umbrella university. The umbrella university is new in that it provides a method for integrating technical and professional studies. It is this method, moreover, that makes it possible to plan an institution in which such integrated training can be done on a scale large enough to establish significant intellectual, social, and financial benefits. There will be difficulties to overcome before this new concept becomes generally accepted, since the separation of teachers and technicians from the universities is deep-rooted. But, as reported by this study, it would appear that the movement has a momentum that will not be stopped.

SUCCESSFUL EDUCATIONAL APPROACHES

This study has directed a spotlight upon a selected group of case studies consisting of institutions of higher education that have made successful efforts at educational development. From them we have extracted certain principles and lessons comprising guidelines to success, which we describe at the end of each study. In this more general report, only the main elements or conditions for a successful approach are outlined and the recent significant moves in the direction of educational innovation discussed.

Main Conditions for Success

Whenever educational institutions have contributed to development, integrated planning and careful preparation and discussion have been found. For a program to succeed, there must be a well-worked-out and carefully elaborated plan. The case studies of the University Centre for Health Sciences in Cameroon and the Ethiopian University Service Program illustrate this prerequisite.

The presence of competent, dynamic, and committed leadership is another critical and decisive factor. Wherever it has been present, there has been movement toward the implementation of the objectives of the plan; where absent, its lack has thwarted the achievement of what may have been worthy objectives. This element has been especially evident in Cameroon, in Ahmadu Bello University in Nigeria, in Ethiopia, and in Tanzania. (In the latter case, the influence of the president of the republic has never been far from the educational scene.)

Staff development has been a prerequisite for educational development in every case we have studied. The development of staff in university-level institutions requires a long period of preparation and patient assistance over an even longer time span. Whereas staff development in the past has necessitated training abroad, the growth of postgraduate institutions in Africa should facilitate local strengthening of the faculty.

Political support remains an absolutely vital condition for success in educational development. Where it is present, the fruits of a strong educational program can be realized. If it is absent, even the most imaginative, well-planned, and well-led educational program will fail.

New and Innovative Programs

In the study of university program development, it is clear that African universities are now offering programs that are far outside the classical definition of the university as implanted in the late 1950s or early 1960s. The following examples are relevant:

1. Comprehensive programs, or the parallel training in the same institution of professionals (doctors or engineers, for example) with technicians at senior, middle, and elementary levels. Not only are such programs economical in terms of training facilities and staff but, more important, they also exhibit a functional approach, with the formation of development teams that can undertake all the important aspects of field activities. The approach so far has been used most effectively in the health sciences, but it is equally applicable to rural development, development engineering, and agricultural training. The programs of Tanzania, Cameroon, and Ethiopia provide specific illustrations of these several cases.

2. Specific service courses at nonuniversity levels, such as short courses in automotive repair, instructor training for library programs, and a multitude of agricultural demonstration and practical courses, as offered by faculties of engineering, education, and agriculture.

3. Extension and summer programs, where university courses are offered in the evenings and during vacations, using university faculty teaching at university standard. In some countries, such as Nigeria (northern) and Ethiopia, such courses have been very important in the upgrading of teachers and civil servants. The reinvigoration and improvement of continuing education divisions in African universities are being taken seriously by university and government leaders.

4. Practical service-study programs as a required component of the students' educational experience. Work-study programs, already widely known elsewhere as sandwich courses or cooperative programs, have only just begun to develop in African universities and other institutions of higher education, partly because limited industrial development offers too few program opportunities. They are, however, high on the agenda of many of the universities visited and can be expected to develop over the next few years.

5. University research institutes, which have undertaken, and are undertaking, policy-oriented research activities on problems often jointly identified and selected in order of priority by university-government committees. Consultancy centers, where members of the university staff are available for a small fee for consultation on technical, commercial, and professional problems, also have developed in a number of institutions, particularly through faculties of engineering and agriculture.

6. The year-round university, which stays open throughout the year for both service and instruction. The year-round program is already realized in several of the institutions studied. Such a concept represents a radical departure from the European tradition that gave rise to the long vacation.

SOME CHARACTERISTICS OF DEVELOPMENT-ORIENTED
UNIVERSITIES

It would be presumptuous to assume that we have pinpointed all or even most of the characteristics of the development-oriented universities of Africa. The following are some of the indicators, drawn mainly from the institutions included in our cases, but also from those institutions briefly visited by team members. In some cases, certain characteristics have been emphasized or sharpened by participants at the final workshop of the African regional team held at the University of Yaoundé, Cameroon. With a far more comprehensive and inclusive study of the institutions of higher learning in Africa, one could attempt to provide several more of the necessary elements of development-oriented universities. This list of indicators is not expected to give rise to carbon copies but only to serve as a background document for discussions and as a point of departure.

The elements are expressed in question form. Although no one single institution may respond positively to all the questions, those institutions that give the larger number of positive replies may be judged to be more development-oriented than the others.

1. Is the university development plan integrated with or closely allied to the national development plan? Are university staff members, collectively or sectorally, involved in the formulation and evaluation of the national plan? Do mechanisms exist to assess the production and the effective and proper use of graduates? Are university staff members, individually, in groups, or collectively, formally or informally, participating in the formulation of policies? (Or are staff members merely followers, implementers, or critics of new policies?)

2. Are university leaders openly committed to the building of a development-oriented university or institution? Is the staff equally committed on this issue? Are the university leaders supported by the political authorities of the nation? Is there an effective mechanism to facilitate good working relationships between the university and the government? Is it functional?

3. Is the university seen as an investment on behalf of the taxpayers, the people? Is the university committed to the values of excellence, sacrifice, service, work, and greater social justice, rather than those of elitism? Is it innovative? Does it contribute to the liberation of the African mind? Does it make the African more self-reliant?

4. Is the program of study formulated, organized, and delivered to reflect the needs of the society and the nation?

5. Does the medical and health personnel training emphasize the provision of essential health services to the rural and urban population?

Does the university attempt to train the health team together within one institution? Does it practice integrated thematic teaching? Are the teaching hospitals and other health centers built, equipped, and organized in such a way that they could easily be duplicated or used as models by the graduates in other provincial and urban centers?

6. Do the courses of study offered and the methods of training used in technological schools prepare the graduates to tackle directly pressing development problems whose solution will contribute to the improvement of the lives of the people? For example, are there courses in transportation, conservation and management of water, design and building of low-cost rural and urban housing, and rural electrification? Are the agricultural schools organized to teach, conduct research, and serve in such a way that they contribute directly to the productivity of the farmer and therefore to the improvement of his life? Have consultancy centers and services been established where staff members are readily available for advice on the technical, commercial, and professional problems of the people, particularly through such faculties as technology and agriculture?

7. Are organized and continuing efforts being made by schools of education and the university to improve the rest of the educational system through educational research and curriculum development, textbook preparation and revision, in-service training for those involved in the running of the school system, and the provision of expertise in committees and commissions when needed?

8. Is the university concerned and involved not only with the preservation of the nation's cultures but also with their improvement and renovation?

9. Has the university a strong extension service program? Does it attempt to open the university to the communities far away from the physical location of the campus through extramural continuing education, correspondence courses, short and long seminars and workshops, radio education, and provincial branch centers?

10. Does the university provide service-study, work-study, or other practical education for the students, thus linking education with life and living and with production? Are university staff, administration, and students at work in the field for a part of the academic year, giving urgently needed and useful service to communities in one or more fields of the students' specialization?

11. Are university staff members undertaking research and publication not only to discover and advance the frontiers of knowledge but also to make teaching more pertinent to students? Have research institutes been established to undertake policy-oriented research activities? Is rural development being promoted not only through attempts to meet basic human needs but also through development research in economic, political, administrative, and cultural areas by inter-

disciplinary teams? Are research policies for research institutes developed and research priorities set by government-university committees or boards?

12. Does the university provide comprehensive technical and professional studies in which technicians and professionals learn to understand and appreciate each other's role in the development process?

13. Is the university training, or conscious of the need to train, educational management specialists; rural and local development personnel; general educational planners; measurement, testing, and project evaluation experts; and farmers' cooperative specialists?

14. Has the university a well-conceived staff development program? Does the staff development program encourage or require the writing of research papers on local or comparable problems? Does it require staff to serve in government, quasi-government, or private agencies in order to acquire practical, real-life experiences?

15. Is the university or higher education system coordinated and supervised to avoid unnecessary overlap or duplication? Is the university providing positive leadership in this area?

16. Is the university conscious of its role of contributing to the strengthening of African unity and international solidarity by encouraging staff, student, and publication exchange? Does it, in one way or another, encourage its staff and a section of its students to be equipped, at the very least, with an understanding of both French and English, or, better still, to be functionally bilingual in them, and perhaps in some other important language?

HIGHER EDUCATION AND EXTERNAL ASSISTANCE

The Past

The main lines of foreign assistance to higher education for development have shifted in three important respects. In the beginning, educational assistance was characterized by a one-way flow of African students to foreign universities for undergraduate education. With the growth of institutions for undergraduate education in Africa, this form of assistance has already fallen off or is likely to fall off sharply in the future. In the second stage, early in the period of institution building, external assistance brought foreign scholars to African universities. At the outset, with only a limited number of Africans trained to professorial level, expatriate scholars were given long-term appointments in many of the key academic positions in Africa. Little by little, the need for assistance of this kind, at least on a large scale, has declined. Future visiting professorial appointments are likely to be in well-specified and limited fields. In the third phase, there was an economic orientation to certain forms of external assistance for educational development. The building up of markets was a consideration of some donors. With the growing stress on human development in the emerging universities, this emphasis has become less apparent, and individual and social well-being is seen as more central to educational assistance. Thus external assistance for educational development today is more likely to be connected with the central aims of the developing society.

External assistance for education is entering a healthier and more creative period than ever before. The imaginative marshaling of aid to support development-oriented universities in Africa by African governments, international organizations, and private and other donors might well be the turning point of university development strategy in Africa. It is also an opprotunity to distinguish sincere, committed, and genuine friends from superficial ones with neocolonial aims.

The development of higher education in Africa, then, is largely a by-product of political independence, a product of the post-1950s era. It is interesting to observe that, while African countries were engaged in establishing universities, Unesco convened a conference in 1962 in Tananarive, Madagascar, to look into the overall development strategy of African universities, including the problems and ways and means of adapting their curricula to African needs. Some ten years later, the Association of African Universities convened a workshop at Accra, Ghana, with participation by interested universities and members of the association. The workshop undertook a comprehensive review and discussion of the issues of adapting higher education in Africa. Between the two meetings, little was done on a continental scale. There were individual efforts in which African universities were studied and assisted by international organizations, private foundations, and professional associations, but their scope was limited.

The major positive and lasting contribution that assisting agencies and foundations have made to the universities appears to be the development of overall infrastructures, particularly in the field of human resource development. With the initial task of institution building substantially completed, and with the availability of a core of permanent committed and competent indigenous staff, donor agencies are enabled to reassess their assistance philosophy with a view to helping the local staff to be more productive, active, and involved in the development process of their respective communities and societies. How this support should and can be deployed needs further thinking and consultation, and has been a major focus of our study.

The Future

As universities are in different stages of development, it is hardly possible, nor is it wise, to suggest a uniform method of assistance. In planning assistance and areas of cooperation, it may be worthwhile to bear in mind some of the fundamental criteria that should guide action. In Africa, internal and external assistance should be directed to the establishment and/or strengthening of the training, research, and consultant-service capacity and capability of African institutions. As there are several instances of attempts by universities to find genuine solutions to and be deeply involved in the problems of development, assistance could strengthen such innovative activities and positive orientations. One study that could well be strengthened by assistance is consideration of the intimate relationship of cultural factors and the process of development—which are the constraining and which the facilitating elements of the different cultures in relation to development in Africa?

It is clear that the strengthening of higher education in Africa, while being a concern of donor agencies, is primarily the task and responsibility of the countries themselves. This report and, in particular, the recommendations concerning areas of assistance, is addressed, therefore, to the countries of Africa that fortunately have come to see the importance of education in clearer terms. [4] The suggestions are also addressed to the Organization of African Unity, the Economic Commission for Africa, the Association of African Universities, and the African and Malagasy Council on Higher Education. It is hoped that these regional organizations will take the opportunity to make use of the findings of the team, discuss them, and consider ways and means of implementing them in practice.

Institutions with strong leadership tend to be good not in one area or discipline alone but in several areas. Indeed, the strength of a university results from the interrelationship of its parts, which support and reinforce one another. For this reason, attention must be given to overall institutional development. Educational management, in particular, should not be neglected, and assistance should also be given to integrated planning, library development, and educational technology. The role that faculties of law and administration can play needs consideration. It is important to note that narrow disciplinary training may not meet the national need for educated leaders; a different and more broadly based problem-oriented approach is called for.

Universities are expensive institutions. They might shift some or all of the expenses to students, supplementing tuition with loans or scholarships, but this proposal needs further investigation in the context of general educational planning and management. Greater attention to administrative, financial, and overall educational management is called for.

Because of the heavy cost involved in establishing and running universities in Africa and because their financing is a heavy charge on the government, there is a serious need to examine university-government relationships. In this connection it is suggested that this study and other reports on African higher education could be considered for discussion at the Unesco 1976 Regional Conference of African Ministers of Education. It would be a good idea if such discussion were preceded by special meetings sponsored by the Association of African Universities or the Organization of African Unity, in which university administrators, university staff, and government representatives participated to formulate the general lines of further university development in Africa and the contribution of the university to the development efforts of the society it finds itself in. Careful advance preparation for these meetings and further case writing would be highly desirable. Here the donor agencies that have supported the project up to now could be helpful.

Areas of Assistance

There are five areas that are particularly deserving of support: educational research and curriculum development; promotion of rural development through research; development and application of technology in agriculture, health, and engineering; extension and continuing education activities of universities; and further areas of study, including the structure, organization, and management of African universities, the social commitment and political opinions of students, the development of nonuniversity institutions in Africa, educational management, women's education, communications, postgraduate programs, and the open university.

Educational Research and Curriculum Development

Education is probably the most important activity and concern of Africa. Governments have shown their support by contributing as much as 20 to 30 percent of their national budgets to education. At the same time, they are not satisfied with the kind of education they have. It would seem self-evident that changes in educational policies would be more successful, realistic, and productive if they were backed by the results of purposeful research. Unfortunately, the quantity and quality of educational research are still far from adequate. A major effort to raise the level of such research is urgently needed and recommended.

Support should be given to the few existing centers, or a new structure should be created for the coordination and improvement of educational research institutions in Africa. This effort should have the highest priority.

Promoting Rural Development Through Research

There are institutions of research under different names in Africa: development research institutes, institutes for economic and social research, economic research bureaus. In one way or another, all are interested in making their contribution to the socioeconomic development of their countries through research, publication, and training. They are the result of the fact that, in most of Africa, the concern for rural transformation, for improving the lot of the underprivileged, and for providing (at least at a minimal level) equality of opportunity is widespread. These institutions could be made centers of research and publication, working hand-in-hand with the government and other development agencies. They should be coordinated and assisted in a systematic and continuing manner, which is not the case at present. It would seem that expanded support in this area would give productive results.

The tendency to consider cultural studies as superfluous and unnecessary is questioned. The whole area of traditional attitudes as facilitating or constraining elements vis-à-vis development is significant and presents serious issues that cannot be bypassed. The question of how and to what extent studies of this nature could or should be associated with institutes of development research, or whether they should be pursued in small but viable institutes for cultural studies, needs to be resolved.

The Development and Application of Technology in Agriculture, Health, and Engineering

An area of special weakness in Africa is the practical, down-to-earth use of technology to improve life and living. How can the university's expertise be used so that it provides consultancy, research, and other services to small-scale businesses, industries, and others that may need help? The recent trend, exemplified in Ibadan, Kumasi, Zambia, and Addis Ababa, toward establishing centers or institutes for the application of scientific and technological research to development, including the formal and informal interdisciplinary study teams at Dar es Salaam and Nairobi Universities, needs to be investigated and methods of assistance devised. It is urgent that technology come to the rescue of the rural citizen, including rural women.

We have not answered the question as to which is the best approach, and discussion of how one encourages and supports the selected approach is also very much called for. In establishing or making use of technology centers in different parts of the region, a long-range assistance strategy needs to be constructed with a view to ensuring ultimate financial self-sufficiency. Mechanisms of consultation and coordination should be established. At the same time, the popularization of science, including the development of scientific and technological museums illustrating scientific concepts and principles, ought to be given serious attention. The need to publicize science and technology is more urgent in Africa, at its current state of scientific and technological development, than in the developed world. Schoolchildren and the average citizen need to be exposed to science and technology day in and day out. Support and recognition should be given to pilot programs in health and agriculture that make use of the new technology, especially if the pilot program is aimed at reaching neglected sections of the population, both rural and urban.

Extension and Continuing Education Activities of Universities

More and more universities in Africa are organizing courses, seminars, and workshops on a continuing basis for surrounding communities. They are scheduling the programs during evenings, Saturdays, and summer vacations and are instituting correspondence programs and programs on the air. Consultants' services could help expand the horizon of the universities' understanding of their role in this field. Assistance with staff and materials and with design and construction of appropriate buildings would also be most helpful.

Further Areas of Study

The African team has identified various areas in African higher education that merit additional study. These include:

1. The structure, organization, and management of African universities. A careful investigation into the suitability, applicability, and relevance of their structure would be appropriate. In this connection, a study of the governance of universities in Africa and their relationships with their governments is urgently needed.

2. Social commitment and student opinion. Students who have received higher education are very important prospective servants and leaders in their countries. Their social and political orientation needs some careful thinking. The related questions of who goes to the university and why and the other side of the coin—the wise and effective utilization of graduates—should be fully investigated.

3. Organization and development of postsecondary nonuniversity institutions in Africa and cooperation between these institutes and the universities.

4. Educational management. Although this has been noted above, the team gives it further emphasis because it has been neglected and because so much depends on sound administration and management. Universities have tended to take over colonial management patterns, and these are inadequate for future needs.

5. Women's education, singled out as an area of neglect in several of the case studies, including Tanzania, which in other respects has advanced far in achieving equality of opportunity. The African team hopes to explore this area further as a phase two activity.

6. Communications, a vital area, with special importance in a multilingual continent such as Africa. In addition to the many local languages, the two international languages, French and English, are important vehicles of education. (The Cameroon case illustrates ways in which effective bilingualism can be pursued.)

However, there are many other aspects to communications apart from the purely linguistic one. Communications also involves the identification and exchange of outstanding scientists and scholars within Africa (J. Ki-Zerbo, secretary-general of the African and Malagasy Council on Higher Education, has proposed a "master African educator" plan patterned after the system used in the United States under the auspices of the National Academy of Sciences and the American Association for the Advancement of Science) and a wider dissemination of scholarly works. An African university press deserves consideration, perhaps including several regional presses, and there is a need for African scholarly journals with broader outreach and coverage. Beyond this, communications includes the relations between educational institutions and society. New relationships are required, calling for a deeper sensitivity to the human needs of nonuniversity people.

7. Postgraduate programs. Such programs will become more and more important, making it possible for young Africans to receive their education within the continent rather than having to go abroad for all their graduate work.

8. The open university. This kind of institution has evolved in other countries as a method of carrying on higher education at all levels. In Africa, where the education of mature adults is a crucial aspect of education, such institutions could fill a no less vital role.

NOTES

1. Unesco, Statistics on Research and Experimental Development in African Countries: Analytical Report (SC/CASTAFRICA), Ref. 1, p. 10.

2. From Final Report of Conference of Ministers of African Member States Responsible for the Application of Science and Technology to Development, held in Dakar from 21st to 30th January, 1974.

3. Julius Nyerere, "Education and Liberation" (opening address), Development Dialogue, 2 (1974): 51.

4. See the several recommendations, in particular, recommendation No. 20, of the Final Report of the Conference of Ministers of African Member States Responsible for the Application of Science and Technology to Development, Unesco, Dakar, 21-30 January, 1974.

11

THE CONCEPT OF DEVELOPMENT

Development is very often viewed as a state or condition that has already been attained, as when, for instance, one speaks of developed nations. Perhaps this view of development is biased in the direction of material or economic performance. Economic efficiency is, of course, an important aspect of development, for it attests to a culture of performance, innovation, and organization. Nevertheless, human communities are not merely machines for producing material objects and related services. A human community is an association of human beings, and the condition of development therefore cannot be rightly viewed except in terms of human welfare or well-being. Indeed, there are instances of nations that are conventionally regarded as developed where the quality of human life or well-being is threatened by degradation of the natural environment, serious inefficacy in the social control of production technology, inequity in the production and sharing of the national wealth, and unsolved ethical or moral difficulties in heterogeneous populations living together.

And so it may be wiser to regard development as a process rather than as an attained stage or condition. Conceived as such, development is necessarily a continuing situation. All the nations on the planet are at some stage of development in this process, although the course of development is not unidirectional, owing to the vast range of aspirations, and constraints, among the various nations.

But even though the development process is not unidirectional, neither is it undefinable. Our view of development includes three elements. Briefly stated, it is the process of increasing, first, modernization of the economy (that is, the production of wealth and the efficient

use and management of resources); second, the efficacy of social
mechanisms in the management of consensus and conflict; and third,
and most important, human well-being in relation to the environment.

Modernization requires the use of appropriate and efficient technology; it therefore implies an openness of mind in the choice of
methods and tools, whether "hardware" or "software." Thus, not only
the economy but also the society as a whole should be modernized, in
the context, of course, of the nation's cultural values. Social efficacy
means that the community is not helpless and can decide and act in the
face of social crises. And our view of development requires that the
ultimate test of national performance be human well-being.

We take this position on human well-being for a number of reasons.
Perspectives such as 2,000 A.D. and Spaceship Earth compel us to be
concerned about the future of the planet as the habitation of humanity.
We are concerned about the condition of the planet because we are concerned about the condition of humanity. Global concerns about the
problems in food, population, and energy touch all nations. Nearer to
home, the unrest from the 1960s to the present has given new urgency
to social problems. Young adults, who constitute so much of the populations in the developing countries, especially in Asia, and who will be
the leaders of the 1980s, have focused attention on the fundamental issues of justice, morality, human dignity, and liberation. These issues
emphasize the need for more attention to human well-being.

Our solicitude for human well-being does not imply that we ignore
other imperatives. We consider that the goal of well-being encom-
passes all spheres of human activity, including those outside the individual, such as the status of the nation and its international
relationships. Human well-being is relative and a balance of various
factors, individual, national, and international. To achieve it, of
course, requires compromise, but compromise cannot be carried
beyond a point; for example, the nation's leaders cannot neglect human
well-being in the pursuit of international power. If the decision makers
are oriented to well-being, they will stop at the right point in such a
pursuit.

Higher education in the service of development can help increase
the capacity of nations to produce more of those material goods that
make human life pleasant and rewarding, but it must also reinforce
concern for justice, morality, and human dignity. Both higher education and development must be regarded as approaches toward the liberation of people from the constraints, for example, of poor health,
ignorance, poverty, unemployment, runaway technology, that prevent
them from realizing their human potential.

The various nations on the planet are assumed to be pursuing the
ideals of humanity in their own ways through structures and processes
that reflect their different histories, cultures, values, and capabilities.

Some will perform better than others. But most nations must still make special efforts to lift the poor to the level of the more comfortable groups. Many countries must solve environmental problems. And all, or almost all, have problems of inequality in the distribution of material goods.

Because well-being includes all people, development must be measured in terms of the degree that each nation attains and secures it for everyone in the nation. Development is attained only when the well-being of every member of the community is achieved and assured.

Reflecting this expanded view of development is the companion concept of social accounting as a measure of national performance. A society may define or prescribe goals or performance targets, but without a measure, confusion may set in even on the issue of the goals themselves. On the other hand, if the measure adopted is not in harmony with national goals, it has a tendency to draw efforts toward its own fulfillment rather than achievement of the goals. If the gross national product, for example, is the measure of performance, production levels tend to be stressed, resources wasted, and distribution of wealth understressed. If social welfare is the goal, program success has a different meaning. It is, therefore, suggested that a social accounting system can be very helpful to a development effort by establishing the standards by which programs are judged.

(A basic "social indicators" scheme, as most social accounting systems are called, involves adoption of a list of areas of social concern, each of which is deemed necessary to individual and community well-being. Then statistical indicators are devised to measure national performance in each area; for example, health and nutrition, learning and skills, income and consumption, employment, capital and non-human resources, housing/utilities and environment, public safety and justice, social mobility, and political values. The result is a composite measure of how well or poorly the nation produces "net beneficial product" or "net national welfare" or some similar well-being aggregate. The NBP or NNW can be disaggregated to indicate how regions or income classes, for example, are faring. Thus, social indicators likewise measure distribution of values. A practical policy application of the system would be the stipulation of a target of X percent GNP increase with the proviso that a significant portion of the increase (say, upward of 50 percent) goes to families earning less than a certain annual income.)

Inasmuch as higher education is not, or ought not to be, viewed as mere training for skills, but must include experiences or insights in decision making and in human values, a social accounting system must consider these objectives in any study of higher education and development. One caveat is necessary in most discussions of higher education (or of any education, for that matter) in relation to large

societal objectives: formal education alone cannot bring about a desired
end (for example, social reform, enlightened electoral decisions, increased productivity, national unity, or justice). Even if the entire
formal education system were deliberately designed and operated to
achieve these societal goals, the prospects of success are sketchy at
best. To attain such goals not only formal education but also a broad
range of nonformal educating agencies, such as the family, civic associations, churches, political parties, unions, government, and economic institutions, must work together.

Even if higher education is oriented to social justice or comprehensive economic planning, it can do little if the government itself does
not deliberately pursue these objectives. Thus, there must be a degree
of consensus in the society about problems and/or objectives, a political will to face those problems and pursue those objectives, and government ability to meet the problems and implement goals.

THE ROLE OF THE UNIVERSITY

The university is the traditional seat of higher education, and,
whether in the advanced or the developing countries, the classical role
of the university—to preserve, transmit, and increase knowledge—
cannot be neglected. In the developing countries of Asia, moreover,
many of which did not have scholarly traditions, these functions must
be pursued more assiduously than ever as part of the process of raising
the level of the nation's intellectual and, therefore, economic, political,
social, and cultural development. Because of pressures from government and society, university scholars may be forced to devote their
research efforts to immediate problems, but even in a developing
country, basic, fundamental research, in the long run, may be more
important to public needs. A university's commitment to intellectual
excellence is its primary and most significant contribution to a developing nation.

Nevertheless, universities in today's circumstances are compelled
to be more than ivory towers. The land-grant colleges in the United
States more than a century ago showed the way for their counterparts
today in the developing countries through their efforts in public service
and extension work. To the three classical functions of the university,
therefore, must be added that of attention to the needs of the community and the nation.

Crucial as universities are to national development, higher education also takes place in institutions below university status: colleges,
technical schools, community colleges, academies, and special institutions of various sorts. Moreover, nonformal education, such as

extension courses, short training programs, and radio and TV series, provide postsecondary education.

In our view, both traditional and nontraditional institutions of higher education must become instruments of national development. The objectives to which higher education must respond have both national and international dimensions, which may be briefly stated as follows.

National objectives include:

1. Focus informed attention on the most serious national problems.

2. Strengthen the capacity to solve urgent local and community problems, such as food and nutrition, health and environment, employment and human resource development, housing, planning, urban in-migration, and equity.

3. Broaden and strengthen the indigenous capacity to absorb and advance science and technology for development; promote accumulation and transfer of skills.

4. Disseminate and apply more effectively existing knowledge as well as art and culture.

5. Promote national integration. The nations of Southeast Asia have moved ahead since independence in the 1940s and 1950s; on the whole, therefore, consolidation of independence has been superseded by the quest for national unity.

International objectives include:

1. Improve the country's position in international markets.

2. Develop capabilities to deal with international problems, such as the monetary system, scientific problems with worldwide sources of knowledge, and the environment.

3. Participate in international dialogues on issues of human well-being and make more effective contributions to the world community of nations through cooperation at the bilateral, regional, and international levels.

THE SOUTHEAST ASIAN REGION

The Southeast Asian region, which is the locale of the case studies presented here, consists of 11 independent nations, from the Philippines in the east to Burma in the west. In 1970, 283 million people lived in this part of the world, with per capita GNP ranging from as high as $1,075 in Brunei and $844 in Singapore to $96 in Indonesia and

$78 in Burma. This is neither the most populous region of the world
nor is it the most backward in terms of national development. (See
Table 5 for detailed economic data on Southeast Asia.)

The five nations of the Association of Southeast Asian Nations
(ASEAN) are perhaps at this stage of time the most developed and the
most homogeneous grouping in the region. Indonesia is the largest in
area and population, 1.9 million square kilometers with 120 million
people; it also has the lowest per capita GNP, $96. The leading island
of Java is densely populated (70 million people), but the outer islands
are sparsely populated. On the other hand, Singapore has 2.2 million
people in an area of 580 square kilometers and has the highest per
capita GNP at $884. In between are Thailand with 40 million people
in 514,000 square kilometers and with a per capita GNP of $210; the
Philippines, also 40 million people in 299,000 square kilometers and
with a per capita GNP of $240; and Malaysia, 12 million people in
332,600 square kilometers and with a per capita GNP of $400. It
appears that in Southeast Asia the larger the area of the country and
the population, the lower the per capita GNP, although, of course, the
relationship is more complex than that.

Except for Thailand, the Southeast Asian nations, until the post-
World War II period, were ruled by metropolitan powers from Europe
and North America. Even Thailand, although nominally independent,
was subject to external pressures during the colonial period, hemmed
in as it was by territories ruled by outside powers. From the second
half of the nineteenth century to the World War II, Thailand was within
the sphere of influence of the United Kingdom. Under colonial rule,
cultural ties were built up in each country with the political suzerain,
and, for good or ill, many aspects of the culture and institutions were
implanted or absorbed. Education especially was influenced by such
cultural ties, which explains the diversity in educational systems,
outlooks, and experiences of the different countries.

Higher Education in Southeast Asia

Two crosscurrents affect higher education in Southeast Asia. On
the one hand, the populace aspires to higher education, as they see in
it, rightly or wrongly, the key to a better life. This aspiration is
probably most intense in Indonesia, but it is also powerful in Thailand
and continues to be strong in the Philippines, where for more than
three generations, with the establishment of a system of mass education in the American colonial period, education has been very open.

But, on the other hand, governments are determined to control
and limit higher education, as in Singapore and, to a lesser degree,

TABLE 5

Basic Economic Data on Southeast Asia

	Total Area (sq. km.) (land area including area under inland waters)	Midyear Population (millions)		Per Capita GNP (U.S. $)			Total Enrollment in Higher Education
		1972	1973	1971	1972	1973b	1970
Brunei	5,770	0.12f	n.a.	n.a.	n.a.	n.a.	n.a.
Burma	678,030	28.87	29.56	80	90	90	45,891c,e
Cambodia	181,040	7.15a	7.31a	130	120	120	11,094d
Indonesia	1,904,340	123.12	126.09	80	90	100	221,124e
Laos	236,800	3.11	3.18	120	130	140	517e
Malaysia	332,630	11.0a	11.32a	400	430	480	16,509d
Philippines	300,000	39.04	40.22	240	220	250	622,116d
Singapore	580	2.15	2.19	1,200	1,300	1,490	13,683
Thailand	514,000	38.53	39.74	210	220	240	70,997
South Vietnam	173,810	19.37	19.88	230	170	180	47,021e
North Vietnam	158,750	21.34e	n.a.	n.a.	n.a.	n.a.	n.a.
Southeast Asia	4,327,100	283.69f	n.a.	153e	n.a.	n.a.	—
World	133,920,000	3,632.00f	n.a.	n.a.	n.a.	n.a.	—

Note: n.a.: data not available.
aProjected with the latest annual growth rate.
bFigures for 1973 are preliminary estimates.
cPublic education only.
d1968.
e1969.
f1970.

Sources: Asian Development Bank, Key Indicators of Developing Member Countries of ADB, Vol. 5, no. 2, October 1974. Unesco Regional Office for Education in Asia, Progress of Education in the Asian Region, Statistical Supplement, Bangkok, 1972.

in Malaysia and in Thailand. The elitist view of higher education is probably a carryover from the colonial era, especially under the British. But it is also justified by governments today on grounds of efficiency: to get the best return on the government's expenditures, to direct the work force where it is needed, to avoid the problem of educated unemployed. The idea of elite higher education also arises because strong governments are loathe to deal with large and often intractable groups of students and intellectuals.

What should be the choice between this yearning for higher education and the government's view of "efficiency"? The fact of the matter is that, despite occasional government pronouncements on restricting higher education, enrollments have been going up faster than population increases. Given the many tasks of development and the pressing need for trained people, it is very difficult to escape the mounting necessity for higher education.

Of course, we do not believe that everyone in the population should be or can be a Ph.D. There are many types of postsecondary education other than scholarly or professional training. Furthermore, a great diversity of institutions and methods, not just universities, can be used to carry out the work of higher education. Likewise, we understand that government restrictions on enrollment may, as in the Philippines, be aimed at raising the quality of postsecondary education where there is already large enrollment at the college level. While there is much efficiency and innovation in higher education in Southeast Asia, some great inefficiencies cannot be overlooked.

A striking lesson in the economic development of those nations that today are considered advanced is that the highest payoff in the wide range of areas of investment has been investment in education. Japan's economic and national development in the late nineteenth and early twentieth centuries is a vivid illustration. Education has a pivotal role, for it is people who develop a country. There is still another lesson: education for national development is a task of generations.

Except perhaps in a recession or depression, a progressive modern society needs all the trained people it can get. Not only are top-level professionals and managers required but a large host of competent supporting staff, as well as persons of varied skills, must also be available. The requisite numbers of such people are difficult to estimate because the quantitative relationships between growth and requirements of trained manpower cannot be derived from historical experience. Although attempts are being made to develop social indicators, there is still a long way to go to understand the link between development and the necessary numbers of higher level people trained for specific development tasks. Nevertheless, for developing countries, the more trained people there are, the better the prospects of developing the society (not just the economy).

That there is a shortage of trained people in Southeast Asian countries is shown in an economic measure: the relatively high compensation that qualified professionals command and the large differential between their salaries and the wages of both unskilled workers and those with some higher education, such as white-collar workers and teachers. There are even countries where the pay is enough to attract expatriates from advanced economies. This situation is paradoxical as well as unhealthy for developing countries with per capita incomes way below those in advanced countries. The reliance on expatriates detracts from another desideratum for most developing nations, namely, intellectual and technical independence through a strong and adequate indigenous professional and technical class.

It should be noted that in many developing countries today there is a large mass of educated unemployed and a tendency toward emigration of skilled professionals, such as doctors. This is true especially in some economies in Asia, which, for various reasons, including government economic and political policy, are growing very slowly. But the Southeast Asian countries are not generally in such a dismal position; growth rates have been at least satisfactory and in some cases gratifying indeed. Furthermore, the evidence, say in the Philippines, is that the problem of educated unemployed is a least partly illusory: the great mass of unemployed are those looking for their first job and once they find that job, they tend to remain employed, or else unemployed college graduates, because they come from a higher income level, choose not to take a job until they find what they consider satisfactory positions.

The surpluses of trained people in certain fields do indicate imbalances and inefficiency in the educational effort as well as inadequate government policies to absorb the output of the educational system. We do not deny that the efforts in higher education should be related to the economy's manpower needs, for example, toward more technicians rather than toward too many graduates in less useful areas, such as humanities. It is our feeling, however, that the educated unemployed in Southeast Asian developing countries represent a temporary stage in development. The fact is that there are in all the Southeast Asian countries shortages not only of managers, entrepreneurs, and people with sophisticated modern technical skills but also of stenographers, clerks, and office superintendents. Under these circumstances, it is certainly better for long-run development to have reserves of trained people rather than a shortage.

In an economy that is growing satisfactorily there should be no fear that there will be problems of placing qualified workers. As the qualifications of the available work force rise, employers, too, raise their qualification standards; where they formerly required elementary school graduates, they now require secondary school graduates.

For the development of the economy and society, a critical mass of "leader elements" is needed: the entrepreneurs, the intellectuals, the professionals, the managers. There are also the political leaders, who provide the nexus between popular aspirations and concerns, on the one hand, and government programs and national policy directions, on the other. The lone charismatic leader-hero and his personal supporters cannot bring about national development without managers of development programs and projects, without entrepreneurs of economic undertakings and of intellectual enterprise, without the support of politically attuned people who feel the popular pulse and feed back opinions and feelings to the top leadership. The nation produces this critical mass primarily through higher education. Higher education, however, must produce not only supporters of a particular political regime but also groups and individuals who provide the nation with alternative policy directions, management concepts, and resource allocation/distribution schemes. The availability of these leader elements is not a luxury but a necessity for development, for they contribute not only to the efficiency of public and private management but also to the openness of society.

One of the goals of modern-day policy is egalitarianism. Education is a potent democratizing element. The more people who are educated, the more people there are who share a common experience. This sharing cannot but lift the level of humanity in the population and strengthen the society.

The egalitarian effect of higher education extends as well to material measures of well-being, that is, the distribution of income in the society. In the first place, higher education is one of the most effective ways of promoting social (and, therefore, economic) mobility. Furthermore, as the supply of professionals and qualified manpower increases, the price (salaries) of these go down. At the other end of the scale, the supply of unskilled workers shrinks relatively and thus their wages go up. The narrowing of the income gap is an historical experience in today's advanced countries and is, in fact, one of the measures of degree of development.

Above all, higher education has a humanistic goal to justify it, even without the economic and political justifications. Man is a rational being, and higher education is a means to the fulfillment of human nature.

SOME CONCLUSIONS

Now, perhaps, a few more immediately pertinent questions may be examined in connection with the need to improve higher education in Southeast Asia.

Age of Institutions

We have found that new institutions are not necessarily more development-oriented than older ones. The University of the Philippines, which opened in 1908, and Thammasat University, which was founded in 1933, are leaders in development education. It is not the age of the institutions that matters; a new institution can just as easily be established to preserve as to change the status quo. Rather, what is crucial is that the concern for development problems is so widespread that institutions can no longer ignore it. Older institutions have created new programs to cope with specific problems; in so doing, they have either recognized or set up new organizations. As for the new institutions, they have responded to the demand, and in some cases have been set up specifically to cater to a need.

Institutions of higher education started to become development-oriented largely in the 1950s and the 1960s when development problems came to a head after independence. Even in Thailand, which had been nominally independent, higher education directed itself increasingly to solving the social and economic problems of the nation.

Cultural Origins of a Country's Higher Education System

The countries studied in connection with this report show different mixes of three cultural influences on Southeast Asia: the traditional cultures, foreign cultural intervention, and modern culture. All but Thailand were colonized, but by different powers. They had different histories and distinct traditional cultures of varying strengths. The occupying powers had diverse motives in setting up the educational systems, especially the universities, during the colonial period. The colleges in the English colonies, for example, were designed to produce well-trained and highly paid public servants rather than executives for the private sector.

In addition, educational patterns reflected the differing cultural origins of the political suzerains; for example, the Dutch and English tended toward the Continental European system of higher education with its elitism and emphasis on specialization, and Thailand, which was oriented toward England, was greatly influenced by that tradition when Chulalongkorn University was established. On the other hand, the American colonial administrators in the Philippines took the charters of the land-grant colleges of the United States for their model when setting up the University of the Philippines; this University, therefore, has had a longer tradition of public service, professional training, and mobility of staff among the academic, government, and private sectors.

In the development of newly independent nations, there is a stage when there are still strong cultural and economic links with the former metropolitan power. Then later the people begin to absorb modes of thought from other countries. The Indonesians, for example, who were ruled by the Dutch, have become more aware of and appreciative of American culture.

It should be noted that cultural influence was two-way; for example, many American universities became more development-oriented after their staff came to this part of the world as Fulbright grantees, on AID programs, and so on.

Amount, Source, and Nature of Previous Assistance

In almost all the successful programs studied here, foreign support (from USAID, the Asian Development Bank, the Rockefeller Foundation, Ford Foundation, the Colombo Plan, Commonwealth scholarships, and others) has been a crucial addition to local resources. Where no foreign aid was received (for example, the Center for Research and Communication in the Philippines), local sources of finance outside the institution itself were and are essential.

The effectiveness of assistance depends on the nature of the assistance agency or cooperating institution no less than on the absorption capacity of the receiver. And just as the program depends on both parties, the aid confers mutual benefits.

Nevertheless, the relationships among donors, cooperating institutions in the donor countries, and recipients do not remain static but evolve from one stage to another. The capacities to assist, on the one hand, and to receive, on the other, change as expertise gets transferred over the years. The aid requirements of Southeast Asian countries in the 1970s are different from what they were in the 1950s and 1960s. Southeast Asian institutions of higher learning have now progressed not only in the level of technological development and sophistication but also in their intellectual independence, their confidence, their ability, and their desire to make decisions for themselves. In the face of such development, much of it brought on by successes in past aid efforts, aid givers cannot maintain the same attitudes and programs, but must search for new ones or, better still, press the recipient countries to frame their own plans and requests for aid to which the donors can respond.

Nevertheless, in the accounting for the amounts of external assistance given, we believe the figures should be placed in perspective.

In reality, much of the aid goes to cooperating institutions in the aid-giving country rather than to the recipient. Furthermore, it is important to avoid intellectual imperialism and academic pork barrelling for the foreigners as well as for the local recipients. Without attention to these and other aspects of the donor-recipient collaboration, the relationship may easily deteriorate.

One conclusion stands out in these various cases of aid: The highest payoff in the aid programs has been in training people. The example of the "Berkeley Mafia" in Indonesia, that is, the economists trained in the United States in a crash program in the 1960s, is a vivid case in point.

Role of Government and Its Attitudes Toward Educational Innovation

It is obvious that the government should follow through on worth-while innovation and that there should also be continuity in government support. We believe, however, that the government should not monopolize the development effort but should encourage conscientious effort by private initiative. The entire nation should be mobilized for national development. No government has a monopoly of wisdom, inventiveness, and effectiveness in higher education, and governments should not deny the society the benefits of private sector initiative. We are impressed by the results forthcoming—the imagination, vigor, and dedication—when government supervision and regulations are flexible, as in the Philippines.

It might be appropriate at this juncture to suggest that donor agencies support governments that attempt to democratize as well as to raise the quality of higher education. Higher education in Southeast Asia is an expensive proposition; in all Southeast Asian countries except the Philippines per capita government expenditure on higher education is higher (sometimes several multiples higher) than per capita gross national product (see Tables 5 and 7). In view of the increasing need for trained high-level manpower for development and of the humanistic goals of higher education, it might be fruitful to assist governments that try to distribute the expenditure on education among a larger number of beneficiaries to help a larger number of the young people. A complementary measure would be some redistribution of the financial burden: both affluent parents and other private sources could share educational costs.

Sources of Innovation or Reform

According to the classic theory of innovation, the process of innovation or reform consists of four steps: the perception of the problem, setting the stage, the act of insight, and critical revision.[1] In the postwar period, developing countries have become aware of problems of poverty and unemployment and the various manifestations of economic, social, and political underdevelopment. This awareness has been the result of external, no less than internal, stimuli. Unfortunately, the time lapse between perception of the problem and innovation can be considerable.

Change or reform comes from individuals. Foreigners, such as members of foreign aid agencies, can introduce innovation, based on their or others' experience abroad. Among the nationals of the country, innovation comes often, although not by any means exclusively, from persons who have had international exposure through such experiences as fellowships for advanced study, international seminars, field trips, or work experience. Assistance to individuals is thus important, and the danger of brain drain can be dealt with by focusing on well-motivated individuals.

Role and Contribution of Faculties

It is not a faculty as a whole that acts to bring about desired change, but individual faculty members and administrators or small groups of faculty and administrators. It is a lamentable fact that generally faculties have not been a source of innovation. Role perception has an important bearing on this situation. Do the faculty members view themselves as scholars writing for the international world or do they want to address themselves to local problems? Again, in some societies, if a rare individual innovates, he runs the risk of ruining his career. Thus, much depends on how the individual perceives his role; the results are different, depending on role perception.

Role of Student Bodies

In our observation students have had little direct effect on innovation or development orientation in higher education, as is perhaps to be expected from so young a cohort in the population. However, they have been instrumental in forcing good teaching by the faculty. Their

TABLE 6

Public Expenditure on Education—Around 1954, 1960, and 1967
(at current market prices)

Country	Year	Currency	Percentage of GNP	Percentage of Total Public Expenditure	Recurring Expenditure (thousands)	Teacher's Salaries as Percentage of Recurring Expenditure	Capital Expenditure (thousands)
Burma	1954[a]	Kyat	1.8	n.a.	n.a.	n.a.	n.a.
	1960		1.6	n.a.	110,564	89.2	1,208
	1967		3.0[d]	16.8	242,109	86.2	15,408
Cambodia	1954	Riel	1.7[d]	n.a.	n.a.	n.a.	n.a.
	1960		n.a.	n.a.	682,365	91.3	81,000
	1966		4.2	22.0	1,264,377	97.3	79,587
Indonesia[1]	1952	Rupiah	1.1[e]	n.a.	600,500	n.a.	312,000
	1960		0.7[f]	n.a.	n.a.	n.a.	n.a.
Laos	1954	Kip	n.a.	n.a.	81,800	81.0	17,000
	1960		n.a.	n.a.	186,000	n.a.	56,000
	1967[b]		n.a.	10.2	1,635,145	76.5	—
	1968[b]		n.a.	9.6	1,529,370	74.3	—
Malaysia Sabah	1954	Malaysian dollar	n.a.	n.a.	n.a.	n.a.	n.a.
	1960		n.a.	n.a.	6,346	88.9	3,253
	1967[g]		n.a.	n.a.	12,309	n.a.	3,886
Sarawak	1955	Malaysian dollar	n.a.	n.a.	5,311	n.a.	806
	1961		n.a.	n.a.	12,266	82.3	3,432
	1967[b]		n.a.	n.a.	24,324	n.a.	5,830
	1968[b]		n.a.	n.a.	25,030	n.a.	3,869

Country	Year	Currency					
West Malaysia	1954	Malaysian dollar	n.a.	n.a.	80,305	n.a.	11,929
	1961		3.4a	n.a.	205,270	74.0	27,310
	1967		5.0	14.6	429,857	76.1	55,342
Philippinesa,c	1954	Peso	n.a.	n.a.	182,156	n.a.	n.a.
	1960		2.6	n.a.	298,077	90.2	18,057
	1967		2.8	n.a.	693,730	87.5	10,229
Singapore	1955	Singapore dollar	n.a.	n.a.	n.a.	n.a.	n.a.
	1959		n.a.	n.a.	59,978	84.5	1,571
	1968		3.6	16.8	146,797	80.4	8,933
Thailand	1954	Baht	2.9	n.a.	816,000	n.a.	11,000
	1959		2.5	n.a.	1,129,875	79.4	104,124
	1968		2.9d	n.a.	2,443,892	80.4	935,461
Vietnam, Republic of	1954	Piastre	n.a.	n.a.	326,001	n.a.	—
	1960a		1.0	n.a.	796,000	n.a.	90,000
	1967a		1.1	5.4	3,721,817	87.3	328,183

Note: n.a.: data not available; — = magnitude nil or negligible.
aMinistry of Education only.
bCentral (or federal) government only.
cNot including expenditure on the third level of education.
dAs percentage of gross domestic product at market prices.
eAs percentage of gross domestic product at factor cost.
fAs percentage of net domestic product at factor cost.
gExpenditure on public education only.

Source: Unesco Regional Office for Education in Asia, Progress of Education in the Asian Region, Statistical Supplement, Bangkok, 1972.

indirect effect has been considerable, too; the students' social consciousness and their drive for progress have forced conservative faculty members to change or to innovate.

Today student groups are demanding greater participation in national policymaking in several Southeast Asian countries. The situation seems hopeful, but up to this point the constructive effects of such changes remain to be seen.

TABLE 7

Unit Recurrent Costs of Education by Level in
Southeast Asian Countries, 1965
(in U.S. dollars)

Country	Per Capita GNP	Unit Recurrent Cost in Level		
		I	II	III
Burma	60	9	20	136
Indonesia	91	11	22	380
Cambodia	118	26	111	212
Malaysia (west)	269	43	82	1,146
Philippines	151	27	71	99
Singapore	544	60	73	874
Thailand	826	116	127	1,030

Source: F. H. Harbison, J. Maruhnic, and J. R. Resnick, Quantitative Analysis of Modernization and Development (Princeton, N.J.: Princeton University Press, 1970).

Outside Financing

We believe there will always be a need for some form of external financing for the very important reason that it is often the most appropriate vehicle for innovation. The case studies are evidence of the catalytic and crucial role of outside financial assistance.

The Link Between Education and Development

It is educated people oriented to development who innovate for development. Not only scholars but also administrators are needed; a local bureaucrat can interfere with and frustrate development efforts even if there are enough development-oriented scholars.

It takes at least 10 or 15 years to build a critical mass of such development-oriented scholars and administrators. If aid is to be effective, aid agencies should support the buildup of that critical group and help keep it intact against such attractions as higher pay and better positions.

Strengthening Effective Programs

Flexibility should be built into an innovative educational program; sometimes a program may be so rigid that it is not replicable. There is also a need for continuous reevaluation and modification of programs. Effective programs require varied and expert personnel resources as well. To meet such needs continuing finance is essential.

Orientation of Education for Development: Rural or Urban?

Education for development cannot choose between rural or urban orientation. We think this is a false dichotomy. The goals of higher education should be modernization and development, with special attention given to the structure, needs, and manpower of the country concerned. We do agree, however, that under present circumstances, developing countries should give more attention to modernization of rural areas or those regions outside the main cities.

Balancing International and National Responsibilities

Development should be the concern of both international and local scholars; there should be no dichotomy between the quality of scholarship and its focus on local and national needs. We believe there is a need for more competent and committed development-oriented scholars from the developing countries who will have an impact on their counterparts from the developed countries. We foresee such an impact because, while scholars in the developed countries are talking about general problems of development, scholars in the developing countries are actively involved in concrete development programs and will be able to draw on their experiences. We believe the donor agencies could help promote a dialogue between these communities of scholars from the developed and developing worlds. Bilateral, regional, and international cooperation is part of the development thrust in Southeast Asia today.

THE ROLE OF DONORS

The development of higher education in Southeast Asia is now, after independence, a responsibility of the governments and the officials of the nations themselves. If national officials are jealous of this responsibility, then it is important that they do their homework in regard to their countries' education; that they think through the problems, make the plans, raise as much local funding as possible, and identify the areas where foreign aid is needed. Donor agencies should respect the prerogative of national officials to determine their own requirements. With this approach, the donor institutions would not only be more effective in public relations terms but, in addition, would be in a better position to decide how to assist.

Donors tend to think of all developing countries as homogeneous and consequently that institutions and programs can be transferred automatically from one country to another. Countries differ, however, even within Southeast Asia; there are different mixes of history, cultures, and institutions. Before they go to a particular country, therefore, foreign experts should try to understand the local mores and culture, which are often more sophisticated than they appear.

Furthermore, it would be helpful for donors to remember that a nation goes through different economic, social, and educational stages of development. Aid, therefore, must be designed in terms of the present and future development of the country's educational system. Too often foreign experts think in terms of the 1950s or 1960s rather than of the 1970s or 1980s.

The types of technical assistance and expert advice needed by Southeast Asian countries in the 1970s are different from those in the earlier day. In the 1950s, the higher education systems of many Asian countries were rudimentary, whereas in the 1970s the education systems not only are much larger but are also more complex and the numbers of qualified people locally available are greater. In the typical Asian university, for example, there are fewer expatriate Ph.D.s and more native Ph.D.s. In these circumstances, local institutions need higher caliber and generally more mature foreign experts and visiting professors who can guide and inspire local staff.

Finally, both local educators and officials and aid givers should be reminded that higher education, while it contributes materially to national development, cannot by itself achieve all the good things to which a nation aspires.

Successes in integrating higher education and development, often made possible by external assistance, are leading to "second-generation" problems, that is, the efforts are being copied elsewhere, and even in the original sites, the educational programs have moved

up to successive and sometimes more complicated stages. These
problems, although they denote progress, call for fresh efforts. The
donor agencies will still have a part to play in their solution.

At the very least, the aid institutions can help promote awareness
of successful efforts to link higher education and development. Workshops and seminars are useful for disseminating such knowledge; individuals learn from others' experience and meetings may trigger
insights that lead to solution of problems.

We have pointed out the importance of outside donors in acting as
catalysts in development efforts and the value derived from foreign
training of individuals. But we also have a warning: While donors
should have freedom to choose where they will put their money, they
have a responsibility, too. Through their fellowships and aid they can
influence and improve or unbalance and distort the development of
institutions.

THE CASE STUDIES

The case studies presented here have been chosen not only to in-
struct but also to reflect the diversity in educational tradition in attitudes toward the private sector and in approaches to mass education
versus selectivity in Southeast Asia. To some extent, the cases reflect
the forces of their societies at this moment in history. The case studies are not exhaustive; throughout Southeast Asia, many imaginative
programs are being carried out to link higher education with national
development efforts. Nor are the cases always unique to the countries
in which they are set. Thailand, for example, has rural development
projects carried out by students and Singapore is improving technical
education. Our choice of these cases does not mean that these countries are the only ones in which such efforts are to be found. Rather,
the programs were chosen in their specific locales because they illustrate the kind of program common to the region as a whole while re-
taining valuable local flavor.

It should be noted also that not all Southeast Asian countries are
represented in the case studies. Finally, any conclusions to be derived
from the studies may or may not apply to all countries or to the entire
region.

The first case study, the University of Malaya, deals with the
normative role that an institution of higher education plays; that is, it
examines how a university helps society define values and purposes
and promotes these. This University is the oldest, the largest, and
still the most prestigious in Malaysia. In this country a multiracial
society is making its way toward national unity, and the University

reflects the society. The case describes a university that cannot move faster than the society because the society cannot yet settle basic issues. The University of Malaya is responding to the demands of the society rather than leading it by opening up more educational opportunities for Malays.

The studies of Gadjah Mada University and the Maeklong Project are of operational programs, that is, programs that apply knowledge to the solution of development problems. Gadjah Mada University in Jogjakarta in central Java was the first university established by the Indonesian Republic. It is, therefore, considered one of the leaders in university development; it is, moreover, setting a pattern of cooperation with the government authorities in the region. Since it is not in the capital (Jakarta), Gadjah Mada is less subject than the University of Indonesia to the raiding of faculty and the pressures to serve immediate needs and can thus develop in its own way. But the study shows how the process of building up a true university takes time, perhaps even generations, in a setting that is not ripe for it; if the seed is to grow, the ground must be prepared and the seed nurtured carefully.

Furthermore, Gadjah Mada illustrates a clash of cultures and educational approaches: the Indonesian oral tradition, the Continental European university model, and the United States land-grant college approach. Yet this university shows how even a young institution can engage in research and public service activities that make its other functions meaningful. It also vindicates foreign aid to universities, as it is precisely those faculties that have benefited from external assistance that are providing models for other faculties to emulate.

The Maeklong Integrated Rural Development Project in Thailand brings together three of the leading Thai universities in an integrated effort in rural development. These three institutions have received assistance to strengthen their various competencies: Kasetsart University in agricultural sciences, Mahidol in medicine, and Thammasat in social sciences. Each has carried on extension and public service activities of its own, but now they have joined for rural development in the Maeklong region northwest of Bangkok. It is a pioneer effort both because of the interuniversity cooperation and because of the multidisciplinary approach; a project team consisting of trained university graduates from differing disciplines lives in a chosen rural area. Furthermore, it is a departure from established modes of doing things, at least for Mahidol University, which is generally oriented toward United States health care delivery systems. The effort is still experimental and unproven, but it has already succeeded in getting three strong institutions to collaborate, strengthening each other in the the process.

The training role of institutions of higher education, that is, preparing effective contributors to national development, is brought out
in the case studies done in Singapore and the Philippines, two countries
different in educational approach, but both doing commendable jobs.
Ngee Ann Technical College is examined in relation to the middle-level
manpower training schemes of Singapore. Singapore has a tough-
minded and rational government that has examined the country's manpower needs and has decided to emphasize technical-level education
more than university education. Ngee Ann Technical College accepted
a downgrading of its status from a degree-granting level to a certificate
level, and yet, in so doing, has actually lifted itself up by raising the
quality of its technical education.

Finally, there is the Philippines, which among the countries of
Southeast Asia has the most trained manpower. But the Philippines is
not content with present efforts and is expanding its offerings in graduate education to include the retraining of experienced executives. It is
also unique in the way both the public and private sectors have responded to the country's educational needs. Three institutions engaged
in manpower training for economic development are described: the
Development Academy of the Philippines, the Asian Institute of Management, and the Center for Research and Communication. These are
second-generation institutions in the sense that they build on a relatively advanced educational network and draw on a large manpower
pool. All require from their students work experience either before
enrollment or during the course of study. They offer different study
programs and all engage in research and public service activities.

It is fair to say that all the institutions studied are veering toward
the United States land-grant model of a university. The leaders of the
institutions have seen and have copied Western institutional models,
and yet these innovative individuals remain true to their own cultures
and nations.

THE ASIAN REGIONAL TEAM

The Asian regional team is an independent group chosen by the
regional director for Asia, Dr. Puey Ungphakorn. Members served
in their individual capacities. The work, however, was undertaken in
cooperation with at least two semiofficial Southeast Asian organizations
involved in higher education for development, the Regional Institute for
Higher Education Development (RIHED), which is based in Singapore,
and the Association of Southeast Asian Institutions of Higher Learning
(ASAIHL), with its secretariat in Bangkok. In the case of RIHED, the

cooperation was formally noted by the chairman and board of the Institute. The secretariat of ASAIHL established a working relationship with the team and made its research and publications available.

NOTE

1. Abbot Payton Usher, A History of Mechanical Inventions (Cambridge, Mass.: Harvard University Press, 1954), pp. 523, 526. Schumpeter held similar views. See Joseph A. Schumpeter, The Theory of Economic Development (Cambridge, Mass.: Harvard University Press, 1934).

12

THE CONCEPT OF DEVELOPMENT

In the past, development was generally understood as a measurable and material stage of growth reached by some societies while others were struggling to climb to a similar point on the ladder. The maximum development goals of OECD (Organization for Economic Cooperation and Development) countries in the 1960s were tied to an increase in their gross national products. Many reached the goal and some surpassed it, but disappointment set in about what they had accomplished, and they began to doubt whether they were indeed becoming more "developed." In turn, the developing countries came to doubt that advancement was to be measured by how much they resembled the developed countries and learned that one-dimensional growth was a mixed blessing.

At the beginning of the 1970s, the ministers of development of the OECD countries themselves announced that growth is not an end in itself but mainly a means to create better living conditions and called attention to development's qualitative aspects. Throughout the world, social well-being began to compete with economic growth as the most important goal of society. Development meant using economic, social, technological, and political means to improve the quality of life rather than merely enlarging the gross national product. Development, it was suggested, is more than growth; indeed, growth sometimes aggravates the problems of development. Progress is not simply getting more of what a society has accumulated. It also has its social and human content.

Leaders in Latin America, as well as in the rest of the developing world, have shared this new way of thinking about development.

Part of the International Strategy for Development, approved by the
United Nations General Assembly on October 24, 1970, was assumed
by the Latin American regional organization CEPAL as a guideline for
evaluating development in Latin American countries. It states:

> Since the goal of development is to provide for everyone
> the opportunity for better living conditions, it is essential
> to achieve a more equitable distribution of income and
> wealth in order to promote social justice and efficiency
> in production, raise employment levels substantially,
> secure a higher level of income and broaden and improve
> means of education, sanitation, nutrition, housing, and
> social service and safeguard environment. Hence, the
> qualitative and structural social changes should occur
> simultaneously with the rapid economic growth and exist-
> ing differences—regional, sectorial and social—should be
> reduced substantially. These goals are at the same time
> determinant factors and final results of development.
> Therefore, they should be considered as integral parts
> of the same dynamic process and require a united approach.

The new concept of development, however, varies in its application
from country to country, depending on stages of poverty or growth and
on social and national values. Just as developing countries should not
try to duplicate the history of industrialized countries, so individual
countries and regions should not seek to imitate too closely other
country models. In both cases, however, nations can learn from
others' mistakes and successes.

In this study, our concept of development, while not ignoring material development, is essentially related to the quality of life. We do
not pretend to define development for each country, but seek only to
describe the framework as we see it and have applied it to examples
of higher education for development within the region.

In Latin America, social well-being as the aim of development
includes the ideas of change, equality, and independence, as well as
individual development and dignity. While each country must set its
own objectives and plan its own strategies for reaching them, each
country and region can help others to achieve common goals. In an
interdependent and interrelated world, a problem in one country affects others, and all countries have a role to play in its solution.

HIGHER EDUCATION AND DEVELOPMENT

The university is crucial to development. In its teaching role it provides formal training for men and women. It prepares the country's leaders and skilled individuals who will influence national development. The university is part of the community's conscience and serves as an instrument for social improvement. As a cultural institution, the university must be balanced between reflection and action, between the spiritual and the material, the humanistic and the scientific-technical. It must help define the nation's identity and educate individuals who understand their own culture as well as that of other peoples. As a part of a wider system of education, it must be related to other educational levels.

Higher education today must give the student some awareness not only of his rights but also of his responsibilities and obligations to the well-being of the society in which he lives. Above all, it must help him see that community welfare depends on the welfare of individuals; the community is not an abstraction and the individual is not merely a "resource" for development but rather the reason for development.

If Latin American countries are to achieve better living conditions they must build five major capacities, and higher education within these countries must be judged by how well it develops them: (1) the capacity to comprehend, define, and give priorities to society's needs and aspirations; (2) the capacity to comprehend and define the problems that arise in the process of meeting these social needs and aspirations; (3) the capacity to formulate various alternatives for solving problems; (4) the capacity to apply appropriate technology to alternative solutions; (5) the capacity to select and apply the various mechanisms, strategies, and policies to solve these problems.

This study has sought cases in which postsecondary institutions are contributing to the development process both by forming future leaders and by solving urgent community problems. We have been looking not merely for university development or community service but rather for a new type of education in which teaching, research, and service are interrelated and in which educational goals are linked to social needs.

To understand the programs, accomplishments, and goals of the institutions we have described in the case studies, it is well to remember the historical, social, and political conditions they confront.

On the positive side, the circumstances of higher education in Latin America would seem favorable, at least as compared with many other areas of the world. If longevity could be equated with development, Latin American higher education would be highly advanced. As the region of the Western Hemisphere first colonized by Europeans,

Latin America contains the oldest universities in the Americas, several dating from the early sixteenth century. The national capitals all boast major centers of learning, and almost all secondary cities have their own local institutions. State and private colleges are widely dispersed throughout the larger nations—Mexico, Colombia, Peru, Brazil, Argentina, and Chile—and most of the other countries. Altogether, there are now an estimated 1,000 universities or affiliates in Latin America,[1] a higher ratio of institutions of higher education to population than Africa and Asia have.

In addition, a greater proportion of youth of university age, 6.7 percent in 1970, attend academic courses in Latin America than in Asia and Africa, and the proportion more than doubled during the 1960s. Some modern and impressive university complexes, such as the national institutions in Mexico City, Rio de Janeiro, and Buenos Aires, throng with tens of thousands of students. As the numbers of students have increased, new academic institutions have appeared, especially in the private sector where vocational and technical subjects are emphasized. The number of such institutions more than doubled between 1960 and 1970, from 11 percent of the total to 23 percent.

Although Latin America has been hospitable to foreign scholars who occupy teaching positions in its institutions, the institutions do not depend on them; the region does not lack its own supply of professors, at least in the more traditional subjects. Taken as a whole, therefore, it can be said that Latin America's higher education has developed considerably in the sense of growth of physical plant, staff, and student body, placing it next to the so-called developed world in its quantitative aspects.

It must be confessed, however, that much of higher education in Latin America is inadequate. Many of our Latin American institutions are groping in a haze of speculation and ideological and theoretical discussions that evade reality and the search for specific data necessary to cope with immediate problems.

Latin American students have been activists for decades while their counterparts in other continents passed serenely through their schooling. This student activism, with its notable political ingredient, is a distinctive social phenomenon of Latin America that must be recognized in any consideration of higher education. The constant pressure from students to modernize and broaden the role of the university also bears directly on the importance of the turn toward higher education for development; the students' idealistic goals and realistic concerns need to be tended and their energies need to be utilized constructively.

Educators seeking the pedagogic and institutional changes necessary to bring Latin American higher education into the development process confront a number of barriers: a feudal heritage, the traditional conservatism of our institutions, the entrenchment of vested interests, the mixed effects of previous reforms, and the politics of student activism. Perhaps most difficult to conform to traditional ideas are the concepts underlying higher education for development, that society is a whole rather than a collection of parts, that the university has a responsibility to the whole rather than to a select segment, and that higher education should become an outgoing active participant in programs serving society as a whole.

In addressing themselves to higher education for development, therefore, the institutions which we have chosen and surveyed in this study deserve recognition for their initiative, not easily undertaken, and for their direction, not easily pursued. These five institutions suggest several routes that may be taken by higher education for development. Many other institutions in Latin America are looking and moving in the same direction.

LATIN AMERICAN DEVELOPMENT PRIORITIES

In selecting the case studies, the Latin American team used a list of development priorities based on a series of studies carried out by the United Nations Economic Commission for Latin America, CEPAL. The team looked for ways in which postsecondary institutions were confronting any of these priorities. Such a list might also be used as a guide for universities that seek to apply the skills and knowledge of higher education to social needs. The urgent problems of Latin America include population, urbanization, environment, employment, income distribution, extension of social services, and housing.

Population

The rate of population growth in Latin American nations ranges from 1.5 to 3.4 percent, with an overall average annual rate of 2.8 percent, relatively high in comparison with other regions of the world (only South Asia has a growth rate this high). (According to a 1972 United Nations report, annual population growth rates for 1965-1970 were 1.8 percent in East Asia, 2.8 percent in South Asia, 0.8 percent in Europe, 2.6 percent in Africa, and 1.2 percent in North America.) Programs and policies must be formulated to cope with population growth and demographic shifts, with changes in the labor market, with overcrowded cities, and with the soaring demand for higher education. With over 50 percent of Latin Americans under 25 years of age, enrollment in institutions of higher education increased at an average rate of almost 10 percent from 1960 to 1970; where there were 2.6 university students per 1,000 population in 1955, 13 per 1,000 are projected for 1980, a fivefold increase in a quarter of a century.

Urbanization

Latin American cities, like the universities, have been transformed by the explosion in population and the impact of development. They have become the magnets of commerce and enterprise, attracting job seekers principally from smaller towns and rural areas, and the major centers have almost doubled every decade. During the 1970s, city dwellers will increase by 65 percent, an addition of 75 million inhabitants. Higher education will both feel the effect of urbanization and have the opportunity to affect policy regarding it. There are short supplies of city planners, statisticians, surveyors, draftsmen, social workers, accountants, civil engineers, capable clerical workers, nurses, paramedical technicians, and public administrators. Urban problems require not only manpower, however, but also strategies for combining skills and knowledge from various disciplines into effective community action.

Human Environment

If higher education is to affect the quality of life as well as the economic growth in its society, it must meet the challenges of poverty, poor health, and blighted living conditions. In densely populated areas people suffer from overcrowding, squalor, air pollution, traffic congestion, and inadequate housing. They lack parks, recreation facilities, good sanitation, and job skills. In the countryside, land deteriorates and farmers use a limited and polluted water supply. Higher education is, in a number of instances, supplying technology and interdisciplinary efforts to solve environmental problems and is fostering the social and scientific research on which such efforts must rest.

Employment

Unemployment in Latin America is increasing as the result of a number of interrelated forces. Population growth rates and migration

from the countryside to the city have swelled the number of unskilled
urban workers. At the same time modern capital-intensive technology
has been imported from the industrial countries and is absorbing less
rather than more unskilled manpower; there is a shortage of semiskilled and skilled workers. Postsecondary institutions in a number
of cases should address themselves both to the shortage of trained
people and to the economic dislocations. By adjusting curriculum,
counseling students, and assisting community job-training programs,
such institutions can also better orient higher education to social need.

Income Distribution

According to the U.N. Economic Commission for Latin America,[2]
the lowest 20 percent of all income-receiving units in Latin America
in the early 1960s shared approximately 3 percent of the total income,
while the highest 5 percent income group accounted for about 33 percent of the total income, creating a sharp contrast between the per
capita income of each group: $60 for the first and $2,600 for the
second. (In the United States these same income groups received 4.6
and 20 percent ot total income.) Educational opportunities are closely
related to income.

Extension of Social Services

In all Latin American countries, social services financed with
public funds have been increasing. While countries, states, and regions differ, this expansion has generally created new demands that
are difficult to meet. How should funds be allocated? What should be
the priorities of such services as education, health, recreation, and
social security?

Education requires a delicate balance of the three levels: primary,
secondary, and higher. In all but one of the Latin American countries,
higher education has expanded more rapidly than primary education
and continues to have the highest increase. To justify its support,
higher education must help meet the needs of the other levels and of
the systems as a whole. In one case study, the University of Antioquia
in Colombia sought to increase attendance at rural schools through
flexible schedules and teaching techniques.

Health and nutrition conditions in Latin America greatly improved
in the 1960s, the general mortality rate dropping from 10.4 per 1,000
in 1960 to 8.8 in 1970. Infant mortality has been significantly reduced.

Such endemic diseases as yellow fever, smallpox, plague, and typhus are declining or have disappeared. These gains are largely due to the extension of potable water and sewage services and to measures of preventive medicine. There have been notable increases in the numbers of health centers, hospitals, and medical personnel. In terms of social expenditures, health follows only education in public disbursements.

The health of the region, however, varies widely between rural and urban areas; an estimated 37 percent of those living in rural areas and small communities still do not have access to basic health services. Although it has been brought under some control, communicable disease is still a serious health problem in Latin America, and a large portion of the population still does not have sufficient food or water. In many countries the protein-calorie intake of the majority of its population is below international standards.

Traditionally, higher education in Latin America has given major attention to philosophy and letters (liberal arts) and the field of medicine has been an important modernizing element. A number of universities, illustrated by the case studies of Colombia and Brazil, have brought their capacities more directly to bear on the specific problems of their region through research training and the design of health delivery systems for less privileged areas. Some, like the National Agrarian University in Peru, have also attacked the problem of food supply by providing technical help to owners of small and medium-sized farms.

The proportion of population covered by social security systems in Latin America continues to increase, although there is a great difference among countries. Again, the systems tend to overlook rural and lower class workers, although gains have been made in extending the coverage to a larger proportion of the rural population, including sugar workers in Brazil, banana workers in Panama, and seasonal farm workers and small landholders in Mexico.

Housing

Population growth and urbanization have counteracted most government efforts to improve housing. In both rural and urban areas, people with low incomes pay high rents for inadequate dwellings. Although both national and local governments have channeled large proportions of their resources into housing in the 1960s, massive housing needs persist.

THE LATIN AMERICAN PROGRAMS

A different problem was tackled in each one of the cases studied (see Appendix C). The selection of cases was made according to previously established requirements. Furthermore, samples of different types of institutions were obtained: in Peru, a national, specialized university; in Brazil, a national (federal) provincial university; in Colombia, two provincial (public or state) universities; and, in Mexico, an institute or private university. The institutions also differ in age: the Universities of Antioquia and Bahia (counting from the date their faculties were established) are the oldest; next are the National Agrarian University of Peru, the Monterrey Institute of Technology, and the University of Valle (Colombia), which is the youngest.

Programs started as a result of different factors: strong government influence in the case of Peru; almost completely private action in Monterrey (Mexico), and joint government-university efforts in Antioquia, Valle, and Bahia. The largest number of students participated in Peru; in the remaining cases, most of the activities were carried out by professors.

During the selection and subsequently during the study of the cases, it was evident that in order to develop an effective social program the institution had to have a critical mass of staff members and administrators in at least one of its areas to initiate community research and service activities. Such a nucleus within the institution can radiate the spirit of community service throughout the entire institution and eventually influence other institutions of higher education within and outside the country.

Development of Programs

Most of the projects were based on a well-defined program focused on a specific problem. As community projects progressed, participants became more aware of the complexity and interrelatedness of problems and the need to bring in other disciplines. The project described in the University of Valle case study, for example, started as a way to give medical students experience with the health problems of a low-income urban family and community in Cali (Siloé). Later, it was expanded with the assistance of other disciplines to a rural area (Candelaria) and eventually become a system for delivery of health services to a densely populated area of a provincial capital city. The experience gained was utilized for the establishment of multidisciplinary programs at other universities in Colombia. It has influenced national health programs and served as a model for a similar program implemented at the Federal University of Bahia in Brazil, a more comprehensive institution than that at Valle.

The research and extension program in industrial development at the Monterrey Institute of Technology and Advanced Studies achieved similar results. It has served government regional agencies and private corporations, and was expanded to such related areas as education, agriculture, sanitation, and industry.

We believe that the university should be primarily an agent of development, but its role cannot simply be that of rendering service for the sake of service itself. Its roles in community development projects are to produce or test a "model," which must be used to improve the training of its students, and to support research that can be reproduced to benefit other communities. It should not supplant public or private social agencies. Its fundamental objective is forming the country's leaders.

Innovation and the Individual

A program is generally started by one individual who promotes it and dedicates all his time and abilities to it. The program's success depends fundamentally on the competence, motivation, and dedication of this person. It is he who creates an atmosphere of enthusiasm and builds a group of able people from whom his successors can emerge. All the cases studied have been initiated by a devoted leader. Those with leadership qualities should, therefore, be identified and provided with good training, since future programs for university development will depend on them to a large extent.

All the cases described are innovative in the sense that they seek effective, economical, and practical programs to meet the priority needs of Latin America. Institutions should stimulate this search for new horizons, for ways to turn ideas into reality, for new techniques and administrative systems, and for better utilization of funds. The programs and their directors will set the example for others in the institution.

Role of the Professors

The professors' participation in community development programs is closely related to their effectiveness as teachers and researchers. Well-designed service activities give relevance to their teaching and

promote research, which in turn nurtures teaching. Most of the staff
who initiate and carry out these programs are full-time professors.
As they become absorbed in service activities, however, they may
limit their teaching role for lack of time or because they are involved
in administrative duties. Several rectors and deans have warned of
this danger. To avoid it, administration of the program must be
planned carefully, spreading responsibility among several persons.

Role of the Students

If the program is to serve as a means of training, students must
participate. Sometimes students are shocked or anguished by the realities they meet; they identify so completely with the needs of those
whom they are serving (as happened in the University of Valle's family
program) that they may lose objectivity and hamper improvement efforts. Sometimes their activities have a political overtone, as in the
Peruvian case, when opposition arose from the fact that the program
was government-sponsored. It is important, nevertheless, for students to become acquainted with community needs and to feel that they
can help solve these problems.

As community activities become more complex and multidisciplinary, however, undergraduate students participate less. The project's
only contribution to teaching then becomes its influence on the curriculum or on the expertise of the professors. At the University of Valle,
undergraduate student participation decreased, and, in other cases,
participation is limited almost exclusively to graduate students; in the
Monterrey case, student participation is almost nonexistent. The
Peruvian project is an exception; student participation is numerous
and very satisfactory.

Role of the Community

Service programs should have community participation not only
to establish community needs but also to achieve a community's collaboration in the solution of its problems. Such participation varies
a great deal, but most of the programs studied succeeded in achieving
it. In the National Agrarian University project, professors and students live in the community, and the community thus shares actively
in the program. Community participation was important in the early
phase of the University of Valle project and remains so in the teaching
or extension aspects of the current program. The One-Teacher School

and the Individualized Instruction and Flexible Schooling programs carried out at the University of Antioquia relied heavily on community support and interest, especially in the Flexible Schooling project where parents agree to see that their children study at home on the days they are not in school. In the program in Brazil, community members help diagnose problems, but so far they have not participated in deciding on solutions. In the case of the program of the Monterrey Institute of Technology, industrial clients have varying relationships, but aside from training programs, workers and community residents take little part in the programs.

Administration

The institutions of higher education generally have handled the programs' administration. The administration of universities, particularly public institutions, however, is unwieldy, and programs sponsored by government agencies face special inconveniences, such as rigid procedures, excessive controls, delay in paying expenses, and difficulties in hiring personnel above certain levels. These problems force some of the institutions to look for other ways to conduct community programs more efficiently and more flexibly. Private foundations are managing most of the funds for the programs at Valle and in Peru. The Antioquia programs are financed through an official decentralized institute with special authorization from a committee of the rector's office. CEDUR, at Bahia is financed by PROPED, an almost autonomous organization supported by the rector of the University. Monterrey is a private institution and undoubtedly has the most efficient administration of all the projects.

One of the most serious problems faced in the administration of programs is that directors also have to serve as promoters, financers, paymasters, professors, and public relations officers. A director who must carry out this number of tasks has little time or energy for teaching, which is therefore often discontinued. More efficient forms of administration must be found.

Evaluation

All the programs studied have tried to evaluate their activities, but, because the problems are complex and the programs lack resources to carry out their plans, the evaluations have not been thorough. On the other hand, there are few good indicators with which to evaluate social programs that seek well-being rather than economic growth. This situation, in conjunction with the lack of cost data, makes it difficult to establish a cost-benefit ratio. Better cost studies are needed for the future.

Relations with Government

All the programs have been carried out in cooperation with government—directly sponsored and financed by government, as in the Peru case, through a decentralized institute, as in the Antioquia case, closely linked in planning and execution, as in the Valle and Bahia cases, or undertaking specific studies for government, as in the Monterrey case. In some way connected, government can more easily continue the pilot project on a larger scale. There is a danger, however, that the institution may become merely an arm of the government or turn into a simple service agency. The university is well equipped to serve as consultant, researcher, or evaluator. It can design and test samples, but it is not in a position to, nor should it, provide direct, massive routine service. Nevertheless, to ensure wide coverage, the program should have close relationships with the government, taking, at the same time, certain essential precautions.

Relations with Private Enterprise

Except for Monterrey, none of the institutions studied has had significant relations with private enterprise. In most places, local private foundations have helped with the management of funds and have provided financial assistance. Good relations with private business or industry, however, are particularly important in countries where private enterprise influences employment.

The case studies at the National Agrarian University of Peru and the Monterrey Institute of Technology show that effective programs for development can be either entirely governmental or entirely private. In either situation, university autonomy may be affected, by government interference or by an exclusive private influence.

Other Educational Levels

Several case studies are related directly or indirectly to other educational levels. Development programs must disseminate informa-

tion, involving nonformal or adult education in the cases of health
service delivery systems (University of Valle), urban development
(Federal University of Bahia), and technical agricultural assistance
(National Agrarian University at La Molina). In the One-Teacher
School program and in the Individualized Instruction and Flexible
Schooling program (University of Antioquia), the projects not only seek
to solve a fundamental problem (primary education in rural areas) but
also offer programmed activities for parents to help them cooperate
with the school. In Monterrey, courses are organized for factory personnel as well as for graduate students. In these cases, the university
has the opportunity to introduce innovations within the formal system,
as well as to participate in nonformal education.

Foreign Aid

All programs, except that of the National Agrarian University at
La Molina, have received directly or indirectly substantial financial
assistance from international agencies. All the institutions studied,
including La Molina, likewise have received and continue to receive
foreign collaboration from different sources. Difficulties in securing
funds in Latin America make foreign aid vital for the initiation of most
programs. Outside funds have served to promote community programs
and have played an important role in their execution.

If the university is to become an agent of development and change,
it must receive assistance in its efforts to solve social problems and
to show that community service is an essential part of higher education.
Assistance is also needed to promote research and experimentation
and to upgrade project administrators and personnel. In the end, the
success of the projects is ensured by the individuals concerned. Indeed, foreign donors usually grant aid to a project when they are impressed by the quality of the person who directs or promotes it.

Both staff and students, however, resist assistance that they
suspect has strings attached and is given to further special social
purposes. Thus, the purpose for which assistance is given must be
clear. Most universities prefer to receive assistance directly without
conditions. Many agencies, however, would rather grant assistance
through special and more easily managed institutes. Making donations
through a government institute, as in the case of ICOLPE (the Colombian Institute of Pedagogy) in Antioquia, should be explored further,
especially if the institute provides administrative capacity and guarantees effective management of the program. In Antioquia, such assistance promoted so much government interest that it had to be curbed
so that the project would not be overextended. Using a government

institute, nevertheless, can add red tape, since another official comp-troller is involved.

Aid can also be given through international organizations or foundations established by such organizations, for example, the Pan American Foundation. While such foundations are not often used as intermediate agencies and sometimes have rather inflexible systems, they cannot be suspected of trying to impose the ideas of other countries.

Several countries require all donations to be approved by the national government. This requirement makes procedures more difficult and delays approval. Political pressures within the government can also create barriers to outside funding.

The projects studied constitute a nucleus of promising experiments. There are also programs in other institutions that might affect both the institutions and the educational system. To produce greater impact, however, they need more financial assistance.

REQUIREMENTS FOR DEVELOPMENT PROGRAMS

Having studied the cases at several higher education institutions, we can point out some of the required and/or desirable conditions for an effective program for development. They include the following points:

1. The program must seek to meet the needs of the people, especially of the majority poor. If possible, it should form part of a national or regional social development plan based on an inventory of needs and priorities.

2. The program must be run by someone who cares deeply about it and must also have the enthusiastic cooperation of the higher education institution that sponsors it.

3. Several interrelated disciplines should participate in solving the problems the program attacks.

4. The program should have the joint support of the higher education institution and of another agency, government or private.

5. Professors, students, and community must participate actively, and the program must be incorporated within the teaching structure of the institution.

6. The project must be planned in advance and must keep records of its activities and evaluate them regularly.

7. There must be adequate financial resources. Local funds should be available to match external aid.

8. Well-organized administrative and accounting divisions should free the director for teaching and research activities.

SUGGESTIONS FOR THE FUTURE

The network of Latin American educators formed during this study has created a new communications system; it should be preserved and enlarged as a first step in establishing the concept of higher education for development. The classic concept of a university is being questioned, and institutions must be encouraged to modify the university learning structure and assume a commitment to the needs of the community. Not only the developing countries but also the developed countries have reasons to doubt that economic progress automatically leads to social well-being. Knowing what other institutions and countries are doing can give courage to university innovators.

The cases studied do not, of course, deal with all development priorities. Our study does not cover all countries of Latin America nor all kinds of institutions of higher education. We have not been able to include large national multiuniversities and institutes nor other public or private social development agencies.

It is important to continue this work, combining study of more countries and kinds of institutions with more intensive analysis of the kinds of projects and institutions already partially explored. It would be frustrating to see these investigations discontinued or assistance removed from the institutions that are preparing the way. The great Spanish poet Machado said: "Caminante, no hay camino, se hace camino al andar." ("Traveler, there is no road, the road is made while traveling.") In these cases, at least, the road is being built.

We would like to suggest the following ways to encourage education for development in Latin America:

1. Use the present study by publicizing it and analyzing it in round-table discussions and seminars and by exchanging information on the different programs being carried out in the various countries and continents.

2. Help implement some of the programs studied according to the development priorities of the countries concerned.

3. Extend the study by increasing the number of cases of innovative institutions, of national universities or nonuniversity institutions, of institutes, of countries in different stages of economic development, and of projects dealing with other Latin American priorities, such as income distribution, housing, and regional inventories of needs.

4. Study more intensively issues such as government-university relations, university-private sector relationships, administration, finance and accounting of community projects, and cost-benefit relations.

There are many questions still to be answered; indeed, they have multiplied as the program advanced. Like someone looking down from a high hill, we are becoming aware of a larger panorama and finding a wider and more challenging universe. We hope to help others see at least part of what we see.

NOTES

1. The figure may be exaggerated. Some institutions call themselves universities although most instruction is at secondary level. See The University in Society: An International Dialogue (New York: Institute of International Education, 1974), p. xv.

2. United Nations, ECLA, Income Distribution in Latin America, 1971. Quoted in "Economic and Social Progress in Latin America: Annual Report 1972," Inter-American Development Bank, Washington, D.C., p. 8.

PROJECT STAFF,
REGIONAL TEAMS,
TASK FORCE MEMBERS,
AND CORRESPONDING MEMBERS

J. Ki-Zerbo, secretary-general,
African and Malagasy Council for
Higher Education, Ouagadougou,
Upper Volta

F. Mbassi-Manga, dean, Faculty
of Letters and Social Sciences,
University of Yaoundé, Yaoundé,
Cameroon

Mohamed Omer Beshir, professor,
Institute of African and Asian
Studies, University of Khartoum,
Khartoum, Sudan

*Frank Bowles, former university
planning officer, Haile Selassie
I University, Addis Ababa,
Ethiopia

Mulageta Wodajo (Ethiopia), Education Department, World Bank,
Washington, D.C., United States

A. Ngu, vice-chancellor, University
of Yaoundé, Yaoundé, Cameroon

Consultants   David Court, Institute for Development Studies, University of
Nairobi, Kenya

A. Babs Fafunwa, dean, Faculty of
Education, University of Ife,
Nigeria

---

*Died May 1975.

ASIAN REGIONAL TEAM

Director   Puey Ungphakorn, rector, Tham-
                                     masat University, Bangkok,
                                     Thailand; member of the National
                                     Assembly of Thailand

Deputy director   Sippanondha Ketudat, acting deputy
                                     secretary-general, National Edu-
                                     cation Commission of Thailand;
                                     member of the National Assembly
                                     of Thailand

Other team members   Amado A. Castro, professor of
                                     economics, University of the
                                     Philippines, Quezon City, Philip-
                                     pines

                                 O. D. Corpuz, president, University
                                     of the Philippines, Diliman; presi-
                                     dent, Development Academy of the
                                     Philippines

                                 Yip Yat Hoong, deputy vice-
                                     chancellor, University of Malaya,
                                     Kuala Lumpur, Malaysia
                                 Later replaced by
                                 V. Selvaratnam, lecturer in soci-
                                     ology, Rural Development Division,
                                     University of Malaya, Kuala
                                     Lumpur, Malaysia

                                 Amnuay Tapingkae, director,
                                     Regional Institute of Higher Edu-
                                     cation and Development, Singapore

Consultants   Soedjatmoko, National Development
                                     Planning Agency, Indonesia

LATIN AMERICAN REGIONAL TEAM

Director

Alfonso Ocampo Londono, president, Fundación para el Desarollo Industrial, Cali, Colombia

Deputy director

Rene Corradine, Universidad del Valle, Cali, Colombia

Other team members

Carlos Tunnermann Bernheim, former rector, Universidad Nacional Autonoma de Nicaragua, Leon, Nicaragua

Pablo Willstatter, Institute for Educational Development, Lima, Peru

Alvaro Aranquibel Equi, former chief of planning office, Universidad del Oriente, Cumana, Venezuela

Dr. Gabriel Velazquez Palau, Rockefeller Foundation representative, Universidade da Bahïa, Salvador, Brazil

Consultants

Farzam Arbab, Rockefeller Foundation representative, Cali, Colombia

Frances Foland, fellow, Institute of Current World Affairs. New York, N.Y., United States

Carlos Medellin, Asociacion Colombiana de Universidades, Bogota, Colombia

Henrique Tono Trucco, regional director, Centro Internacional de Investigaciones para el Desarrollo, Bogotá, Colombia

Ramon de Zubiria, ex-rector,
Universidad de los Andes, Bogotá,
Colombia

Rafael Rivas, ex-dean, Universidad
del Valle and Universidad de los
Andes, Bogotá, Colombia

Agustin Lombana, academic dean,
Faculty of Interdisciplinary Studies,
Universidad Pontificia Javeriana,
Bogotá, Colombia

Alberto Alvarado, Fondo Colombiano
de Investigaciones Cientificas y
Proyectos Especiales "Francisco
José de Caldas," Bogotá, Colombia

Beverly B. Cordry, director of
research, Phoenix College,
Phoenix, Arizona, United States

Carlos Vidalon, International Bank
for Reconstruction and Development, Washington, D.C., United
States

TASK FORCE MEMBERS

Duncan Ballantine

Director, Education Department,
International Bank for Reconstruction and Development

Jacques Grunewald

Conseiller des Affaires Etrangères,
Section des Etudes Générales,
Ministère des Affaires Etrangères,
France

A. R. MacKinnon

Special Advisor, Policy Branch,
Canadian International Development
Agency

William T. Mashler	Director, Division for Global and Interregional Projects, United Nations Development Programme
D. Najman	Director, Department of Higher Education and the Training of Educational Personnel, Unesco
Robert Schmeding	Deputy Director, Office of Education and Human Resources, Bureau for Technical Assistance, U.S. Agency for International Development
later replaced by James B. Chandler	Director, Office of Education and Human Resources, Bureau for Technical Assistance, U.S. Agency for International Development
Tarlok Singh	Deputy Executive Director, United Nations Children's Fund
later replaced by Newton Bowles	Deputy Director, Programme Division, United Nations Children's Fund
J E C Thornton	Chief Education Adviser, Ministry of Overseas Development, United Kingdom
Michael P. Todaro	Associate Director, Social Sciences, Rockefeller Foundation
later replaced by R. Kirby Davidson	Deputy Director, Social Sciences, Rockefeller Foundation
F. Champion Ward	Program Advisor in Education, International Division, Ford Foundation
Alfred C. Wolf	Program Advisor to the President, Inter-American Development Bank
Ruth K. Zagorin	Director, Social Sciences and Human Resources, International Development Research Centre, Canada

CORRESPONDING MEMBERS

Robert L. Clodius

Project Administrator, MUCIA, University of Wiscon, Madison, Wisconsin, United States

Carl K. Eicher

Department of Agricultural Economics, Michigan State University, East Lansing, Michigan, United States

Robert F. Goheen

President, Council on Foundations, New York, New York, United States

John Hannah

Executive Director, World Food Council, United Nations, New York, United States

J. George Harrar

Former President, Rockefeller Foundation, New York, New York, United States

The Rev. Theodore M. Hesburgh

President, University of Notre Dame, Notre Dame, Indiana, United States

John F. Hilliard

Consultant, USAID, Bethesda, Maryland, United States

Choh-Ming Li

Vice-Chancellor, Chinese University of Hong Kong, Shatin, New Territories, Hong Kong

Helen M. Muller

New York, New York, United States, and Geneva, Switzerland

*Harry K. Newburn

Arizona State University, Tempe, Arizona, United States

---

*Died August 1974.

Arthur T. Porter

Vice-Chancellor, University of Sierra Leone, Freetown, Sierra Leone

R. Cranford Pratt

Professor of Political Science, University of Toronto, Toronto, Canada

The Hon. Carlos P. Romulo

Secretary of Foreign Affairs, Government of the Philippines, Manila, Philippines

Vernon Ruttan

President, Agricultural Development Council, Singapore

Sir Philip Sherlock

Secretary-General, Association of Caribbean Universities and Research Institutes, Kingston, Jamaica

Soedjatmoko

National Development Planning Agency, Indonesia

Clifton R. Wharton, Jr.

President, Michigan State University, East Lansing, Michigan, United States

Herman B Wells

Chancellor, Indiana University, Bloomington, Indiana, United States

Gilbert F. White

University of Colorado, Boulder, Colorado, United States

Ahmednagar College, India, 36, 108-10; Center for Studies in Rural Development, 109; Rural Life Development and Research Project, 108
Aklilu Habte, 19, 35, 39, 209
Alvarado, Alberto, 213
Amnuay Tapingkae, 211
Antioquia State, Colombia, 24, 125
Antioquia, University of, Colombia, 24, 25, 41, 63, 125-27, 131, 195, 197, 200, 201, 202; Department of Research and Extension, 24; Faculty of Education, 24, 125-27; One-Teacher School Program, 24, 125-26, 199, 202; Program on Individualized Instruction and Flexible Schooling, 25, 126-27, 131, 200, 202
Aranquibel Equí, Alvaro, 212
Arbab, Farzam, 212
Argentina, 192
Asia, 3, 4, 19, 28, 35, 116, 143, 153, 166-88, 192
Asian Development Bank (ADB), 120, 177
Asian Institute of Management (AIM), Philippines, 28, 43, 50, 114, 115-17, 187
Asian Report, 9, 10, 28, 29, 42, 45-46, 49, 166-88
Asian Team, 9, 12, 26, 187-88
Asian Vegetable Research and Development Center, Taiwan (AVRDC), 34
Association of African Universities, 143, 159, 160, 161
Association of Southeast Asian Institutions of Higher Learning (ASAIHL), Bangkok, 187-88
Association of Southeast Asian Nations (ASEAN), 171
Ateneo de Manila University, Philippines, 115-16
Audu, I., 209

Bahasa Malaysia, 41, 112-13
Bahia, Brazil, 20, 56 (see also, Federal University of Bahía)
Ballantine, Duncan, 213

access to higher education, 16, 28, 63, 96, 99, 107, 119, 163
Accra, Ghana, 159
Accra, University of, Ghana, 148
Addis Ababa University, Ethiopia, 19, 23, 33, 38, 63, 92-94, 148, 162; College of Agriculture, 23; Ethiopian University Service, 37, 92-93, 154; Faculty of Education, 23, 94; Faculty of Sciences, 23; Institute of Building Technology, 92; Institute of Development Research, 19, 38; Public Health College, 92; School of Social Work, 93; University College, 92
adult education, 7, 17, 19, 25, 202
Africa, 3, 4, 8, 9, 19, 35, 61, 63, 89, 139-65, 192
African and Malagasy Council on Higher Education, 160
African Report, 40, 46, 47, 48, 49, 63, 139-65
African Team, 11, 148-49, 156
Agency for International Development, United States (USAID), 3, 21, 50, 51, 90, 111, 126, 177, 214
Agricultural Development Council (ADC), United States, 111
agricultural programs, 7, 11, 15, 17, 18-19, 25, 30, 35, 95, 97, 101, 105, 110-11, 120-21, 122, 133-35, 148, 155, 157, 161, 162-63, 196, 202
Ahmadu Bello University, Nigeria, 19, 21, 23, 39, 41, 56, 57, 63, 100-02, 148, 150, 154; Abdullahi Bayero College, 100; Arabic and Islamic Studies Division, 100; Center for Nigerian Cultural Studies, 102; Division for Agricultural and Livestock Services Training, 100; Extension Research Liaison Service, 100, 101; Faculty of Education, 23; health extension program, 21; Institute for Agricultural Research and Special Services, 19, 41, 100, 101; Institute of Administration, 41, 100, 101; Institute of Education, 23, 41, 100, 101

Bangkok, Thailand, 19, 50, 121
Bellagio, Italy, 139
Beshir, Mohamed Omer, 210
bilingualism, 21-92, 139, 158, 164
Bimazubute, Gilles, 26
Bombay, University of, India, 109
Botswana, 23, 87-89; Ministry of Education, 23
Botswana, Lesotho and Swaziland, University of, (UBLS), 23, 47, 63, 87-89, 139, 148, 150; College of Agriculture, 88; Faculty of Education, 88
Bowles, Frank, 10, 46, 79, 210
Bowles, Newton, 214
Bradley, William, 16
Brazil, 56, 192, 196, 197, 200 (see also, Federal University of Bahía); Ministry of Education and Culture, 56; Secretary of Agriculture, 56; Secretary of Public Health, 123; Treasury Department, 56
Brunei, 170
Buenos Aires, Argentina, 192
Bujumbura, University of, Burundi, 148
Bureau of Research Allocation and Land Use (see, Dar es Salaam, University of)
Burma, 170
Burundi, 26

Cairo—Khartoum branch, University of, Sudan, 104, 105
Cali, Colombia, 20, 127, 197 (see also, Valle, University of); Municipal Health Service, 128
Camargo, Lleras, 11
Cameroon, 13, 30, 37, 38, 41, 50, 51, 54, 58, 89-92, 139, 154, 155, 164 (see also, Yaoundé, University of); National Planning Commission, 21, 58, 90
Canada, 88
Canadian International Development Agency (CIDA), 21, 51, 90, 213
Candelaria, Colombia, 20, 127, 129, 197
Castro, Amado A., 211
Catholic Seminary, Poona, 109
Cauca University, Colombia, 131
CEDUR (see, Federal University of Bahia)
Center for Research and Communication (CRC), Philippines, 43, 114, 117-18, 177, 187
Center for Studies in Rural Development (see, Ahmednagar College)

Center for Urban Development (see, Federal University of Bahía)
Centro Internacional de Agricultura Tropical (CIAT), Colombia, 34
Chandler, James B., 214
Chile, 192
China, 10, 13
Chinese, 113, 119
Chinese University of Hong Kong, 35
Chulalongkorn University, Thailand, 176
Clodius, Robert L., 215
Colombia, 11, 25, 30, 37, 50, 129-31, 192, 196 (see also, Antioquia, University of, and Valle, University of); Ministry of Education, 126; Ministry of Health, 30, 128; Secretary of Education, State of Antioquia, 24, 125, 126; Secretary of Education, State of Sucre, 24, 126
Colombian Institute for the Development of Higher Education, 126
Colombian Institute of Pedagogy, 126
Colombo Plan, 177
community attitudes, 12, 68-69, 124, 134, 145, 199-200
community relations, 32, 56, 128, 134
community service, 18, 25, 35-37, 40, 92-94, 100-02, 108-10, 120-22, 155, 157, 163, 169, 186, 187, 191, 195-96, 197, 198
comprehensive programs, 153, 155, 158
consultancy services, 7, 17, 29, 60, 94-96, 100, 114, 132, 155, 157, 160, 162-63
Coombs, Philip H., 4
Cordry, Beverly B., 213
Corpuz, O. D., 211
Corradine, René, 212
costs, 9, 10, 62, 99, 103, 114, 130, 147, 160-61, 178, 182, 201
Council of Social Development (see, Gadjah Mada University)
Court, David, 44N, 210
Creole, 99
Cuba, 10
cultural values, 6, 102, 112-13, 147, 157, 160, 162, 167, 171, 176-77, 186, 191
curriculum, 16, 22, 23, 32, 33, 37, 38, 51, 60, 70-71, 100-01, 106, 127, 145, 148, 150, 159, 161-62

Dakar, Senegal, 148

Dakar, University of, Senegal, 90, 148;
Medical School, 90
Dar es Salaam, University of, Tanzania,
23, 25, 36, 38, 40, 56, 106-07, 148,
153, 162; Bureau of Resource Allo-
cation and Land Use, 40; Economic
Research Bureau, 40; Faculty of
Arts and Social Sciences, 38, 106;
Institute of Adult Education, 25;
Institute of Kiswahili Research, 40
Davidson, R. Kirby, 214
De La Salle College, Philippines, 115-
16
Development Academy of the Philippines
(DAP), 28, 31, 34, 39, 46, 113-15,
187
donor agencies, 1, 14, 48-51, 51-53,
110, 159, 161, 177, 178, 184-85
(see also, Agency for International
Development, CIDA, Ford Founda-
tion, French Foreign Ministry,
IDRC, IBRD, IDB, Rockefeller
Foundation, UNDP, UNICEF,
Unesco)
double-level training, 97 (see also,
umbrella university)
Dutch, 91

East Africa, University of, 106
East Europe, 105
Ecole Normale Supérieure, Mali (see,
Higher Teacher Training School)
Economic Commission for Africa, 160
Economic Research Bureau (see, Dar
es Salaam, University of)
education systems, 17, 22-25, 63, 79-
80, 148, 149, 157, 169, 195, 202
Egypt, 102, 105
Eicher, Carl K., 215
English, 25, 91-92, 112-13, 119, 139,
158, 164
enrollment, 105, 113, 140-45, 173, 192
Equatorial Guinea, 139
Ethiopia, 13, 23, 35, 37, 93-94, 140,
153, 154, 155 (see also, Addis Ababa
University); Ministry of Education,
94
Ethiopian University Service (see, Addis
Ababa University)
Europe, 143, 145, 153, 171
evaluation, 13, 61-62, 73, 115, 125,
126, 132, 183, 200
Evans-Anfom, E., 209
extension programs, 7, 17, 25, 27, 32,
35-37, 56, 93-94, 101, 130-31, 134,

148, 155, 157, 161, 163, 169, 186,
198
Extension Research Liaison Service
(see, Ahmadu Bello University)

faculty attitudes, 12, 38, 56, 66-67,
93, 95, 108, 135, 156, 202
faculty participation, 18, 19, 30, 36-
37, 46, 58-59, 95-96, 111, 121-22,
124, 133, 134-35, 156, 157, 179,
197, 198
Fafunwa, A. Babs, 31N, 210
Federal University of Bahía, Brazil,
20, 24, 33, 38, 39, 41, 46, 51, 58,
61, 63, 123-25, 197, 198, 200, 201,
202; Center for Urban Development
(CEDUR), 20, 123-25, 200; Faculty
of Medicine, 20, 61; University Program of Research and Education for
Development (PROPED), 20, 39, 51,
56, 58, 123-25, 200
financing, 15, 31, 40, 43, 48-51, 52,
76, 96, 114, 116, 125, 126, 131,
134, 161, 182
Foland, Frances, 212
Fonds Aide Coopération (FAC), 21, 51,
90
food and nutrition, 6, 14
Ford Foundation, 51, 87, 101, 111,
115, 116, 118, 123, 126, 177, 214
foreign aid, 158-64, 177-78, 182, 184-
85, 186, 202-03
France, 90; Foreign Ministry, 213
French, 91-92, 99, 139, 158, 164

Gadjah Mada University, Indonesia, 18,
33, 36, 38, 41, 60, 110-11, 186;
Agriculture Complex, 111; Council
of Social Development, 110; Girirejo
Mangunan, 111; Institute of Rural and
Regional Studies, 18, 38, 41, 60,
110, 111; Kulia Kerga Niata
Mahaseiswa Project, 36, 111; Merapi
Slope, 111
German, 91
Ghana, 37 (see also, University of
Science and Technology)
Goheen, Robert F., 215
Goma, L. K. H., 209
government attitudes, 9, 11, 39-42, 48,
56, 58, 69, 87-89, 92, 93, 108-09,
112-13, 114, 117, 124, 129, 134,
145, 154, 160, 169, 171, 178
Graduate Volunteers Service Program
(see, Thammasat University)

Grunewald, Jacques, 213
guidelines, 15, 54-77, 154, 203

Habakkuk, H. J., 6
Haile Selassie I University (see, Addis Ababa University)
Hannah, John, 39, 215
Harrar, J. George, 34, 215
Harvard University, United States, 9, 16; Harvard Business School, 28, 50, 116, 118
Hazen Foundation, 16
health services, 6, 7, 14, 15, 17, 19, 20-22, 25, 30, 33, 37, 38, 39, 51, 89-91, 98, 102, 105, 109, 121, 123-25, 148, 155, 156, 161, 162-63, 196, 197-98, 202
Hesburgh, The Rev. Theodore M., 215
Higher Teacher Training School, Mali, 26, 97
Hill, F. F., 34
Hilliard, John F., 215
Hulbe, S. K., 108

Ibadan, University of, Nigeria, 8, 25, 90, 162; Extra-Mural Department, 25; Medical School, 90
Ife, University of, Nigeria, 25; Department of Extension Education, 25; Isoy Rural Development Project, 25
India (see, Ahmednagar College)
Indonesia, 9, 170, 171, 177, 178, 186
Indonesia, University of, 186
Industrial University of Santander, Colombia, 131
Institute for Agricultural Research and Special Services (see, Ahmadu Bello University)
Institute for Industrial Research (see, Monterrey Institute)
Institute of Education (see, Ahmadu Bello University)
Institute of Production Management Forecasting, Mali, 98
Institute of Rural and Regional Studies (see, Gadjah Mada University)
institutional models, 18, 32-34, 176
Inter-American Development Bank (IDB), 205N, 214
interdisciplinary studies, 37-39, 47, 50, 60, 95, 106, 111, 121, 124, 125, 131, 162
International Association of Universities, 6

International Bank for Reconstruction and Development (IBRD), 3, 50, 62, 213
International Council for Educational Development (ICED), United States, 3, 4
International Crops Research Institute for the Semi-Arid Tropics, India (ICRISAT), 34
International Development Research Centre, Canada (IDRC), 214
International Institute of Tropical Agriculture (IITA), Nigeria, 34, 101
International Maize and Wheat Improve-
Inter-University Council, United Kingdom, 52
Islamic University of Omdurman, Sudan, 104

Jakarta, 186
Japan, 116, 173
Java, Indonesia, 171
Javeriana University, Colombia, 131; Education at a Distance program, 131
jobs and employment, 17, 25-29
Jogjakarta, Indonesia, 36

Kasetsart University, Thailand, 19, 26, 38, 120-22, 186; Maeklong Integrated Rural Development Program, 19, 30, 33, 36, 38, 41, 46, 50, 55, 60, 61, 120-22, 186
Kellogg Foundation, 51
Khartoum, University of, Sudan, 102-04, 148, 150; Senior Scholars and Research Fellowship Scheme, 102-04
Ki-Zerbo, J., 164, 210
Kumasi, Ghana, 29, 153, 162 (see also, University of Science and Technology)
Kwapong, Alexander, 42, 44N

La Molina, Peru, 18, 36 (see also, National Agrarian University)
land-grant colleges, 9, 16, 169, 176, 186, 187
Latin America, 3, 4, 8, 9, 14, 15, 25, 33, 143, 153, 189-205
Latin American Report, 41, 42, 47, 49, 189-205
Latin American Team, 193

leadership, 18, 29, 39, 45-47, 48, 52, 75, 108, 124, 154, 160, 175, 191, 198
Lesotho, 87-89 (see also, Botswana, Lesotho and Swaziland, University of)
Lesotho, National University of, 89
Lesotho, University of Botswana, Lesotho and Swaziland (see, Botswana, Lesotho and Swaziland, University of)
Li, Choh-Mind, 31N, 35, 215
Limb, Philip, 35
literacy, 19, 25, 92, 96, 109, 122, 139, 140
Lombana, Agustin, 213
London Polytechnic Institute, United Kingdom, 58, 120
London, University of, United Kingdom, 102
Los Andes, University of, Colombia, 131
Los Baños, Philippines, 34

MacKinnon, A. R., 213
Machado, 204
Maeklong Integrated Rural Development Program (see, Kasetsart, Mahidol or Thammasat Universities)
Mahidol University, Thailand, 19, 26, 38, 120-22, 186; Maeklong Integrated Rural Development Program, 19, 30, 33, 36, 38, 41, 46, 50, 55, 60, 61, 120-22, 186
Malawi, University of, 150
Malaya, University of, Malaysia, 26, 41, 112-13, 185
Malaysia, 9, 112-13, 116, 171, 173, 185 (see also, Malaya, University of)
Mali, 26, 41, 96-98, 140, 148; Production Ministry, 97
management of programs, 69-70, 150, 160, 161, 163, 200
management training, 113-18, 131-33, 187
Mandarin (see, Chinese)
manpower training, 7, 9, 17, 25-29, 33, 41, 61, 72-73, 87-89, 98-99, 104, 106-07, 113-18, 119-20, 150, 187
Mashler, William T., 214
mass education, 9, 61, 171
Massachusetts Institute of Technology, United States, 15
Mauritius, 26, 62, 139; Ministry of Agriculture, 98-99

Mauritius, University of, 27, 58, 98-99, 148; College of Agriculture, 98; School of Administration, 98-99; School of Agriculture, 98; School of Industrial Technology, 98-99
Mbassi-Manga, F., 210
Medellin, Carlos, 212
Medical School, Mali, 26, 98
Mexico, 27, 192, 196, 197 (see also, Monterrey Institute of Technology and Advanced Studies)
Mexico City, Mexico, 192
Middle East, 9
Midwest Universities Consortium for International Activities (MUCIA), United States, 111
Mmari, G., 209
Monekosso, G. L., 149, 209
Monterrey, Mexico, 27
Monterrey Institute of Technology and Advanced Studies, Mexico, 7, 15, 26, 27, 30, 33, 36, 41, 43, 55, 58, 62, 131-33, 197, 198, 199, 200, 201, 202; Division of Engineering and Architecture, 30, 132; Institute for Industrial Research, 131; Research and Extension Program, 43, 131-33
Mook, Telfer, 108
Msekwa, Pius, 209
Mulageta Wodajo, 210
Muller, Helen M., 215

Nairobi, University of, Kenya, 33, 148, 162; Development Institute, 33
Najman, D., 214
National Agrarian University, Peru, 7, 11, 18, 30, 33, 35, 36, 41, 49, 55, 133-35, 196, 197, 199, 201, 202; Transferal of Technology Program, 11, 18, 30, 36, 55, 56, 133-35
National Community Action, Colombia, 126
National Engineering School, Mali, 26, 97
National Federation of Coffee Growers, Colombia, 126
National School of Public Administration, Mali, 26, 97; Institute of Production Management, 98
National University, Bogotá, Colombia, 131
Netherlands, 176, 177
Newburn, Harry K., 215

Ngee Ann Technical College, Singapore,
    16, 26, 33, 35, 41, 43, 55, 58, 60,
    119-20, 187
Ngu, A., 210
Nigeria, 8, 40, 155 (see also, Ahmadu
    Bello University); Ministry of Agri-
    culture, 101
Nigeria, University of, 25
North America, 143, 171
Nyerere, Julius, 9, 12, 44N, 165N

Ocampo Londoño, Alfonso, 212
One-Teacher School Program (see,
    Antioquia, University of)
Organization for Economic Cooperation
    and Development (OECD), 189
Organization of African Unity, 160, 161
Overseas Development, Ministry of,
    United Kingdom, 90
Oxford University, United Kingdom, 6

Pan American Federation of Faculties
    of Medicine, 128
Pan American Foundation, 203
Panama, 196
parallel training, 17, 155
Perkins, James A., 4
Peru, 11, 13, 30, 35, 56, 192, 197,
    199, 200, 201 (see also, National
    Agrarian University); Agrarian
    Reform Act, 11, 18, 56; Ministry of
    Agriculture, 18, 30, 56, 133, 134
Peters, John, 108
Philippines, 9, 27, 43, 113-18, 170,
    171, 173, 174, 176, 178, 187 (see
    also, AIM, CRC, DAP); National
    Economic and Development Authority,
    114
Philippines Executive Academy, 114,
    115
Philippines, University of the, 34, 115,
    176; Institute of Public Administration,
    114
Pius XII Catholic College, Lesotho, 87
Poona University, India, 109
Porter, Arthur T., 216
Portuguese, 91, 139
postgraduate training, 161
Pratt, R. Cranford, 44N, 216
primary education, 7, 22, 23, 24, 25,
    63, 96-97, 100-01, 124, 125-27, 195,
    202
private enterprise, relations with, 43,
    114, 118, 120, 131-33, 162-63, 201

Program of Research and Education for
    Development (see, Federal University
    of Bahía)
PRIMOPS (see, Valle, University of)
Program on Individualized Instruction
    and Flexible Schooling (see, Antioquia,
    University of)
Programs for Systems of Health Services
    Delivery (see, Valle, University of)
PROPED (see, Federal University of
    Bahía)
Puey Ungphakorn, 13, 36, 187, 211

Regional Conference of African Ministers
    of Education, 161
regional directors, 4
Regional Institute for Higher Education
    Development (RIHED), Singapore,
    187-88
regional reports, 8, 17
Regional Teaching Centers, Mali, 97
relations with business and industry,
    43-44, 48, 59-60, 94-96, 114-18,
    131-33
research, 27, 30, 32, 33, 39, 41, 50,
    94-96, 101-02, 106-07, 114, 117-18,
    121, 130-31, 147, 150, 155, 157, 160,
    161-62, 169, 186, 187
Research and Extension Program (see,
    Monterrey Institute)
resistance, 12
Reston, James, 11
Rhodesia, 139
Rio de Janeiro, Brazil, 192
Rivas, Rafael, 213
Rockefeller Foundation, 51, 52, 111,
    122, 123, 177, 214; International
    Health Division, 52
Roma, Lesotho, 88, 89
Romulo, Carlos P., 216
rural development, 17, 18-19, 21, 24,
    25, 30, 31, 33, 35-37, 89-91, 92-94,
    108-10, 110-11, 120-22, 125-27,
    133-35, 155, 161, 162, 183, 185,
    194, 202
Rural Economic Research Unit (see,
    Ahmadu Bello University)
Rural Polytechnic Institute, Mali, 26,
    60, 97
Ruttan, Vernon, 216

Salisbury, Harrison, 4
Samaru, Nigeria, 100
Schmeding, Robert, 214

School of Administration (see, Mauritius,
    University of)
School of Agriculture (see, Mauritius,
    University of)
School of Industrial Technology (see,
    Mauritius, University of)
secondary education, 7, 22, 24, 26, 63,
    96-97
Secondary Teacher Training School,
    Mali, 97
Selvaratnem, V., 211
Sherlock, Sir Philip, 216
Siloé, Colombia, 20, 37, 127, 129, 197
Singapore, 10, 26, 27, 41, 116, 119-20,
    170, 185, 187 (see also, Ngee Ann
    Technical College); Ministry of
    Finance, 41
Singapore, University of, 26
Singh, Tarlok, 214
Sippanondha Ketudat, 211
social indicators, 168, 173
Soedjatmoko, 22, 33, 211, 216
South Africa, Republic of, 139
South Africa, University of, 87
South Asia, 9
Southeast Asia, 9, 28, 170, 171
Southeast Asian Science Foundation, 117
Spanish, 91, 139
staff development, 15, 21, 46, 49, 51,
    52, 58, 102-04, 130, 148, 150, 154,
    158, 192
student attitudes, 12, 35, 37, 38, 57,
    64-65, 93, 134, 145, 163, 202
student participation, 10, 18, 19, 30,
    35-37, 46, 57, 58-59, 92-94, 94-95,
    106, 108-10, 111, 121-22, 124, 134-
    35, 157, 179, 182, 197, 199
Sucre, Colombia, 24
Sudan, 104-05 (see also, Khartoum,
    University of)
Suharto, 111
Swaneng High School, Botswana, 23
Swaziland, 87-89 (see also, Botswana,
    Lesotho, and Swaziland, University
    of)
Swaziland, University of Botswana,
    Lesotho and Swaziland (see, Botswana,
    Lesotho and Swaziland, University of)
Sy, Tidiane, 209

Taiwan, 116
Tamil, 113
Tananarive, Madagascar, 159

Tanzania, 9, 10, 12, 26, 40, 42, 154,
    155, 164 (see also, Dar es Salaam,
    University of)
Task Force, 3, 4, 213-14
teacher training, 22, 23, 24, 39, 63,
    100-01, 104, 105, 118, 125-27,
    151-52, 152-53, 155
technician training, 7, 63, 89-91, 97,
    98-99, 103, 104, 105, 114, 119-20,
    151-52, 152-53, 155, 158, 185, 187
Technological University of Pereira,
    Colombia, 131; Open University
    Program, 131
Technology Consultancy Centre (see,
    University of Science and Technology)
Thailand, 9, 13, 26, 30, 35, 171, 173,
    176, 185 (see also, Kasetsart,
    Mahidol and Thammasat Universities);
    Ministry of Agriculture, 121
Thammasat University, Thailand, 19,
    26, 36, 37, 38, 120-22, 176, 186;
    Graduate Volunteers Service Pro-
    gram, 37, 121; Maeklong Integrated
    Rural Development Program, 19, 30,
    33, 36, 38, 41, 46, 50, 55, 60, 61,
    120-22, 186
Thornton, J. E. C., 214
Todaro, Michael P., 214
Toh Chin Chye, 26
Tono Trucco, Henrique, 212
Transferal of Technology Program (see,
    National Agrarian University)
Tulane University, United States, 127;
    Family Health Foundation, 127
Tunnerman Bernheim, Carlos, 212
Tuskegee Institute, United States, 16

umbrella university, 9, 21, 38, 94, 105,
    153
unemployment, 6, 9, 104, 152, 174,
    194
Unesco, 23, 25, 27, 51, 96, 100, 159,
    165N, 214
United Church Board of World Ministries,
    108
United Kingdom, 52, 87, 88, 90, 102,
    120, 171, 176; Ministry of Overseas
    Development, 90, 214
United Nations (UN), 190
United Nations Children's Fund
    (UNICEF), 23, 50, 51, 90, 96, 100,
    214
United Nations Development Programme
    (UNDP), 21, 50, 51, 89, 90, 214

United Nations Economic Commission for Latin America (CEPAL or ECLA), 190, 193, 195
United Nations University, 42
United States, 11, 12, 13, 16, 88, 117, 176, 178
university administration, 10
University Centre for Health Sciences (see, Yaoundé, University of)
university-government relations, 6, 7, 8, 9, 11, 15, 39–42, 56, 69, 73–75, 96–98, 100–02, 106–07, 127, 129, 130, 132, 135, 145, 150, 151, 154, 156, 161, 163, 178, 201
University of Science and Technology, Ghana, 29–30, 35, 41, 43, 59, 60, 61, 94–96, 148; Faculty of Agriculture, 94–95; Faculty of Architecture, 94; Faculty of Art, 94; Faculty of Engineering, 94; Faculty of Pharmacy, 94; Faculty of Science, 94; Faculty of Social Studies, 94; Technology Consultancy Centre, 29–30, 36, 60, 61, 95–96; Voluntary Technology Group, 59, 61, 95
urban development, 17, 20, 31, 38, 123–25, 127–29, 183, 194, 202

Valle, University of, Colombia, 10, 11, 20, 22, 33, 37, 38, 41, 46, 127–29, 197–98, 199, 200, 201, 202; Division of Health, 127–28; Faculty of Medicine, 20, 33, 61; Research Program for Systems of Health Services Delivery (PRIMOPS), 20, 22, 30, 50, 127–29
Velasquez Palau, Gabriel, 14, 212

Vidalon, Carlos, 213
Voluntary Technology Group (see, University of Science and Technology)

Ward, F. Champion, 214
Wells, Herman B., 216
West Africa, 16
West Germany, 16
West Indies, 88
Wharton, Clifton R., Jr., 216
White, Gilbert F., 216
Wirtz, Willard, 11, 12
Willstatter, Pablo, 212
Wolf, Alfred C., 214
women, education of, 98, 106, 119, 140, 141, 161, 162, 164
work-study, 12, 17, 35, 38, 43, 57, 59, 92–93, 117, 155, 157
World Bank (see, International Bank for Reconstruction and Development)
World Food Council, 39
World Health Organization (WHO), 21, 51, 58, 89, 90
World Neighbors, 108
Yale University, United States, 16
Yaoundé, University of, Cameroon, 21, 89–92, 148, 149, 153, 156; Department of English, 91; Department of French, 92; Faculty of Arts, 92; Faculty of Law, 92; University Centre for Health Sciences, 21, 30, 37, 38, 41, 50, 51, 58, 89–91, 92, 149, 154
Yip Yat Hoong, 211

Zagorin, Ruth K., 214
Zambia, University of, 162
Zaria, Nigeria, 100
Zubiria, Ramon de, 213

ABOUT THE AUTHORS

KENNETH W. THOMPSON, Director of the Higher Education for Development Program at the International Council for Educational Development is Commonwealth Professor of Government and Foreign Affairs at the University of Virginia. Previously he served as Vice-President of the Rockefeller Foundation. He has written several books about international affairs, including <u>Understanding World Politics</u>, and has articles published in numerous magazines and scholarly journals. Dr. Thompson holds a Ph. D. in Political Science and International Relations from the University of Chicago.

BARBARA R. FOGEL, Assistant Director of the Higher Education for Development Program is now Acting Director of the continuing HED program at the International Council for Educational Development. She is the author of <u>What's the Biggest?</u> and has had articles in numerous journals. She has served in an editorial capacity of the staffs of several periodicals, including <u>Public Opinion Quarterly</u>. Ms. Fogel is a graduate of Smith College.

RELATED TITLES
Published by
Praeger Special Studies

EDUCATION AND DEVELOPMENT RECONSIDERED: The Bellagio
Conference Papers

Ford Foundation/Rockefeller
Foundation
edited by F. Champion Ward

EDUCATIONAL PLANNING AND EXPENDITURE DECISIONS IN
DEVELOPING COUNTRIES: With A Malaysian Case Study

Robert W. McMeekin, Jr.

COMPARATIVE HIGHER EDUCATION ABROAD: Bibliography and
Analysis

Philip G. Altbach

EDUCATIONAL COOPERATION BETWEEN DEVELOPED AND
DEVELOPING COUNTRIES: Policies, Problems, and Innovations

H. M. Phillips

EDUCATION FOR RURAL DEVELOPMENT: Case Studies for Planners

edited by Manzoor Ahmed and
Philip H. Coombs

THE ECONOMICS OF NONFORMAL EDUCATION: Resources,
Costs, and Benefits

Manzoor Ahmed

HIGHER EDUCATION IN DEVELOPING NATIONS: A Selected
Bibliography, 1969-74

Philip G. Altbach and
David H. Kelly